Ideas
for
Britain

Ideas
for
Britain

Ideas
for
Britain

Hugh Salmon

Matador
9 Priory Business Park,
Wistow Road, Kibworth Beauchamp,
Leicestershire. LE8 0RX
Tel: 0116 279 2299
Email: books@troubador.co.uk
Web: www.troubador.co.uk/matador
Twitter: @matadorbooks

ISBN 978 1785898 853

British Library Cataloguing in Publication Data.
A catalogue record for this book is available from the British Library.

Printed and bound by CPI Group (UK) Ltd, Croydon, CR0 4YY
Typeset in 11pt Aldine401 BT by Troubador Publishing Ltd, Leicester, UK

Matador is an imprint of Troubador Publishing Ltd

To the memory of my father

CONTENTS

★   These posts also feature in my book *'Thoughts on Life and Advertising'*.

INTRODUCTION

9 JANUARY 2015

In my day, if you wanted to go to Oxford or Cambridge, you had to stay at school for an extra term - and do a hell of a lot more work. My trouble was that the extra term was the rugby term. Whether this is an excuse for my failure, the fact is I failed.

I was puzzled by this. I hadn't failed at anything else, so how could Oxbridge not want me now? After all, as well as the rugby, I had been captain of the school cricket team and, although the grades weren't great, I had achieved five A levels. And my school must have thought I was clever enough as they put my name down in the first place. Surely there had been a mistake? Sadly not.

My father told me I didn't take my studies seriously enough. He questioned my academic commitment wherever I went to university. If anything, he thought I would work even less hard as sex and drinking would be allowed, and drugs available.

I agreed with my Dad so, from the ages of 18-22, I lived the life in London. I was a car cleaner, a car dealer, a delivery driver and an accountant. I spent the summer of 1979 teaching water-skiing in Corfu.

Then I got lucky.

By the same age as my contemporaries who had taken the academic high road, I knew I wanted to be an adman. I had friends at Ogilvy & Mather (O&M) and Foote, Cone & Belding (FCB). Both offered me jobs as a graduate trainee. I chose O&M.

Two years later, I told my boss about my idea for a music magazine on cassette tape. He loved the idea and asked me if he could help. I said I needed offices, so SFX was launched just along the corridor.

SFX was a great ride but, sadly, we ran out of money and I returned to advertising, as an Account Director at FCB and a Board Director at Kirkwoods. Then, in 1988, when I was 31, Ogilvy got me back to manage the Thailand office, their fourth largest in the world (and possibly their best). After that, and having got married and had our first child, Ogilvy transferred me back to London to oversee the Unilever account.

Then I got unlucky.

The American I was to replace in Ogilvy London announced she would not be going back to New York after all. The job Ogilvy had transferred me back to London to do wasn't there any more. Instead, they wanted me to manage the Middle East region out of Bahrain. But my wife and I did not want to live in Bahrain. And, by this time, I had been approached by Lintas, another Unilever agency, to manage CM:Lintas, with a promise this would lead to my heading up all the Lintas operations in London.

Soon after arriving at CM:Lintas in 1992, I found the Chairman was defrauding the company by diverting money into a personal account elsewhere. He was a crook. I tried to persuade him to stop. He tried to fire me. I reported him to head office. They did fire me. Worse, to cover up the fraud, they told lies about me which I felt affected my reputation in the advertising industry.

This led to a five year litigation in which I wanted to clear my name. I had no idea it would take so long. In 1997, I won the case in 'spectacular' fashion. An executive of Interpublic Group, holding company of Lintas Worldwide, and quoted on the New York Stock Exchange, flew over to London on Concorde, issued a public statement effectively admitting the fraud, made a fulsome apology and paid me £475,000 damages.

In taking on this litigation, I feared I may never work in a multinational advertising agency again and this turned out to be the case. After two years as Managing Director of a small London advertising agency, I established The Salmon Agency in 1999. Soon after this, I began to suffer chronic back pain from an old rugby injury and in time, after four operations, found the active life of managing a business difficult to sustain.

So I started to write as, back in the day, my teachers had thought I could do.

In the hands of the NHS, I witnessed the suffering some people are forced to endure and I began to feel that the understanding of human behaviour and the creative talent I had worked with in advertising could be better applied to improving the lives of the unlucky people in the world.

From 2009-15, a full 'parliamentary period' if you like, I wrote the blog 'A Different Hat' on BrandRepublic.com. I have had no vested interests to protect, no selfish cause to promote. Just a naïve hope that, one day, something I have written might make someone else's life better.

I have re-ordered my posts from chronological order in which they were published to the subject matter to which they relate. In this way, I do hope that, in here somewhere, is something that might make your life a little better too. I have divided my 'blog books' into two:

1. '*Thoughts on Life and Advertising*' is based on my own working life.

2. '*Ideas for Britain*' deals with society on a wider, more political, level.

I hope you enjoy reading them.

Hugh Salmon

16 AUGUST 2016

A BIT ABOUT BREXIT

Since publishing this book as an ebook last year, the EU referendum has exposed the divisions in society I was railing about throughout the 2010-15 coalition parliament. On 16 June 2016, a week before the referendum, I wrote this letter to the Daily Telegraph which was acknowledged but not printed:

SIR –
    In voting whether or not to remain in Europe, it is necessary to define the word 'Europe':
    Before 2004, the sixteen member states of the EU were: Austria, Belgium, Cyprus, Denmark, France, Germany, Greece, Ireland, Italy, Luxembourg, Malta, Netherlands, Portugal, Spain, Sweden, UK.
    Since 2004, the following twelve states have been admitted: Bulgaria, Croatia, Czech Republic, Estonia, Finland, Hungary, Latvia, Lithuania, Poland, Romania, Slovakia, Slovenia.
    As anyone who has seen the Alan Bennett play 'The Lady in the Van' knows,

you can have one person living in your drive but not twenty-eight – especially if you
have very little historic or cultural affinity with the new arrivals.

Europe and the 'EU' are not the same thing.

It is that simple.

This letter was more than a personal view. It was a reflection of what the British public had fed back to me as a parliamentary candidate in 2010 and since. The enlargement of the EU in 2004 was a political cock-up of monumental proportions, possibly catastrophic proportions. If this had not happened, a referendum need never have been called and Britain would still be in the EU.

Hugh

NB By their nature, blog posts feature hyperlinks to other online articles and references. Because this paper copy of these posts cannot include hyperlinks all I can say is that the eBook verison of this book is closer to these blog posts as they were written.

1
ADVERTISING AND MARKETING MATTERS

1.1 How the UK Government ignored the most basic law of advertising

11 October 2013 09:07

The Rt Hon Theresa May, Secretary of State for the Home Office has announced that she wishes to create a 'hostile environment' for illegal migrants to Britain. But early attempts to do this run the risk of alienating those of us who have every right to be here.

In July, the Home Office, led by Ms May, launched an advertising campaign against illegal immigrants to the UK. The chosen message was as follows:

In the UK illegally?
106 arrests last week in your area
GO HOME OR FACE ARREST
Text HOME to 78070 for free advice, and help with travel documents

The media channel used to transmit this message was 'poster vans' which were driven through six London boroughs where, apparently, 'illegal immigrants are likely to be'.

I was one of many who found this to be a particularly tasteless piece of work and posted to this effect on Twitter and LinkedIn. But 224 people felt more strongly than me and complained to the Advertising Standards Authority (ASA) who, this week, ruled:

'The ad must not appear again in its current form. We told the Home Office to ensure that in future they held adequate substantiation for their advertising claims and that qualifications were presented clearly.'

In relation to the phrase 'GO HOME', the ASA weasled as follows:

'We acknowledged that the phrase "GO HOME" was reminiscent of slogans used in the past to attack immigrants to the UK.... We recognised

3

that the poster, and the phrase "GO HOME" in particular, were likely to be distasteful to some in the context of an ad addressed to illegal immigrants.... However, we concluded that the poster was unlikely to cause serious or widespread offence or distress.'

Whatever the ASA have found, who are the people who thought up and created this distasteful piece of work – and who on earth approved it?

Whoever they are, surely they must know that all advertising in the UK must be:

Legal, decent, honest and truthful

The ASA makes no secret of this requirement:

'Our mission is to ensure that advertising in all media is legal, decent, honest and truthful, to the benefit of consumers, business and society.'

'Legal, decent, honest and truthful' is a phrase that was cemented into my mind on the first day of my advertising career. It is the DNA of the UK advertising business.

I will leave it to you to judge whether these posters were 'decent' or 'to the benefit of society' or not, but there is an even more fundamental aspect of advertising of which the Home Office seems to have been ignorant or ignored.

As ever, David Ogilvy said it for me:

'Do not address your readers as though they are gathered together in a stadium. When people read your copy, they are alone.'

This is the most basic law of advertising and one that I have stuck to throughout my career. It is, if you like, in my professional DNA.

It means that, however you define your 'target audience' in terms of the media you select, the content of your message must be such that you would be comfortable to say it to one person – not some amorphous group.

Whether you are in advertising or marketing or the media or are ever anything to do with the communications business, you must remember that any form of communication between human beings is a one-to-one thing.

I cannot over-emphasise how important this is.

So let's re-look at this poster van and consider its 'GO HOME' message as a transmission from the Home Office to one person – alone.

For example, what would happen if Theresa May were to stand outside an underground station in London and – for this is what this poster did – say to passers by on a one-to-one basis in this multi-racial, multi-cultural, cosmopolitan capital city of ours?

'Are you in the UK illegally? GO HOME.'

'Are you in the UK illegally? GO HOME.'

'Are you in the UK illegally? GO HOME.'

It might be that such an approach would not only provoke the 'hostile environment' Theresa May seeks but also a hostile response.

For, if she carried on behaving like this and continued to transmit her slogan to each passer by, she might be arrested by the police for breaching the peace or causing an affray – or even, perhaps, a riot.

And then, subject to the extent of the affray and damage caused, she might even find herself sentenced to a spell in prison.

And which Government Department is responsible for police and prison?

Yes, you've guessed it. The Home Office.

You couldn't make it up, could you?

1.2 BRANDING: UNDERSTANDING THE IMPORTANCE OF TRUST

23 APRIL 2013 09:04

When I joined the advertising business, there was a new buzzword called 'marketing'. Few knew what it meant. At Ogilvy & Mather, where my career was born, we had a guy – yes, one person in the whole agency – whose job was to explain this new concept to our clients.

Now, some people argue, everything is marketing.

In his wonderful, intelligent lecture on screenwriting, Charlie Kaufman said:

> 'They're selling you something. And the world is built on this now. Politics and government are built on this. Corporations are built on this. Interpersonal relationships are built on this.... it has all become marketing.'

In this sense, within the space of my career, marketing has gone from nothing to everything.

That's some journey.

Now, it seems, there is another word that is commonly used and little understood. It is the word 'brand', the application of which is called 'branding'.

What is branding?

There is no easy answer for, as David Ogilvy said:

> 'Brand image is an amalgam of many things – name, packaging, price, style of advertising, and, above all, the nature of the product itself.'

'The nature of a product' can be defined in terms of 'rational' and 'emotional' benefits.

If your clients tell you the truth, rational benefits are easy to identify. The trouble is the rational benefits of a product are often the same as its competitors. Commercial success depends on the identification, and often creation, of emotional points of difference.

I love this part of my job because, to define the emotional values of a brand, you need to understand how human beings think and behave.

And, as I hope you find in all my posts, people are interesting aren't they?

This is why the best way to understand a brand is to think of it as a person, a human being, replete with a complex blend of rational and emotional characteristics.

In life, the way we behave influences other people to like or dislike us on a sliding scale. If you are nice, people like you. If you are horrid, they don't. You may or may not care about this.

But brands do care whether or not you like them, particularly if they want you to buy them.

So what is the one thing brands must do to make you like them? Again, David Ogilvy has the answer. He called it a consumer promise:

'A promise ... is a benefit for the consumer. It pays to promise a benefit which is unique and competitive, and the product must deliver the benefit you promise.'

To deliver a promise, a brand must tell the truth.

And people must trust the brand to do so.

Sadly, it seems, trust is an evaporating characteristic in society today. As I pointed out in my last post, although you and I trust our doctors, politicians don't.

Who, in my life, have I trusted but trust no more?

I won't name individual brands, but here are some of the sectors they are in:

I don't trust cyclists.
I don't trust horse racing.
I don't trust food companies.
I don't trust supermarkets.
I don't trust loyalty cards.
I don't trust marketing.
I don't trust newspapers.
I don't trust banks.
I don't trust business.

I don't trust priests.
I don't trust the police.
I don't trust politicians.★
You?

★   In the online version of this post, each of the categories on this list are hyperlinked to
the reason why I do not trust them.

1.3 IT MAY BE RIGHT. IT MAY BE GOOD. BUT IS IT INTERESTING?

29 JULY 2014 19:26

David Ogilvy said this about advertising:

'You can't bore people into buying your product, you can only interest them into buying it.'

As my advertising career began with Ogilvy, I have been interested in 'interesting' for a very long time.

In today's world, is advertising interesting?

First, as any adman knows, we need to consider the competition which, in terms of interesting, includes all the other things that compete for people's interest.

Next, we need to establish whether there are different levels of interesting? Are all interestings equal? Or are some more interesting than others? How interesting does an interesting have to be to get noticed?

Is there a league table of interesting where, like those tedious research questionnaires, there is 'very interesting' at the top of the table and 'mildly interesting' at the bottom? Or is interesting more ruthless than this? It's interesting or it's not interesting. An interesting can be interesting but it can't be more interesting than another interesting. Is that how it is?

If you are not in, you are out.

Talking of cricket, to Englishmen like me the BBC Radio programme 'Test Match Special' (TMS) defines our Englishness by evoking happy memories of a balmy childhood, a poetic love of language, hazy cricket pitches on gentle village greens and the reassuring sound of willow caressing leather as the ball bumbles and bounds and bubbles to the boundary.

This week, England played India at Lord's, the home of cricket. Here, the imagery reflects a wider, more worldly hue. The Far Pavilions, the Nawab of Pataudi, the flashing blade of Tendulkar, the hustle of Mumbai, the heat of Ganganagar and the chilly foothills of the Western Ghats. A world I have known only in words and pictures. But interesting? Yes, for sure.

This year, I have to confess, and hate to say it, and am aware of the treason of the offence, I have felt a feather of negative thoughts and creeping doubts while listening to TMS. I have begun to feel an increasing banality, a predictability, a repetitiveness I have not heard before.

How can this be?

Is it the prevailing media trend where retired cricketers, captains of their country no less, base their comments on the smug belief that if you did not spend years of your life playing cricket, interesting about cricket you cannot be? These people are beginning to bore me. Sorry.

Lesson One. If people find you interesting, don't take their interest for granted.

In my lifetime, another media institution has emerged. It is the TV arts programme, The South Bank Show. Earlier this summer there was a profile of John Lloyd, legendary producer of Not The Nine O'Clock News, Spitting Image and Blackadder.

I discussed John Lloyd in my book 'Thoughts on Life and Advertising'. You remember. He's the guy who said:

'Intelligence is something you're given. Kindness? That takes effort.'

Interesting thought, eh?

To me, John Lloyd is very interesting. What interests me most about him is his realisation that, as a BBC employee, he was not getting a share in the commercial success of the programmes he was instrumental in creating. He realised he would have to go it alone and create a 'format' which he owned, and could develop and expand and profit from, himself.

And what interests me even more about John Lloyd is that not only did he recognise this need but he had the talent and intelligence and drive to do it.

He created QI.

QI stands for Quite Interesting.

And so I find QI interesting but, as you would expect, only quite interesting. Perhaps this is why I rarely watch it. Don't get me wrong, if nothing else is on, if other people in the room are watching it, I am happy to watch QI. But I am only quite happy. For QI is not very interesting, is it? It is only quite interesting. Actually, sometimes I find QI rather facile and even smug. And facile and smug are not very interesting either, are they? Not interesting at all.

Lesson Two. It is better to be very interesting than quite interesting.

Let's get back to advertising. Is advertising interesting? It should be. David Ogilvy said so.

Attracting my interest, these days, is very difficult. I have admitted my interest in Test Match Special and The South Bank Show. But, these days, I am bombarded with interesting like never before.

I have interesting meetings and interesting telephone calls. I receive interesting email and text messages. I find interesting articles on interesting websites. Interesting people say interesting things and link me to more interesting people and more interesting things on Twitter. My Facebook friends are interesting too. They link me to websites whose reason for being is interesting. I love this priest singing his sermon to Leonard Cohen's 'Hallelujah'. Interesting? Ok, perhaps not. But fun.

And get this. I never do anything without my iPad by my side. It is always with me. Whenever I am reading or watching or listening to anything interesting, I look up any number of thoughts that come to mind. How tall is that lady? Who did she marry? What films was she in? Isn't she dead? Questions such as this were interesting to me at the time but the next day, minutes later even, they become irrelevant and forgotten and no longer interesting at all.

Lesson Three. Do not assume that what you find interesting will interest other people.

There is a lot of interesting about.

Next year, there will be a General Election.

Will it be interesting?

Will the party leaders be interesting?

Will they have interesting things to say?

Will they have interesting new ideas to announce?

Will they develop more interesting ways of advertising themselves to us?

Will they have listened to the wise words of David Ogilvy?

It will be interesting to see, won't it?

1.4 HOW AN ADVERTISING AGENCY COULD HELP DEFEAT ISLAMIC STATE

16 OCTOBER 2014 13:41

On 4 October, Lord Dannatt, who was introduced as a former 'Chief of the General Staff and Head of the Army for several years and knows the Middle East well', was interviewed on BBC Radio 4.

He said:

'We are all united in the fact that the so called Islamic State, and these ISIL fighters, are an abomination and they have got to be confronted and they have got to be faced down'....

This has to be looked at on several levels. Yes, of course there is a military level.....

One is very much on the coalition building. But there are other levels at which we have got to go at this.

Another is the diplomatic and political framework, particularly to get that changed in Iraq and steps are quite helpful there.

But I think the other thing is the mindset. This is – at its worst, its best, its deepest – a battle for minds here.

And although Islamic State and ISIL have got to be destroyed, they also have to be discredited. It's got to be unattractive to young people in this country to want to go and join this movement...

We've got to win that battle for the hearts and minds of decent Muslim people around the world.'

The presenter asked:

'But Governments can't win that battle, can they?'

To which we all know the answer is 'no'. But what politicians – and the military for that matter - can do is engage with people who are experts in changing hearts and minds.

And, it so happens, this is something at which, in London, we are recognised for being the best in the world.

Yes, these experts are called creative advertising agencies.

And yes, I accept what you may think, that much of the job of creative advertising agencies is to persuade people to change their hearts and minds about such items as margarine, confectionary, soft drinks and hamburgers by which human beings are killed in far more subtle ways than having their heads chopped off.

But, as I tried to show in my recent post about Scotland, major multinational companies spend billions of pounds a year in the business of making products people want to buy and shifting them from their factories into people's houses. In many ways, it is what makes the world go round.

Please don't think they do this for nothing or that they are stupid or don't know what they are doing. Far, far more people who left university this summer wanted to join the advertising and communications business than the army.

All these people are very smart and very creative.

Which is just what this problem needs.

And please don't tell me politicians don't know this. When they need professionals to help change the hearts and minds of people in pursuance of their own interests and their own careers, political parties turn to advertising agencies, as the army might have it, like a shot.

So when Lord Dannatt says 'we've got to win that battle for the hearts and minds of decent Muslim people around the world', there's only one answer.

It's on the doorstep mate.

2
BRITAIN MATTERS

2.1 CATCH-22 OF A ROTTEN POLITICAL SYSTEM

13 OCTOBER 2011 08:58

It is legitimate to discuss political parties as brands. After three weeks of Party Conferences, the Liberal Democrats, Labour and Conservative Parties have shown the world their wares and their performance has been open to debate (sic).

I understand the Party Conferences were so overcome by lobbyists and commercial interests that, last week, the Prime Minister was talking to a half-empty hall. Open debate indeed.

Surely the management of the economy, and the good of the people, is fundamentally important to marketing and the marketing services businesses? In a strong economy, consumers spend more money and hence oil the wheels of the economy, which encourages people to spend more. One follows the other. Everybody is better off.

In a weak economy, such as we have now, the opposite applies.

Marketing companies do have an interest in the politics of our country because the decisions taken by these people directly affect our businesses as well as our personal lives.

The trouble is our political system is rotten to the core. It is at best inefficient and incompetent and, at worst, criminal and corrupt.

Never can there have been a time when so many people close to the heart of government have or are facing criminal records.

Extraordinary, isn't it, that Sian Phillips, a young girl with a conviction for 'affray' can be deemed to be unsuitable, and expelled from, something as facile as The X-Factor, yet, as I discussed here, our Prime Minister is surrounded by people who have been arrested or have, or are about to have, criminal records?

Please note that, having studied and discussed the three Party Conferences, I am talking about the whole system, not the individual political parties. None of them has the answer. I am more interested in human behaviour and real people.

In particular, I am interested in the increasing divergence of our society

17

– and, in a world where there is more connectivity than ever before, why there is such a disconnect between the real world and the Westminster Village.

It is not for me, in this post, to examine and define how we should, as a democratic country, move forward. Not only would it be inappropriate but the upstream thinking required would take too long. Furthermore, this is the kind of task I get paid for (as I was for the NHS brand) and don't give away free on the internet.

But, isn't it strange that our three 'main' parties – Liberal Democrat, Labour, Conservative – are all bound by such outdated idealism and anachronistic dogma? If nothing else, this is what their three recent Conferences have revealed.

In the real world, business has had to adapt to change and been forced to innovate like never before.

In this context, aren't we ashamed that we are governed by such an antiquated, shambolic and corrupt political system?

How can we espouse the virtues of democracy in, say, the Middle East, when our own system is so flawed?

Three facts:

1. Just over 1% of the UK population are members of political parties – put together, less than the Caravan Club! *'Can UK political parties be saved from extinction?'* (BBC).
2. Three and a half million people who are eligible to vote do not bother to register to do so. Where art thou Emily Pankhurst?!
3. At the last General Election 2010, the Conservatives won 36% of the vote (307 seats), Labour 29% (258 seats) and the Liberal Democrats 23% (57 seats).

How many of those who voted did so on the merits of the case or by traditional tribal loyalty? How many are die-hard Tories or Labour through and through?

Very few people realised that the whole system is rotten and corrupt, as we now know. Totally unqualified people are responsible for the expenditure of public funds and, as I have seen myself, there is no accountability in the way they do so.

From a simple analysis of the ratio of votes cast to seats gained, you can see why I posted that the AV Referendum was a laughably inept fiasco – but also why I believe, with 59% of votes cast, the Coalition is more representative than would have been the clear majority that was there for the taking by a better-led Conservative Party.

Surely the time has come for a much more fundamental change in our politics – and a more professional and creative approach to the way we manage our country?

Root and branch innovation is required.

But it will not happen – because it cannot happen.

This is why this is such a brilliant week to be celebrating the 50th anniversary of the publication of Joseph Heller's Catch-22, as relevant today as ever it has been.

As the *Sunday Times* said last week:

'We are all in Heller's "conscript army" now. Why do we have a coalition government? Because nobody liked any of them enough to give them power. Why have I lost my job? Because banks didn't understand how to lend money. Isn't that the point of banks?'

Why can't we change the political system?

Because the only people who can change the system are the people who run the system, which is why they won't change the system.

Classic Catch-22.

One day, someone from somewhere will somehow emerge to make things better.

But it will not be a career politician – and certainly none of our lot.

In the meantime, as well as Catch-22, you might find the book that is said to have inspired Mad Men, Joseph Heller's 1974 novel *Something Happened*, worth a read.

It will help you understand what motivates people and how they think and behave.

Unlike our politicians, who haven't got a clue.

2.2 DO WE FACE THE APOCALYPSE: OR ARE WE IN IT?

9 JULY 2012 08:56

Last week, as part of a creative project with First World War themes, I was privileged to meet the writer Nicholas Mosley.

Before we met, I researched Mosley's fascinating life. I did not have time to read his eighteen novels, but I could read some autobiographical work, including his relaxed account of the incident which won him the Military Cross in the Second World War. It seemed to be more force of circumstance than a considered act of bravery. Mosely said:

> 'In war you are given a structure, and you have to obey it – or not.
> In peace you have to find or make a structure, but then why should you obey it?'

About the First World War, Mosely pointed out there had been a feeling of inevitability – that it was 'an apocalypse that had to happen'. And we all know what did happen.

Then he leant back, looked thoughtfully into the air and said, as only an 89-year-old can:

'I wonder what apocalypse we are facing now?'

As far as I know, we do not face an inevitable war with Germany. With the cuts in the armed forces, budget that were announced last week, I am not sure we are ready for war with anybody.

So is there an enemy within?

Politicians have talked about a 'broken society' but should they be looking at themselves?

Is what Mosley would call the 'structure' falling apart? Corruption, immorality and disgrace ooze through every pore: politics, police, the media, banks, the financial markets and business generally have all been shown to be motivated by self-interest and greed. Glaxo Smith Kline were fined $3billion – yes, $3billion – in the US last week.

Here, our discredited politicians decided on a parliamentary rather than judicial enquiry into the banking scandal – a decision which can only have been in their own self-interest (especially after the pathetically inept cross-examination of Bob Diamond by the Treasury Select Committee). Surely we want the best solution to the banking crisis – not the fastest?

The judiciary seems to be the one and only part of our establishment structure that remains upstanding. Even this observation could only be applied to our judges rather than the legal profession as a whole – much of which serves to cover up, justify and profit from the immoral and fraudulent behaviour of 'establishment' figures.

It gets worse. Not only is the structure falling apart but, without a war to rebuild it, there is no one with integrity and respect to do so. It may be that our judges are all we have left.

And even worse. Faced with an austere, hopeless future - alongside a justifiable loss of faith in 'the system' - how much can the people take? Last year, we witnessed widespread rioting, looting and arson. I fear there is more to come.

Nearly a million British soldiers were killed in the First World War.

Is this what they died for?

2.3 OLYMPIC SUCCESS DEFINES A NEW BRITAIN FOR THE 21ST CENTURY

15 AUGUST 2012 08:47

The subject of my first blog post, over three years ago, was 'Convergence and Divergence' *(see 3.1)*. It discussed an observation made, over twenty years ago, at an international business conference by a heavy-hitting American banker, a breed we respected at the time. He said:

'Over time, convergence is more likely than divergence'.

Watching the Olympics, I have asked myself time after time, lap after lap, if he was right. And I have concluded that no, I don't think he was. It seems both have happened. We have converged and we have diverged.

How so?

From a business perspective there has been convergence. These days, all the talk is of the BRIC markets - Brazil, Russia, India and China which, clearly, are all countries. But drill down to their smaller neighbours and multinational businesses group them on a regional basis. World markets are defined, pretty much, by the five continents which make up the five Olympic rings.

Culturally, the nations of the world, as demonstrated at the Olympic opening and closing ceremonies, have diverged. The country that paraded itself as 'Russia Unified Team' in Barcelona twenty years ago is now a cornucopia of different nations; many of which I would struggle to pinpoint on a map but all of which are demonstrably, and rightly, proud of their own cultural identities. Some of these countries are now in the EU, which is why we are not (HS, July 2016)

As individual human beings, it may be that the biggest social change since the first London Olympics in 1908 is that, where we used to think of ourselves as bound by national borders, and fought wars accordingly, we are now much more plural in our sense of identity. We can embrace a multiplicity of racial and cultural backgrounds and all be British.

In this way, the most enduring legacy of these Olympic Games may not be sporting at all.

Historically, the London 2012 Olympics could mark the moment when the British people accepted, at last, what it means to be British and became comfortable with the cultural diversity we embrace – a diversity which is not defined by our place of birth or the colour of our skin but by the way we have behaved over the last two weeks.

It has become openly clear, as we have broadcast to the world, that Great Britain is so much more than a forced amalgam of England, Scotland, Wales and Northern Ireland.

Obviously, Mo Farah is none of these. He was born in Somalia but is as British as any of us. What makes us proud of him, and why he is a modern British icon, is not the refuge we have provided him or his wonderful English accent – but his gracious humility in victory, his love for his family, and the Bolt-like humanity of his publicly embracing 'normal people' in the stadium.

It is the behavioural values that Mo Farah and all our other athletes have shown that has warmed them to our hearts and brought us together as one nation.

In this way a new, Great, Britain has been launched in the last fortnight.

Let's hope other countries in the world – not to mention our own discredited politicians and corrupt business leaders – can show the same spirit of inclusiveness, integrity, equality, tolerance and freedom well before the Olympic Games come back to London.

2.4 WHY THE SCOTS WOULD BE MAD TO VOTE FOR INDEPENDENCE (NOT THAT I CARE)

9 SEPTEMBER 2014 11:34

So, next week the Scots will decide if they want to be independent.

Let me start by declaring a lack of interest in this issue. A complete lack of interest. I think I may be one-eighth Scottish but I really don't care if I have Scottish blood coursing through my veins, or not. It hasn't affected my life either way.

I have been to Scotland a handful of times. I have watched a couple of rugby internationals in Edinburgh and stayed with some friends in the Borders which was good fun. I may have been to Glasgow once to be interviewed on local radio but I really can't remember. Nor can I be bothered to find out. It really doesn't matter either way.

I wonder how many Scots have heard of 'ASEAN'?

ASEAN stands for the 'Association of South East Asian Nations'. It is the Asian equivalent of the EU. And, Scot or not, you need to know about ASEAN. Especially now.

I worked in the ASEAN region over twenty years ago. Thailand to be precise.

In Thailand, I learnt a lesson that I would like to share with the people of Scotland. I am sure the Scots care as much about me as I do about them but, if they are prepared to consider what I have to say, they may agree that they would be mad to vote for independence next week. Not that I care if they do or not. It is nothing to do with me. As I have said.

There is a thing in marketing called *distribution*.

To all the world's major marketing companies, 'distribution' is key to their business. Fundamental.

Now, I know it is easy to be cynical about marketing. Just as it's easy to be cynical about lawyers or accountants. The UK government is even cynical about doctors, for goodness sake *(see 4.1)*.

24

As the writer Charlie Kaufman said: *'it (the world) is all marketing'*.

Take it from me, your life would be a lot worse without marketing. Your quality of life would decrease. You might not survive at all.

The biggest marketing companies in the world are FMCG businesses.

The acronym 'FMCG' stands for fast moving consumer goods. These products are not described as 'fast moving' because they are jet-propelled, or laxatives. They are fast moving because they move fast off the shelves of your local supermarket.

People want them. People buy them. Lots of them. Often. Every day.

Take it from me, the world's major FMCG companies would not bother to manufacture these products without knowing how they are going to distribute them – and working out how many they are going to sell based on how often their customers will buy them.

This is a more exact science than you might think.

And it can lead to more ruthless decisions than you might like.

Let's go back to Thailand. I wish.

For nearly three years (1988-91), in Bangkok, I managed the biggest advertising agency in Asia outside Japan – and Ogilvy & Mather's third biggest office worldwide (bigger than London).

It was the best advertising agency I worked for. This was nothing to do with me. It was because of the Thai people who worked there. During my short tenancy, all I did was help the agency maintain the lofty status it had achieved before I arrived on the scene.

My key role was to enlighten the bosses of our multinational clients, who invariably came from the USA and Europe, on some basic realities of Thailand and the region – and encourage them to focus their investment on this important growth market.

Most of these bosses knew that the populations of China and India were, at the time, about one billion and 800 million people respectively but many of them, in those days, were ignorant of the facts contained in my first, simple PowerPoint slide.

Here's what it said (with more up-to-date numbers):

Populations in South East Asia (2012)
Indonesia – 245 million
Vietnam – 90 million
Philippines – 95 million

Thailand – 64 million
Burma – 64 million
Malaysia – 30 million
Cambodia – 15 million
TOTAL – 603 million (Source: IMF)

These are just some of the countries in ASEAN. There are smaller, less populated countries too. These include Laos and Singapore but, with populations of six and five million respectively, they are not very important, are they?

Now, let's put Scotland into perspective (if you haven't already).

Here are some population figures closer to home:

EU population (2010) – 501 million
UK population (2010) – 62 million
Scotland population (2013) – 5.2 million

We are talking about distribution. Remember?

Whenever you buy something from a shop, someone somewhere has manufactured that product, designed the packaging, printed the packaging, put the packages into boxes, loaded them onto a lorry, carried them to the shop, taken them out of their boxes and put them on shelves in shops and supermarkets up and down the land.

It is hard work making things easy for you to buy.

And, if you are in the business of making things and taking all this trouble to distribute them, it would be natural for you to not only maximise the number of people who have the opportunity to buy your product but, at the same time, minimise the ferrying around required.

Consider this:

Scotland is a relatively large country. And sparse. The land area of Scotland is 30,265 square miles. With roughly the same population, Singapore is 276 square miles.

Have you got that? To distribute your product to five million people in Singapore you drive around town for a day. To distribute your product to five million people in Scotland would take you, what shall we say, three months?

Or shall we put it another way?

In Indonesia, there are 140 million people on the island of Java alone (get that?). The land area of Java is 53,589 square miles. So, in the three months it would take you to drive around Scotland to reach 5.2 million potential customers, you could drive round Java and reach, what shall we say, 80 million?

If you are one of the world's largest and most important marketing companies, and the people of one of the world's smallest and unimportant countries, like Scotland, decide to strike out on their own and, in so doing, make your life more complicated with different rules and regulations, why would you bother with them?

Great Britain – with 62 million people in 88,745 square miles? Maybe.

Scotland alone – with 5.2 million people in 30,265 square miles? Forget it man.

And don't tell me internet and online websites like Amazon, who charge for postage & packaging, will ride over the Highlands to the lonely Scots' rescue.

They are not going to offer free delivery to the Outer Hebrides are they? They are going to charge an independent Scotland an independent, increased rate for p&p, as with any other country.

This *will* happen. You mark my words.

Now, if you are a Scot with half a brain, or have any idea of how the world goes round, you don't need to know any more, do you? You can stop reading this now. I've made my point.

If, however, you feel your reading of Robert the Bruce (really?) or your penchant for wearing kilts or blowing bagpipes will be any way enhanced by being an independent country – let me spell it out for you.

Just as I don't really care whether Scotland is an independent country, the Scots may say they don't care about the world's biggest and important marketing companies.

This would be a naive and, potentially, rather dangerous position.

I have attended meetings where these companies have developed marketing strategies and plans to maximise their sales to the massive populations in Asia. There are too many customers to ignore, aren't there?

And, when it comes to Scotland, surely the opposite will apply?

An independent Scotland will be easy to ignore.

The largest marketing companies in the world include Nestlé, Procter

& Gamble, Coca-Cola, Unilever, PepsiCo, General Mills, Kraft, Kellogg's and Mars.

You use – and buy – their products every day. They include bottled water, tea, coffee, milk, cheese, yoghurt, sugar, cereals, toothpaste, soap, shampoo, hair care, perfume, skin care, deodorants, beauty products, baby care, nappies, sanitary care, biscuits, chocolate, confectionary, soft drinks, juices, fruit, food, chilled food, frozen food, ice cream, snacks, pizza, pasta, butter, margarine, cooking oil, olive oil, sauces, soup, vegetables, baking products, crisps, tortilla chips, washing powder, fabric conditioner, household cleaners, batteries, canned food and pet foods.

There isn't time or space here to list all their brands (Nestlé alone has close to 8,000 brands). Still don't care? Well, Scotland, you didn't know Pepsi own Quaker Oats did you? Or that Quaker Oats, and therefore Pepsi, owns Scott's Porage Oats? In fact, Pepsi own a mill in your country, in Cupar, which you are about to provide an excuse to close down. Them's great oats in the USofA!

Believe me, in the modern world, you cannot live without these companies.

I have no idea whether the world's biggest marketing companies have any fall-back plans for Scotland. No doubt they will wait and see what happens next week.

Nor have I bothered to read and watch the politicians ranting and raving about this referendum. As history has shown, politicians are the last people who can predict the consequences of their actions. Especially politicians who rant and rave.

In fact, I suspect all this is a career move by a politician with a surname one letter from mine. We haven't seen the Scots marching and rioting in the street on this issue, have we? Or anyone jump in front of a galloping horse? Where has all this come from?

Deluded, delusional politicians are a very dangerous breed.

For if, down the line, their politicians persuade the Scots to launch their own currency or, like Ireland, join the Euro, these kind of manoeuvres will add to the inconvenience of Scotland being part of any company's marketing plans and increase the possibility of Scotland being ignored as some irrelevant little outpost.

If the Scots vote for independence or, one might say, *isolation*, making

Scotland too much of a hassle to deal with, the big FMCG companies of the world could easily:

- increase their prices to levels only rich Scots can afford
- not bother to distribute their products to Scotland at all

If this happens, it would result in:

- the shops and supermarket shelves in Scotland becoming empty and deserted
- the Scottish people living a dirty, smelly, hungry life in poverty and misery

I accept that, in this day and age, such desperate repercussions may be unlikely but why risk it? Either way, I have no doubt the costs of living in rural Scotland are bound to increase in an independent Scotland. Independence will give all suppliers an excuse to review their distribution arrangements to maximise their bottom line.

Mark my words, when the time comes, the food, personal care and household product companies of the world will make cold, rational, ruthless business decisions.

There won't be any emotions involved.

They won't care.

2.5 The London Airport Non-Decision Fiasco

6 February 2014

In business, it is essential to be fast on your feet, identifying new opportunities and reacting to threats as quickly as possible.

In public life, decisions are taken far more slowly, if at all, and, often, for all the wrong reasons.

A prime example of this has been the lack of a decision to fulfil the market need for the expansion of London Airport.

Our political leaders have been aware of this issue since well before December 2006, when the Department for Transport 'published a progress report on the strategy' which led, in November 2007, to a public consultation.

The plan was supported by businesses, the aviation industry, the British Chambers of Commerce, the Confederation of British Industry and the Trades Union Congress.

But it was cancelled on 12 May 2010 by the new coalition government.

Instead, in September 2012, an independent commission was established and will report in summer 2015 – just weeks after the next general election.

A couple of weeks ago, there was another row as opposing forces clashed.

What is all the fuss about?

Well, by some quirk of history, the aeroplanes that take off and land at Heathrow Airport fly right over London, our most populous city.

Their noise plays a constant, minute-by-minute, rumbling groan overhead.

The closer to Heathrow they fly, over Vauxhall, Battersea, Wandsworth, Putney, Richmond and onwards and upwards and downwards, the more the rumbling groan becomes a roar and then a boom and then, as they pass over Windsor Castle, a crescendo. What must the Queen think of a Sunday morning? Have you heard the noise Her Majesty has to endure?

Sorry, didn't you hear that?

HAVE YOU HEARD THE NOISE HER MAJESTY HAS TO ENDURE?!

You get the picture.

And, would you believe it, some people think we should build another runway at Heathrow so we can endure even more traffic and – you guessed it – more noise! MORE NOISE!

See?

There are various options under consideration, including Boris Island.

Flushed with his global success at the London Olympics, Boris wants to build a new airport in the Thames Estuary. This way, the noise of the aeroplane traffic is above water rather than people and, in the most public way possible, London can be seen as the vibrant, forward-thinking, prosperous capital city the Olympics revealed us to be.

Inevitably, there are Nimbies on either side:

The anti-Boris Nimbies complain about the bird life that will be affected. The Heathrow-expansion Nimbies rail about more congestion in our green and pleasant land – and, of course, more noise! MORE NOISE! Not again...

Here is the business perspective:

1. Bigger and better airport facilities are a need – not a want. The leaders of 35 of our biggest companies stressed this in a letter to the papers.
2. The opposing views of the Nimbies are not going away. Their objections will not change over time. Although one can understand both sides of the argument, delaying the decision will not sway these people either way. Their positions have been fixed for years.

Well, that is not quite true. A year ago, a helicopter crashed to the ground in Vauxhall, London. The pilot and a pedestrian were killed.

Let this be a warning. The dangers of walking to work on a London pavement should not include the possibility of an aircraft landing on your head. God forbid, a worse accident may one day happen.

This, to me, is the deal breaker. On the balance of all the arguments, the correct decision would be to back the Boris vision and commit to this as soon as possible.

I may be right in this view. I may be wrong.

Either way, a quick decision is vital.

But this can't happen, can it?

Here is the political perspective:

Although Boris Airport is forecast to create 250,000 jobs, there is a need to consider the position of the 200,000 people in the Heathrow area who depend on the airport for their livelihood.

This is an understandable concern and, whichever way it goes, every effort must be made to lessen the impact of this decision on these good people. Having said this, as the new airport would take several years to construct, there is time to develop the support plan they deserve.

In fact, as it has been announced that a new city is required in the South of England, perhaps Heathrow City would be its own, bold option. How about that for an upstream creative idea?

Sorry, I digress.

You do realise, don't you, that it is not the interests of local people that concern our political masters. As ever, their own interests come first.

We know this because it has already happened. The politicians have shown, yet again, that they do not care about anyone other than themselves.

To forecast the way this airport decision will go, you need to analyse the political pressures involved. What constituencies in the Heathrow area do these 200,000 people live in? Are they 'marginal' or are they 'safe'? How could the threat of unemployment of these 200,000 people affect the vote? Which political party would lose seats? Which would gain?

Apparently, the answer is that 'David Cameron is likely to lose seats in constituencies affected by airport expansion'.

So, surprise, surprise, what has our great leader decided to do? Or, rather, not do?

The answer is that, as the Airport Commission will not present their findings until two months after the next general election, David Cameron will not, after a full five years of government, be making a decision on this very important matter at all. Even his own MPs have accused him of 'dithering'.

I am afraid this is just one example of how the imminence of the next general election will override the good governance of Britain until after May 2015.

A sad state of affairs, isn't it?

3

GOVERNMENT
MATTERS

3.1 CONVERGENCE AND DIVERGENCE

13 NOVEMBER 2009 13:59

Two decades ago, I was privileged to attend a conference in Bangkok where the Key Note Speaker was the CEO of a major American Bank. He may even have been The President. Certainly, he was very important. He had a bodyguard and he arrived in his Bank's private plane (as it was private, he probably kept it for himself).

His thesis was that 'Over time, convergence is more likely than divergence'. In other words, all of us would grow closer together – culturally, educationally, religiously, morally, in every way.

I thought this was really clever. The Asian markets were booming, Vietnam was opening up and curious. And certainly there was much more regional awareness. Asian countries knew much more about what was happening in their region than we did in Europe. Above all, there was massive demand for 'international' products and brands.

Two weeks ago, I read 'A Week in December' by Sebastian Faulks. Set in modern-day Britain, the book exposes a society that couldn't be more polarised – culturally, educationally, religiously or morally, in every way.

So what are the media and marketing industries doing to help overcome this divergence?

After all, every year a select few of the cream of British youth yearn for jobs in marketing and advertising – and they learn how to communicate vital messages to the consumer population.

Hardly surprisingly, in a competitive world, these messages are designed to divide rather than unite – brand v brand, service v service, product v product, Pepsi v Coke for pity's sake. We create USP's which are, by definition, unique. They are different.

Now, just look at the divergent tabs along the top of the Brand Republic Home Page – advertising, creative, design, digital, direct marketing, market research, marketing, media, public relations and sales promotion.

With all this skill and expertise and amazing creative talent, as a society, can't we bring these divergent specialisms together to communicate the things that we all agree on and that should, but don't, bind us – right and wrong, the importance of education, respect for others, 'do as you would be done by', tolerance, kindness, freedom?

Only this week, at the Berlin Wall, Angela Merkel talked about "the incredible gift of freedom".

So, who is working to help our communities converge rather than diverge? It certainly is not the 'main' political parties. Over the next few months, they are going to be electioneering at us. They'll be dressing up in red and yellow and blue and green. What a great party it is all going to be.

The trouble is that at the end of it all, whoever wins, we will have endured months of these people telling us how much they can change things and how *DIFFERENT* they are (they had better be).

Talking of colourful people, I once (and only once) attended the Annual NABS Boxing Dinner. A worthy charity to be sure, but this was one sick evening. We all dressed up in our finest and converged to watch some impoverished kids beat the hell out of each other while the media glitterati drank their brandy, smoked their cigars and cheered the lads on. If you were sitting close enough to the ring, you got splattered with blood.

And then, just to ram home the difference between the rich and the poor, a bidding war started between the clients and agencies for the free space various media channels had put up for grabs. Hundreds of thousands of pounds were raised. A bloody fortune.

Thankfully, and inevitably, NABS moved on to newer, more tasteful events. But, without running off with NABS' main income stream, can't this fund-raising principle be applied to society on a wider level?

On 26 October, Warren Buffet said on the BBC:

"Most of the rich people in the United States, and probably in the UK too, would not have done quite as well as if they had lived in Bangladesh or some place like that. They may think they did it all by themselves but society has done an awful lot for them. And if you get the chance to live in a very rich society then you ought to have a taxation system and a personal value system where you believe that a lot of that ought to go back to the people who got the short straws in life".

The technology designed to bring us together is driving us apart.

Surely this new technology, which all of us are using as communications, tools, will have freed up more 'spare media space' than ever?

So in this divergent world, can't we, as a business sector, including clients and agencies, be more creative about using our talents and resources to define and create messaging which might help overcome the divisions in the society we live in?

From time to time, in the trade press, I have seen hypothetical lists of 'teams of all the talents'.

Why can't we do this for real and bring our resources and our skills together to communicate the importance of the values that *UNITE* us?

Wouldn't this be a great brief?

3.2 THE CONSERVATIVES MAY BE DOING THE RIGHT THING, BUT IN THE WRONG WAY

29 OCTOBER 2010 07:25

With all these massive changes in our social welfare system going on, I wonder if they are being communicated with honesty and, in particular, if the Conservative element of the Coalition couldn't be transmitting their message in a less damaging way to their brand?

Here's my story (sorry it's another long one):

In 2007, a professional contact, who has become a personal friend of mine, happened to be appointed to head up one of the Study Review Groups in Iain Duncan Smith's Centre for Social Justice.

He asked me if I would run my eye over his team's final report. I won't say which one but it is an area of society in which I have some experience and expertise. And I like to think he asked me because he would value the wisdom of my input.

Anyway, once I had read the report, which ran to several hundred pages, we met to discuss my response. Overall, it was a very worthy piece of work on which I had a few minor comments.

I would like to emphasise that I was not a member of the Conservative Party and I am not now, but I am prepared to believe that Iain Duncan Smith is an innately good man and that what he was trying to achieve was genuine and for the overall public good, particularly the underclass in our society that rarely appears in our target audience profiles in the commercial world.

And, to give him his due, as an ex-leader of the Conservative Party, Duncan Smith could have spent his time making money on the after-dinner speaking circuit. But he didn't. He got downbeat and dirty and tried to understand the real world out there. As a human being, as much as a politician, I admire him for that (not that they have PR'd it very well).

However, when we met, I did say to my friend that, as and when a General Election was called, there would be an over-arching barrier for all of Duncan Smith's Social Review Groups to overcome.

This would be the deeply entrenched views held by many of the electorate about the Conservative Party and that these views would provoke a response that would override any specific policies, however worthy, just because they came from the Tories.

I advised that there was a communications challenge for the Conservatives to present themselves in a new light and, as a brand, to persuade people to throw away their old prejudices and re-consider the Tories in order for Duncan Smith's initiatives to be accepted more readily and objectively and on their own merits.

As a non-member of the Conservative or any other political party, I felt, from a professional point of view – if they were a client, if you like – that this would be an interesting intellectual challenge (and, ok I admit it, a bit of a pitch).

My friend suggested I submit my views to the Central Office of the Party, which I did.

So here is the verbatim presentation I provided, converted word-for-word, from a PowerPoint presentation. Sorry it is rather long, and please note it was written three years ago, but it leads to a couple of points I would like to make at the end which I think are influencing the current national debate.

I will separate out the presentation by lines of asterisks so you can go straight to the end, if you like:

★★★

HOW TO WIN THE NEXT ELECTION.
PRESENTATION TO THE CONSERVATIVES.
(THE SALMON AGENCY. DECEMBER 2007)

BACKGROUND

Historically (until 'New Labour'?), it was much easier to differentiate between Conservative and Labour. There were much clearer ideological differences between the two parties – and these differences were much easier to define: tax, privatisation etc.

Now the two parties aren't seen to be very different at all: they both fight for the same 'Centre Ground.'

To this day, New Labour harps back to the record of the Conservative

Governments from 1979-1997. Yet, despite this, many of the policies of that period have been accepted, maintained and developed by Labour *(see Appendix)*.

If the ideological wars are over, it was the Conservatives who won them. This is the *truth*.

What is now called 'the centre ground' is where Conservatives have been all along – Labour had to move position, not the other way round. Brazenly, New Labour have stolen the Conservative position – and are being allowed to get away with it! This cannot be allowed to happen.....

What next?

The Conservatives have the right to claim:

i)   that the Conservatives who won the 'ideological war' – the Conservatives were right all along
ii) that Labour, particularly Gordon Brown, have been forced to abandon all their past, socialist, principles
iii) that Labour had to move to what is now called the 'Centre Ground' (which, ideologically, has always been the Conservative position)
iv) that Labour don't know HOW to govern Britain now they are there
v)   that, having won the ideological war, the Conservatives will now define a new politics to drive Britain (and the world) forward into the 21st century.

This is an inexorable logical flow. The question is, how to do it?

The 6 'C's (of Conservative Communications)

We believe the Conservatives have 6 'C's to consider:

- Cynicism
- Context
- Competitiveness
- Clarity
- Creativity
- Confidence

And that the following six pages will help the Conservatives win the next election......

Cynicism

Many of the electorate are cynical about the Conservatives (particularly in regard to the role of the State Sector in health and education and 'caring' for the needy).

Cynicism is an emotion which will not be overcome by rational arguments, particularly when presented as 'policy proposals.'

(Consumer insight – people are not interested in policies. Policies are boring, politicians do them).

Cynicism will not be overcome when presented in the negative.

(Consumer insight – people are not interested in 'broken societies', they want positive messages).

Cynicism and suspicion can be overcome by:

- the personal charisma of a particular leader
- an outstanding track record of delivery by one party (or, by default, by the chaotic state of the other)
- creating a simple, easy-to-understand over-arching context

Context

The Conservatives have a unique opportunity to take the high ground of British, and perhaps even international, politics.

Britain – and the rest of the world – exists as a market economy in a world market.

The old, socialist agenda was wrong – the Conservatives were right (sic).

The Conservatives have the right to claim this victory – and should be proud of it.

BUT... the price that has been paid by the anti-socialist, 'market economy' victory is electoral cynicism that Conservativism is a 'money-means-all' philosophy.

This can be overcome by a simple, easy-to-understand over-arching context:

- by claiming victory against the old, socialist agenda
- by building on this undeniable truth
- by re-defining the role of Government in a modern 'market economy'
- and so establishing a competitive point of difference against Labour....

Competitiveness

The percentage of the electorate bothering to vote is decreasing. They find it increasingly difficult to differentiate between the parties. Some generalisations:

- 'politicians' speak in a language people don't understand
- people aren't interested in 'policies'
- especially when parties steal them from each other
- the major parties are seeking the same 'centre ground'
- and are seen to be largely interchangeable
- a competitive point of difference is staring the Conservatives in the face:

"ROLE OF GOVERNMENT"

Clarity

There is a massive gap between Conservatives and Labour here:

- it is NOT the Government or a Minister's job to give you a flu jab
- it is NOT the Government or a Minister's job to teach your child to read
- it is NOT the Government or a Minister's job to arrest the local thief

GORDON BROWN THINKS IT IS!

It *IS* the Government's job to *ENABLE* these things (not *CONTROL* them). And to do so efficiently and effectively.

There is an opportunity (a need?) for the Conservatives to ruthlessly examine every aspect of society and define the part Government has to play in it. In fact, through the Policy Groups, most of the work is already being done...

Creativity

The work of each of the Policy Groups could be presented more creatively i.e....

- more different (unique)
- more relevant
- more engaging

By applying one, simple over-arching context: "ROLE OF GOVERNMENT"

This is where The Salmon Agency can help by bringing fresh, creative thinking to each of the Policy Groups within this context. We already have some new ideas we can bring to the party.

And thus help the Conservatives become a party of positive change by presenting:

- a clear point of difference vs Labour
- an unarguable, rational reason to vote Conservative
- an exciting vision of a new, world-leading Britain
- and the emotional reward that we can all be part of a new future

Confidence

Right across society, the Policy Groups are doing a *FANTASTIC* job identifying problems ('a broken society') and producing 'policies' to overcome them, but:

- people don't care about policies (they don't see them as 'solutions')

- and Labour can steal them

People want principles and values. So, it would be more *POSITIVE* to communicate that the Conservatives:

i)   have an unqualified commitment to the State sector, especially in defined areas e.g. Health, Education, Protection etc (needs discussion)
ii) are absolutely committed to helping the poor and the needy, whoever they are and wherever they may be
iii) have ruthlessly interrogated every aspect of society and identified who:
    • need the help and protection of more effective Government
    • would benefit from the freedom of less intrusive Government

And thus make more of the electorate *FEEL* confident enough to vote Conservative.

Conclusion

1. Create clear space between Conservative and Labour.
2. Take the moral and economic high ground by claiming victory over the old, socialist ideologies propounded by Labour (especially Gordon Brown).
3. Promise the electorate a new, exciting future for Britain (and the developed world).
4. Reassure the electorate that the Conservatives care about each and every UK citizen, including the poor, unhealthy and needy, and have thought through the way 'The State' can help every single one of them...
   ...BY...
5. Understanding and re-defining the 'Role of Government' in today's market economy
6. Re-thinking and re-presenting the work of the Policy Groups in this context (including fresh, 'upstream' creative thinking applied by The Salmon Agency)
7. Developing a new, over-arching communications strategy based on principles (not 'policies')
8. And so presenting a new 'vision' to make the Conservatives (and David Cameron) a more relevant, more attractive – and more electable – alternative to Labour.

Appendix

From 'How to Get Rich' (2007) by Felix Dennis (Britain's '36th Richest Person'):

> *"I have little time for many of Margaret Thatcher's policies....But she smashed the union's grip on Britain's economy and helped create a climate in which denationalisation of major industries became the cry for Socialist, Liberal and Conservative alike. And if you don't like my reading of history, ask Tony Blair ....*
>
> *... I, and many thousands like me, will always be grateful to the old handbag for bringing the sweet aroma of competition to what, after all, is a nation of shopkeepers ...*
>
> *...I am a Labour man born and bred. I will die voting Labour. It's a tribal thing ...*
>
> *...Even so, that lack of competition nearly ruined Britain...it brought*

us to the edge of an abyss from which I doubt we would have crawled out in my lifetime. Thatcher dragged us back from the brink and nobody knows that better than the current Labour administration. After all, they stole many of her and John Major's policies, and made them their own. Very successfully, too.

Now that's how to handle competition!"

★★★

So that was my presentation.

It was submitted to Steve Hilton and Andy Coulson and their PAs. Steve Hilton agreed to a meeting but I couldn't make the proposed date. I was on a photographic shoot in The Bahamas – well, you have to put your existing clients first, don't you? And, by the time I had come back from the sun, he had gone cold on me.

Since then, the Conservatives have launched their 'Big Society' initiative. How closely is that related to re-defining the 'Role of Government'? I will leave it to you to decide.

So why do I, four years later, bring all this up again?

Well, I am concerned that the Coalition are using the deficit bequeathed to them as an excuse for making social changes they were planning to introduce anyway.

For example, take this week's housing benefit announcement, presented as 'necessary cuts'.

An ex-colleague of mine has business interests in Barbados. Twice now, he has flown, in the luxury and comfort of a Business Class seat, next to a guy who holidays in Barbados six times a year but lives in a council house back home.

Now, I suspect Iain Duncan Smith spotted that there are people like this and, as I think most of us would agree, there is something about it that is not quite right.

But, by wrapping what should and could have been all the positive 'Big Society' ('Role of Government') social changes into some sort of response to the deficit they inherited is not only negative and dishonest but will result in the following:

1. Those who want to think of the Conservatives as cold and calculating

will continue to do so. The Tories, especially the rather freaky George Osborne (look at his face as he sits behind David Cameron at PMQS!), have failed to show what they would call 'the common touch'.

2. The Liberal Democrats will realise that they have been conned (sic) and that the Conservatives have used the deficit to force through some of these radical social changes under the guise of deficit cuts.

3. When the LibDems do realise they have been conned, the survival of the Coalition will be under threat, which will be a pity because I like it.

4. Further divisions in an increasingly divided society.

Surely before charging into these savage cuts, which will affect our businesses and homes, it would have been better management to capitalise and monetise:

i)   the savings and inefficiencies identified by Sir Philip Green
ii) the sale of unneeded physical assets, especially 'Government' property,
iii) the forward value ('securitisation'?) of the Bank shares we now hold?

And *then* cut.

By managing the 'business of Britain' in this way, the Conservatives could have made a positive out of a negative by communicating that cutting was the last, not the first, resort – just as their most diehard critics would expect their natural Tory instincts to be.

As it is, I fear the human effect of a keen but over-enthusiastic new Conservative-led Government will result, at best, in unnecessary suffering and, at worst, social chaos.

I do think that all this could have been avoided by researching these issues and thinking them through (strategy) and then communicating them in a more thoughtful, understanding and humane way (execution).

I hope I am wrong.

3.3 'ROLE OF GOVERNMENT' IN A CAPITALIST SOCIETY

20 JANUARY 2012 15:12

I cannot believe our politicians have only just realised that the 'Role of Government' in a capitalist society is the most fundamental problem they need to solve.

It shows an extraordinary lack of leadership and vision.

I can say this, rather immodestly, because it is exactly what I told them over four years ago – long before the last General Election. Here's my story....

In 2007, a professional contact, who had become a personal friend, was appointed to head up one of the Study Review Groups in Iain Duncan Smith's 'Centre for Social Justice'.

He asked me if I would run my eye over his team's final report. I won't say which but it concerned an aspect of society in which I have some experience and expertise. Once I had done this, we met to discuss my thoughts. Overall, I felt he had developed a very worthy piece of work on which I had a few minor comments.

I would like to emphasise that I was not a member of the Conservative Party and I am not now. But I am prepared to believe that Iain Duncan Smith is an innately good man and that what he was trying to achieve was genuine and for the overall public good, particularly the underclass in our society that never appear in our target audience profiles in the commercial world.

To give him his due, as an ex-leader of the Conservative Party, Duncan Smith could have spent his time making money on the after-dinner speaking circuit. But he didn't. He got downbeat and dirty and tried to understand the real world out there. As a human being, as much as a politician, I admire him for that.

However, I told my friend that, by General Election time, there would be an over-arching barrier for all Duncan Smith's Social Review Groups to overcome.

This would be the deeply entrenched views held by many of the electorate about the Conservative Party and, worse, that the strength of these views would provoke a response that would override any specific policies – however worthy – just because they came from 'Tories'.

I said there was a communications need for the Conservatives to present themselves in a new light – to urge people to throw away entrenched prejudices and re-evaluate the Tories in order for Duncan Smith's initiatives to be accepted more readily, objectively and on merit.

As a non-member of the Conservative or any other political party, I felt, from a professional point of view – i.e. as if they were a client of my strategic marketing agency – that this would be an interesting challenge (and, I admit it, a commercial pitch).

My friend suggested I submit my views to the Central Office of the Party, which I did. I posted the complete presentation on Brand Republic in October 2010 in a blog entitled: 'The Conservatives may be doing the right thing, but in the wrong way' *(see 3.2)*.

In short, my presentation (in 2007, remember) called for a complete re-think of the 'Role of Government' in society today. I argued that the Conservatives had won the ideological wars between socialism and capitalism. Now all they had to do was work out how capitalism could work towards a fairer society in a modern free-market economy.

My presentation was submitted to Steve Hilton and Andy Coulson and their PAs. Steve Hilton agreed to a meeting but I couldn't make the proposed date. I was on a photographic shoot in The Bahamas (well, you have to look after the day job first, don't you?). By the time I had come back from the sun, Hilton had gone cold. We never met.

Imagine my surprise when – yesterday – yes, yesterday! – I read that the Prime Minister used the very words 'Role of Government' in the context of 'a long-awaited speech on capitalism'.

Has he only just thought about this? Didn't he read my presentation? What does this bloke Hilton do all day?!

For this is the issue that is going to define the difference between our political parties from now until the next General Election. Well, not from now. Actually since 2007 when, if he had done what I had told him, Cameron might well have won an outright majority at the General Election in 2010.

I know it is immodest to say so but, because the Conservatives did not bother to work out the 'Role of Government' in the modern world, and the consequent need for they themselves to change within this environment, the human effect of a keen but over-enthusiastic Government has been unnecessary suffering and social chaos.

It is very frustrating that, back in 2007 and again in 2010, I told them this would happen.

Now, years too late, a vital debate has begun.

Hey-ho.

3.4 WHY DON'T LABOUR LAUNCH AN 'UNEMPLOYED UNION' AND A 'DISABLED UNION'?

14 MARCH 2011 09:14

Only a year ago I was out there electioneering as an Independent Candidate in the last General Election *(see Appendix I)*.

In short, alongside many other Independents, I thought the MPs' expenses scandal was an issue that called into account their personal – and collective – integrity.

Surely they could not have each, individually, worked out that they were able to evade Capital Gains Tax by 'flipping' their houses? Did not one of them think of raising a hand to say there was something wrong in this behaviour? Unbelievable. Criminal.

Anyway, as I have a proven and demonstrable track record of financial integrity, I decided to stand up and be counted. At least it would be an interesting experience. And we achieved the local issue for which I campaigned, which pleases me.

During the experience, three Insights emerged which are relevant today:

1. In the political world, they really cannot predict what will happen at an Election. In the event, this is what happened. No one foresaw the Coalition – apart from the exit polls, which were not believed until they were proved right.

2. Within the electorate, many voters are driven by traditional, tribal loyalties. One Labour diehard told me his father would never forgive him if he didn't vote Labour. 'Doesn't he think the world might have changed?' I asked. 'Dunno, he's been dead for 25 years' he replied.

3. The extremes of the Conservative and Labour parties are extremely unsavoury.

I attended a Conservative meeting where I met someone who blamed our economic woes on the Jews. I witnessed Labour tribalism that was physically intimidating *(see 19.3)*.

Below, I will reveal an Insight I have on the middle ground of these two parties.

So, why am I reverting to last year's General Election now, especially – and rightly - when world events are so much at the fore?

Well, the vote on the AV electoral system is less than eight weeks away and, with our interest much directed at Libya and Japan today, I hope you realise what is about to hit you very soon.

This referendum is the glue that has been holding the Liberal Democrats, and hence the Coalition, together. The Liberals have been campaigning, praying and begging for proportional representation since founding of the Electoral Reform Society in 1884.

They would rather the Single Transferable Vote (STV) but, hey-ho, AV would be a massive step in the right direction.

Behind the scenes, since the Coalition came together last year, Nick Clegg has urged and cajoled his party to hang on through every compromising principle, every Conservative balls-up and all Cameron's smug arrogance – all for this referendum. It was Clegg's one big trump card in the Coalition Agreement.

And it is about to happen.

If there is a 'no' vote, there is no way the left-leaning, humane and socially-caring of the LibDem MPs will support the Stalinistic cuts that the Tories have been making. They won't be able to look their constituents in the face, or live with their broken promises, any longer – as the Coalition and their leader have forced them to do.

If there is a 'yes' vote, despite their recent by-election embarrassment, the best chance of the LibDems achieving more seats through the AV system will be the sooner the better. The longer they leave it, the more the economy will recover and the more Labour will get their act together (which they haven't yet, which is why the Labour peers tried to filibuster this Referendum Bill in the Lords).

But, actually, if Labour act quickly and think more strategically, then now may be their best opportunity to regain power (within, I hope, another Coalition).

Here's how it goes.

The perceived wisdom is that Iraq will define Tony Blair's 10 years as Prime Minister.

What if we refuse to accept this analysis?

I am a huge admirer of M&C Saatchi's positioning 'brutal simplicity of thought', so please bear with me through some brutally simple thinking.

First, let us propose that the Thatcher years were not defined by coal miners' strikes or the Falklands war or the Poll Tax.

Let us assume that history will define Thatcherism as the victory of free market economics over socialism. The wall came down. It's as brutally simple as that.

Now let us propose that the Blair years were not defined by the abolition of Clause 4, the Iraq War or the shallowness of New Labour.

And let us assume that history will define Blairism as proof that there is a role for Government (the 'State', if you like) even in free market economies. That simple.

And taking these two consecutive eras, let us question where that leaves us now?

It leaves us in a massive financial mess that is probably not as much Labour's fault as the Tories purport it to be (because the rest of the world is suffering too) and worse than Labour will admit to (although 'there isn't any money left' is pretty bad).

And it leaves us not knowing how the financial wealth generated by a service-driven free-market economy (as opposed to a manufacturing-based economy) can spread wealth down to the underclass in our society that is poorly educated, badly behaved, hopelessly deprived and disgracefully ignored by the rest of us.

This is Labour's opportunity.

I said I would return to an Insight on the 'middle ground' of the Conservative and Labour parties.

The irreversible belief among reasonable-thinking Conservatives is that Labour have always been, and will always be, financially irresponsible. They will spend money on 'the State' that the State does not have.

The irreversible belief among reasonable-thinking Labour supporters is that Tories always put money before people. They have no humanity. They don't care.

This position, I am afraid, is one that the Conservatives, with all their

Old Etonians, multi-millionaires and family trust funds, have already shown to be the case.

So now is the time for Labour to pounce.

Labour have just a few weeks to develop a strategy that delivers just two things:

1. They can manage the economy.

2. They care.

The first challenge will be hard to overcome but they do have a case. They can say they have learnt their lessons, admit they did overspend, emphasise they did not foresee the global economic breakdown and, I am afraid, put Gordon Brown out to dry (and probably Ed Balls, although that may be too executional for now).

The second, and I would argue, is a more important yet more achievable strategy.

Today, millions of people, including public sector workers (even the police and armed forces for goodness sake!) are really suffering under these Conservative cuts. These people don't give a toss about the global economy. They have families to feed, children to educate, relatives to care for and homes and TV licences to pay for.

Labour should disrupt and undermine the Coalition more directly and aggressively.

They should develop innovative solutions that build on their heritage and pull at the heartstrings of their traditional supporters in a way that only Labour can.

In my career, I have learnt that it is unwise to give away upstream thinking and creative ideas for free. If you do, hold the best bit back. The jobsworth who nicks your ideas will foul up the execution of your strategic thinking and steal what should have been your high ground.

As previously discussed, I did this on a professional basis (and as a non-party-member) for the Conservatives in 2007 (see 3.2). For free, I submitted a document to Steve Hilton's office that challenged the 'Role of Government' in modern society.

This, I believe, led to the current Big Society initiative (a potentially Big Idea that, sadly, has been poorly, and anti-socially, executed).

However, as I have given the Tories something for free, I will give this to Labour:

1. As we have moved from a manufacturing to service-led economy, your traditional support within the Trade Unions has become less influential.
2. As we have developed into a service economy, more people have more money. The problem that has emerged is, at the same time, more people have less money. These people are likely to be condemned to a lifetime of unemployment, despair and hopelessness. In only a year, the Tories continue to show they don't care about this. (Iain Duncan Smith had a chance but he has blown it by his ruthless approach).
3. The Labour Party should take their undeniable heritage and develop a strategy to help these people by launching the equivalent of an 'Unemployed People's Union' and a 'Disabled Person's Union'.

Who is fighting these people's corner? I mean really standing up for them, pulling them together and aggressively, not advisedly (as in the Citizen's Advice Bureau), arguing their case at the highest level of Government?

Clearly, it would be bad government for one Government Department to fight against another so, de facto, this will force a simpler, fairer system across society.

Clearly, these Unions will not be funded by the 'members', but by the State. Having said that, it could be argued that these people are more vulnerable than any workers' union. After all, they cannot go on strike. They have no leverage. They just have to accept the ruthless treatment of a ruthless Government.

But they do have a vote. Enter Labour.

If you are unemployed or disabled, Labour and these Unions will be there to help you fill in those forms you don't understand and, more importantly, defend your rights. There will be high-profile public figures to fight your corner and develop innovative ideas to help dig you out of the hole you are in.

Fixing the state we are in can certainly be done in a more caring and humane way. There are lots of brutally simple thoughts and creative ideas just dying to take on this challenge. Those are for later.

4
HEALTH MATTERS

4.1 NHS REFORM: CAN YOUR DOCTOR BE TRUSTED OR NOT?

3 APRIL 2013 09:02

In what may be my most read post to date, DLA Disgrace *(see 6.2)*, I discussed the shameful process that our Government inflicts on the disabled people in our community. It is outsourced to ATOS – 'an international information technology services company'.

Do you know what this means?

It means the Government does not trust your doctor.

How so?

Well, until the Government started paying ATOS to do the job, they trusted your doctor's evidence that your disability was as you were claiming it to be.

Not any more. The Government would rather trust ATOS.

Surely, if doctors provide false declarations on behalf of their patients, they should be named and shamed and punished just as severely as those 'disabled' people who fiddle the system? Wouldn't such an outcome deter rogue doctors from providing false evidence?

For some reason, we don't read about these doctors. Yet they must exist or we would not need this inhuman ATOS technology for the Government to rely on instead.

Given this, is it not strange that, this week, a new law has come into force whereby Primary Care Trusts (sic) and Strategic Health Authorities have been replaced by several hundred 'Clinical Commissioning Groups' run by – you've guessed it – your doctor?!

4.2 NHS – A 'SICK' FUTURE

8 JUNE 2011 08:04

I have a dilemma. As 'A Different Hat' on www.BrandRepublic.com, this is my 100th post.

So I want to make it really special. I want to write about the NHS. Because the NHS is really, really special. And I have an 'upstream' creative solution that may secure its future.

But when I saw a full-page article on the NHS this week, even I could not face reading a full page of political treacle. This is my dilemma.

So here goes.

I know a lot about the NHS – personally and professionally. I was paid to do a project on the NHS brand. It wasn't my highest-paid gig. But it was possibly my most important. Because I value the NHS. And I did a great job *(see 5.4)*.

But the Department of Health were a tricky client. One of the managers said I didn't understand the NHS brand (yes, me). 'Why?' I asked. 'Because you have the wrong pantone colour on your rough layouts'. I'm not joking. Civil servants as ignorant as this manage the biggest 'brand' in the country.

The NHS employs over a million people, although that figure may have been cut by the Government by now. Ah, the Government. Within a few weeks of coalescing, they announced dramatic NHS reforms. Or, rather, the Right Honourable Andrew Lansley CBE MP did. On 10 July 2010 he launched 'Equity and Excellence: Liberating the NHS'.

There was no research and no 'piloting'. Why bother?

Mr Lansley's dad worked for the NHS for 30 years. So he just did it. Except he didn't. On 4 April 2011, he was 'isolated' (another medical term). His reforms were put on 'pause'. That's a weird way to manage a business let alone a country.

And certainly not 'progressive'. By the way, what is 'progressive'? How can 'pause' be 'progressive'? Doesn't the word 'progressive' imply some sort of forward movement?

Anyway, this week, Mr Lansley tried to rescue ('progress'?) his career. He wrote an article called 'Why the health service needs surgery'. Note the word 'why' – not 'how'.

'How' will come from some people called the NHS Future Forum. They have conducted 'an intensive period of listening and engagement'. For which read 'we've done what we should have done in the first place'.

Their report is due this month. They have a big problem to overcome. The cost of the NHS will increase from £130bn in 2015 to £260bn in 2030.

Let me make you a promise. Whatever the NHS Future Forum says, one outcome is guaranteed. This is the important bit.

The solution will require 'competition' – which some will call 'privatisation'. For some, especially Old Labour, NHS 'privatisation' is not acceptable. They will make a hell of a fuss (except they won't be able to, see below).

There's an American billionaire called Stephen Schwarzman. He made his money from a private equity company called Blackstone. Blackstone bought Southern Cross, the UK's biggest care home operator. Southern Cross is in financial doo-doo. But not Mr Schwarzman.

This is why private companies making money out of sick Brits just isn't on. This is the dogma.

People cannot get rich on our getting sick (I sympathise with this). Especially as it is a marketing (perception/creative) not a 'policy' issue. But, as I will show, this dogma is out-dated and irrelevant.

The Right Honourable Andrew Lansley CBE MP didn't work this out. Which is why he was sent to the isolation ward last year.

Like Ms Spelman and her forests *(see 18.7)*, he was too thick to think it through.

Having gathered the Future Forum evidence, what will Government do? What will be their creative solution? Well, without knowing it, the last Labour Government had the answer. First, let's step back and look at the bigger picture.

Socialism, like the Berlin Wall, has bitten the dust. We live in a world of 'free market economies'. But we now know that we cannot let 'free' markets run uncontrolled.

As we have seen in the banking crisis, there is a 'Role for Government'. I bank with NatWest, owned by RBS, 84% owned by the taxpayer (us).

But do I blame the Government for any issues with NatWest? Of course not. I go to my local Manager. Unlike the NHS, the Government do not manage NatWest. We – you and me – just own it. And it seems to be doing OK (now).

So here is my solution.

Let private companies manage NHS services. Feel free. Tender.

In return, we want 30% of the equity and a seat on the board. Our directors will not be civil servants but experienced businessmen. They will abide by a strict public-service code. And be accountable for our best interests, financially and in delivery.

It is pretty much what the Labour Government did with the Banks. By their own actions, Labour have overcome their old socialist position. This will make 'NHS privatisation' easier to sell to the country at large. Because we can make 30% of the money Mr Schwarzman has earnt. And then pay less tax.

Did you watch those New Bounce kids on Britain's Got Talent? They said meeting the Queen would be 'sick'.

Apparently, in the modern vernacular, 'sick' is good.

So let's look forward to a sick future for the NHS.

4.3 HOW THE BANKS CAN SAVE THE NHS

27 FEBRUARY 2012 18:23

In June last year, I posted an Insight to solve the NHS problem which, given the cost of the NHS is forecast to increase from £130bn in 2015 to £260bn in 2030, is a big one.

At the time, David Cameron had stepped in and put the Bill on 'pause'.

This must have been a bore to Health Secretary, Andrew Lansley, who had dreamt up a Bill without, it seems, due research or consultation with the medical profession.

Today, we now find this Bill, more formally the Health and Social Care Bill, is back in 'forward' mode or, more accurately, 'slow forward' mode.

This may be due to the fact that it has become so long, so complex and so unwieldy that apparently only Mr Lansley understands it.

In my experience, the complexity and incomprehensibility of a problem is in inverse proportion to the effectiveness of its solution, especially when politicians are involved.

So what was wrong with my idea?

Well, I do not think there was anything wrong with it at all. In fact, I believe it is more pertinent now than it was when I revealed it last June. That is why I would like to remind you of it now.

Before I do this, and by way of keeping you in suspense, let us try and identify the core issue.

For, as is quite often the case, if you can digest all the verbiage and argy-bargy down to one core insight – or even one word – then it becomes possible to re-build the issue in a much simpler way. To this end, as you may know, I am a great believer in Lord Saatchi's mantra 'Brutal Simplicity of Thought'.

In the case of Mr Lansley's Health and Safety Bill, there is one word around which all our confused and inadequate politicians are dancing.

And that word is *competition*. They just cannot get their heads round it.

The LibDems are against competition in the NHS. This must be true because the Daily Mail says so. Labour are sort of against competition in principle but they cannot say so because they introduced it when they were in Government. The Conservatives believe in competition but they are trying to find a set of words that says so but does not say so, if you follow.

So they are all dancing on the head of a pin, and discussing forestfuls of paper called a Bill (and what a bill!) because none of them are prepared to say what they really mean.

Let's go back to the word 'competition' and see what all the fuss is about.

Well, again, it is simple. What they don't want is private companies making loads of money out of public funds as, for example, some care homes have done – and especially not out of the public's ill health (i.e. the NHS).

So here is my thought. Haven't the Banks provided the answer? As I said last year:

> 'Socialism, like the Berlin Wall, has bitten the dust. We live in a world of 'free market economies'. But we now know that we cannot let 'free' markets run uncontrolled.
>
> As we have seen in the banking crisis, there is a 'Role for Government'. I bank with NatWest, owned by RBS, 84% owned by the taxpayer (us).
>
> But do I blame the Government for any issues with NatWest? Of course not. I go to my local Manager. Unlike the NHS, the Government do not manage NatWest. We – you and me – just own it. And it seems to be doing OK (now).
>
> So here is my solution.
>
> Let private companies manage NHS services. Feel free. Tender. In return, we want 30% of the equity and a seat on the board. Our directors will not be civil servants but experienced businessmen. They will abide by a strict public-service code. And be accountable for our best interests, financially and in delivery.'

Do you know what happened after I posted this? A very senior Tory contacted me and said:

> 'I love the idea but the problem is finding large enough talented populations in Government who understand business and in business who

want to work in Government! Also let's not forget that drugs companies, builders and most of the medical profession make money from sickness.'

I did not reply to these two objections.

To the first, I would say that I am not aware of any trouble recruiting Mr Hester for RBS. I am sure, with the right financial motivation, businessmen would be queuing up to run such companies – especially as business 'sales' would be served up to them on a plate. All that would be required would be efficient management rather than chasing customers.

To the second point, if our politicians and civil servants really cannot find a way of defining the difference between a public service and a plumber, then we all need to see the doctor.

So there you go. Don't worry about 'competition' in the NHS. Just invite commercial operations to tender for the business and, in return, demand a piece of the action.

How long should that take to work out?

4.4 NHS – GOVERNMENT ENGAGES WITH STRATEGIC MARKETING AT LAST

21 JANUARY 2011 08:49

My first ever blog as 'A Different Hat' on this site was posted on 13 November 2009. It was called 'Convergence and Divergence'. *(see 3.1)*
   After setting up my core thesis, I said:

> *'….the technology designed to bring us together is driving us apart. Surely this new technology, which all of us are using as communications tools, will have freed up more 'spare media space' than ever?*
>
> *So in this divergent world, can't we, as a business sector, including clients and agencies, be more creative about using our talents and resources to define and create messaging which might help overcome the divisions in the society we live in?*
>
> *From time to time in the trade press, I have seen hypothetical lists of "teams of all the talents".*
>
> *Why can't we do this for real and bring our resources and our skills together to communicate the importance of the values that UNITE us? Wouldn't this be a great brief?'*

So, on www.BrandRepublic.com last week, I was delighted to read an article headed 'Sorrell and Wight to inform COI review' – which said:

> *'The Government has formed a roundtable of experts including WPP chief executive Sir Martin Sorrell, Engine Group chairman Robin Wight and Channel 4 chief executive David Abraham to advise on its review of the future of COI.*
>
> *Francis Maude, the Cabinet Office minister, said: "The Government needs to be far more innovative in thinking about how it can best deliver incredibly important public information messages.*
>
> *"We need to incorporate the latest ideas from initiatives such as the Ad-Council in the US and the latest thinking from experts such as our Behavioural Insight "nudge" Team.'*

As discussed in last week's post ('Coalition? They're all over the place!') they call this Nudge Team the BIT –

I admit that the brief to this 'roundtable of experts' does not seem one which will change the world, but – at last – the UK Government seems ready to engage with the marketing and communications industry in a more 'upstream' way.

Many times, particularly in Campaign magazine, have I read about the virtues of the COI (Advertiser of the Year 2009, no less) and I absolutely 100% accept that they are all very professional people who do an excellent job.

My issue has been not with the COI itself but the briefs they are given and the role they have played in society. My feeling is that the COI – which, of course, is not their fault – have been asked to produce campaigns that are tactical rather than strategic. Wear a seatbelt. Don't drink and drive. Catch it. Bin it. Kill it.

Of course, politicians don't use the word 'strategy'. They use the word 'policy'.

And the Government are not allowed to use the COI to communicate policies. 'Policies' are, by nature and definition, party political.

So, as soon as public money is used to present any Government initiative including, for example, the reasons we have gone to war, the Opposition are up in arms and start shouting and waving paper around in the House of Commons. They say that, because they hold the opposite view (which they have to because that is why they are called the Opposition), the Government should not use public money in this way.

I think this is mad.

Take this week as an example.

Do any of us have a clue what the new structural reforms of the NHS are all about?

What does abolishing Primary Care Trusts and empowering GPs really mean?

Is this change for change's sake?

Or is it just to save money?

What about people who depend on the NHS, not only for their jobs (1.3million of them, no less) but as patients?

How will they be affected?

Are they worried?

What has been done to overcome their concerns?

To what extent have their concerns been considered?

If the NHS was a commercial business with the whole population as its customers, would it have communicated these fundamental changes in this way?

My answer – and I know a bit about the NHS – is a resounding NO.

It is my hypothesis that many of those who need the NHS most are the least likely to know the answers to these questions. This is unkind, uncaring and inhumane.

All we have heard has been yah-boo politics and posturing and people taking sides and, frankly, as a patient – a customer – I don't care about all this.

I just want to get better. I want the NHS to care for me. How will these changes achieve that?

I think this is a major problem for us as a society. For better or for worse, the UK Government are not allowed to use 'public funds' to explain what and why they are doing – even at the expense of the concerns, and day-to-day livelihood, of the British people.

The reason they are not allowed to do this is because the opposition would want to have their say too.

Well, I am sorry, but this just cannot be right.

The Government is the Government. Whether it is this political party or that political party, or a combination of two political parties, and whether you like them or not, in the modern world, the people whose lives the decisions of the Government will affect deserve to have the 'policies' that affect them explained simply and clearly and in a manner they understand.

Furthermore, the effect of these policies on the people they affect needs to be considered earlier in the process. Further upstream. To use Francis Maude's own language, what human behavioural insights have informed these policies?

Frankly, for as long as they are in power, subject to passing laws through Parliament in due process and in the proper way, the Government are going to do these things whatever the Opposition might say.

The Opposition can shout and scream in the House of Commons, they can bleat in the media and write books and articles and oppose as much as they like. This applies to any Opposition. It is a constitutional, not party political, point.

So please, let's be grown up about this, and empower the Government of the day to engage with the experts as, at last, they have now started to do and, subject to proper financial scrutiny (possibly by an all-party Parliamentary committee), allocate the funds required to the use of the best possible strategic, media, communications and creative skills available.

In this way, they will be able to transmit these 'policies' to the people whose lives they will affect rationally, emotionally, creatively, effectively – and professionally.

Let's face it, the Government are going to do what they are going to do anyway. It doesn't help for the people whose lives they affect to be left divided, unsure and confused.

I hope this newly appointed group from the top of our industry can put their own political allegiances to one side (if they have any) and start this ball rolling – leading, hopefully, one day, to a more united, more convergent, more caring and more humane society.

The politicians might not like it but we, the people of this country, are their constituency – and we are more important than they are.

5
HOW TO SOLVE THE NHS PROBLEM

5.1 ISOLATE 'CARE' FROM 'CURE'

19 NOVEMBER 2014 9:04

This is the first in a short series of posts about the NHS.

As a country, the NHS is the biggest issue we face. If we leave it to the politicians – you know, the people who don't know that invoices for £1.7billion are coming through the door – the NHS could bankrupt us.

Bizarrely, we all know this could happen.

But no one knows what to do about it – or has the guts to take the decisions that need taking.

There are two irreconcilable forces:

'Free at the point of delivery' is *economically unaffordable*. There is a 'funding gap' which is predicted to rise to £30billion by 2020 and £60billion by 2025.

'Private sector funding' is *politically unacceptable*. What a furore Farage caused last week by his suggestion that the NHS be managed by a 'US style insurance based system'!

So.

Creative thinking is required.

But, as the most creative country in the world, have we engaged our most talented creative thinkers to develop new ideas to resolve this dilemma?

Er, no.

As ever, all manner of 'stakeholders' have had a say but our best creative brains – the people most qualified to crack this problem – are left in the cold.

So, as someone who has become a bit of an expert in the NHS over the last ten years, I am going to apply some 'upstream creative thinking' to all this and sort it out myself. No, really. Please don't worry. It's no problem. Really it isn't. It's what I do.

First, I must urge the nation to reconsider my posts of 6 June 2011 and 27 February 2012:

How the Banks can save the NHS (see 4.2)

NHS – a 'sick' future (see 4.3)

These posts show that – if properly thought through – private sector funding could be introduced to the NHS without losing control of quality of service (or, more pertinently to some, without making other people, especially foreigners, rich at the UK taxpayer's expense).

There is no doubt that, like RBS and the NatWest, 'shared ownership' would be a better way.

Let's park that thought.

Why be better when you could be even better?

Is there a yet more radical, more creative, solution?

If so, where to start?

When facing creative challenges like this, the hard work comes at the beginning. It is necessary to ruthlessly examine all the facts, to be objective about all the vested interests and to dig deep, and then deeper still, in search of *the truth*.

You will find all creative people go through this process – musicians, artists, scientists and, yes, even advertising people. To achieve greatness in their chosen fields, they all need to ruthlessly interrogate the truth they seek in order to present their reinterpretation in an original way.

So what is the truth behind the NHS 'problem'?

How did it get like this?

Well, like all things which are true, once you find the truth, it seems ludicrously simple. You wonder how human beings have allowed things to become so complicated.

Because of this, in the case of the NHS, I do not need to take you through all the boring background arguments, the tedious political posturing.

For you know the truth already.

The truth is that, for the NHS to have survived so long, it has, by definition, been doomed.

Here's how it is:

The more people you 'cure', the more you have to 'care' for.

As medical science has advanced, it follows that people who can now be treated and 'cured' today, would, in previous generations, not have been cured and would not have survived. They would have died. And, because they would have died, they would not need to be cared for.

Thus, to a large extent by its own success, the NHS, which started life as a treatment based 'medical service' for people who are ill, has become an extended 'care service' for people who are not as ill as they were.

Because of medical science, some people who need care need it on a very long term basis. And it is this that the NHS cannot afford.

Thus, the creative solution for the NHS is to redefine itself in terms of *treatment* and *care*.

This thought may seem simple.

It is also very radical.

Once you have taken it on board, further creative thinking can be developed so that both of these elements of healthcare ('health' and 'care') can be redefined and restructured, medically and financially, to achieve a national health service that works – and that we can afford.

5.2 WHOLESALE ENGAGEMENT WITH CHARITY SECTOR

28 NOVEMBER 2014 9:11

Last time, I discussed the need for the NHS to differentiate between 'treatment' and 'care'. In the last week, three stories have emerged to support this view:

1. *'Families are being told they have seven days to find their relative a space in a care home – or risk being taken to court'* (Daily Mail)
   Dr Paul Flynn, chairman of the British Medical Association's consultant committee, said: 'Pressure on NHS services is at a critical point and cracks are beginning to appear.'

2. *'Care for people with learning disabilities is 'failing', report says'* (BBC News)
   Simon Stevens, NHS England Chief Executive, said: 'radical changes are needed in NHS and social care.'

3. *'Private equity giant Terra Firma looking to break up Four Seasons Care Homes'* (City AM).
   Terra Firma bought Four Seasons from Royal Bank of Scotland for £825million two years ago. Now: 'The plan would see the company divided into three: an arm to deal with NHS patients; one to handle paying customers; and another to focus on brain injuries and mental health.'

I do not understand this. Why the distinction between 'NHS patients' and 'paying customers'? Shouldn't the level of care be the same?

All in all, based on this week's news alone, I think we can say NHS care is a mess.

THE NHS – 'TREATMENT' AND 'CARE'
Society in the 21st Century has developed to the extent that 'care' is our fastest growing, and most expensive, social need.

As an issue, 'care' needs to be addressed far more radically and creatively than it is now.

Further, as discussed in my last post, the better the NHS is at 'treatment', the more 'care' it will create.

Is the role of the NHS to 'care' for all of us all of the time for all time?

Is this what it was set up to achieve?

There are people who think that, because it is called the National 'Health' Service, the NHS should focus on keeping people healthy – *avoiding*, rather than treating, illness. I have met people in the Department of Health who hold this view.

In one sense it makes sense. The healthier we are, the less likely we are to get sick.

But surely this misses the point? The NHS was not established to be some sort of national health club. The NHS is 'doctors and nurses' – not 'fitness instructors' and 'nutritionists'.

In a interesting lecture, 'The Origins of the NHS', by Professor Virginia Berridge, she made it clear that the original aim of the NHS was pure and simple – 'better access to hospital treatment':

'Then came the Labour victory of 1945 and the NHS Act of May 1946. Bevan espoused the nationalisation of the hospitals (state ownership and control under appointed local bodies) rather than local authority control which had been Labour Party policy until then.'

This is what we want the NHS for:

- when we feel sick, to see a GP (quickly and efficiently)
- if we need to go to hospital, to go to hospital (quickly and efficiently)
- in emergency, to get to A&E (quickly and efficiently)

The job of the NHS is to make sick people better – to provide 'treatment' – not to be some sort of all-encompassing health care advisor and provider.

THE NATIONAL CARE SERVICE (NCS)

So, what to do with patients who have needed 'treatment', but now need 'care'?

We spend £110billion a year on the NHS but, when it comes to 'care', as the Chief Executive of NHS England said: 'radical change is needed.'

I am calling for the launch of a new 'National Care Service (NCS)' in Britain.
And a wholesale engagement with the 'charity' sector.
How come?

ENGAGEMENT WITH CHARITIES

We Brits are a very charitable people.

'Charity UK' is an extraordinary thing. We have 164,097 charities. Total funds raised is over £60billion a year – enough to fill the hole in the NHS budget for the next ten years.

Online you can find a list of our top 1,000 charities. They are an eclectic bunch. Amongst them are Macmillan Cancer Support, the Alzheimer's Society, the Stroke Association and Age UK.

If you had any of these illnesses – following your treatment by the NHS – wouldn't you rather be cared for by specialists in the field and alongside other patients with the same problems as you?

For all the major illnesses – cancer, dementia, diabetes etc – I would like to see specialist centres of excellence – and care homes if necessary – managed by charities on a national and local basis.

These would be independent of the NHS and, like the NHS, not-for-profit but, unlike the NHS, with the professionalism and expertise of any top commercial organisation.

Funding? Please do not be put off. I will discuss funding in my next two posts.

I have bold, new, creative, society-changing ideas to reveal.

CHARITY IN THE UK

According to the Charities Commission, our top 1.2% of charities are responsible for 69.4% of funds raised.

Amazingly, the bottom 75% of all UK charities raise only 3.4% of total funds. Or, to put it another way, the smallest 123,179 charities raise £2.172billion. Whereas the top 1,990 charities had an annual income to Sept 2014 of £44.68billion, no less.

These larger charities are managed by highly qualified professionals who would do a far better and more efficient job in managing 'care' than the mess we have now.

They are highly qualified professionals managing not-for-profit organisations.

This is what we need.

Funding? Please do not be put off. I will discuss funding in my next two posts.

I have bold, new, creative, society-changing ideas to reveal.

DEPARTMENT OF CHARITIES AND CARE (DOCC)

I propose a radical new initiative which, in its boldness and ambition, may be as great as the foundation of the NHS itself.

I am calling for the launch of a new Government Ministry to be called Department of Charities and Care (DOCC).

The new 'National Care Service' (NCS) would report in to DOCC, just as the NHS reports in to the Department of Health (DOH).

If this creates 'competition' and 'tension' between the two NHS and NCS services and the two DOH and DOCC departments, then so much the better. They won't like it, but the DOH and the NHS need to be challenged by better organised, professionally managed 'competitors'. From competition, accountability and improved performance must ensue.

Funding? Please do not be put off yet. I will discuss funding in my next two posts.

I have bold, new, creative, society-changing ideas to reveal.

5.3 GIVE IS BETTER THAN TAKE

3 DECEMBER 2014 8:50

Since I started this blog, I have promoted my view that, in society, we are all consumers – and that professional marketing and advertising, and 'upstream creative thinking', could be better employed for the good of society as a whole. All of us.

In 2008, a new book about marketing theory called 'Nudge' was published. It showed how 'behavioural insights' could influence human behaviour.

In 2010, a 'Nudge Unit' was established at the Cabinet Office 'to use behavioural economics and market signals to persuade citizens to behave in a more socially integrated way.'

In 2014, the 'Nudge Unit' was 'part-privatised'.

Critics such as Dr Tammy Boyce of The King's Fund, said: 'We need to move away from short-term, politically motivated initiatives such as the 'nudging people' idea, which are not based on any good evidence and don't help people make long-term behaviour changes.'

Well, I hope Dr Boyce and The King's Fund will like the nudge I am about to reveal.

Why?

One word: funding.

SEPARATE 'TREATMENT' FROM 'CARE'

In my last two posts, I proposed splitting the NHS into two services:

- 'treatment' would remain the responsibility of the NHS.
- 'care' would be the responsibility of a newly launched 'National Care Service' (NCS).

The reason for needing to do this is clear:

The post-war Bevan model, where the NHS is funded by National Insurance contributions, is bust. As currently financed, the NHS is doomed. New thinking is required. So is new money.

I propose that delivery of new National Care Service be managed by the charity sector, financed by both central government money and charitable donations.

Why?

One word: funding.

A BEHAVIOURAL INSIGHT APPLIED TO THE NHS

When you think about it, the NHS has a hospital curtain around it.

Walk around and you don't see much NHS do you? Step inside a hospital and there's all sorts going on. Inside GP surgeries, the walls are swathed in NHS posters and leaflets. Outside, there are hardly any.

And yes, after a successful operation, you may have paid for the NHS through taxation, but have you ever donated money back by way of thanks to the heroic doctors and nurses who treated you?

You haven't have you?

This needs to change.

As I showed in my last post, in Britain we are a very charitable people. Our charities raise over £60billion a year.

The NHS is funded by taxation which the UK Government *take* from working people. On the other hand, people *give* to charity.

We need to encourage the spirit of giving into the 'care' of our people.

Why?

One word: funding.

A CALL TO 'CHARITISE' ALL NHS CARE SERVICES

Privatising NHS services is politically sensitive. I am not calling for privatisation.

I am calling for all NHS care services to be split off from the NHS and 'charitised'.

This would require them to be managed by independent charities in the not-for-profit charitable sector and overseen by the new 'National Care Service' (NCS) and thus by the new 'Department of Charities and Care' (DOCC).

Why?

One word: funding.

The National Care Service (NCS)

'Treatment' would be provided by the NHS; it would continue to be 'free at the point of delivery'; and it would continue to be funded by central taxation.

'Care' would be provided by the new National Care Service (NCS) and managed by specialist charities in specific areas of medical speciality i.e. 'cancer', 'strokes', 'paraplegia', 'age' etc.

Like 'treatment', 'care' will also be 'free at the point of delivery' and funded by a combination of central taxation and charitable donations. If you can afford the care you need, you will be asked to make a donation – but you won't be forced to.

Raising money from charitable donations to the NCS will become a major national initiative. Everyone, the whole population, will be asked to contribute in one way or another, in terms of time and/or money, including – perhaps especially – the very rich.

Nudge the Rich

I know some very rich people. In fact, if over £100million counts, some obscenely rich people. They are not thieves. Nor are they evil. Most of them are driven. Many of them are socially aware. Some of them even do good things for other people.

All of them are obsessed by earning money. None like giving it away. When asked to do so, they apply the same rigour, and forensic eye for detail, to spending money as they did to earning it.

Very rich people don't like paying tax. Why would they? Knowing money as they do, they can see the inefficiencies in the way public funds are managed and spent and wasted away.

Like it or not, very wealthy people are very smart people. Smarter than our politicians. Not such good degrees, perhaps. But smarter. More nous. And harder. More ruthless. Over-tax them and you will turn them away. Engage with them, cuddle up to them, and you have more of a chance.

One idea would be to provide an income tax option for highest rate tax payers whereby, rather than pay tax at 45%, they are given the option of paying 30% as long as they match that sum with a donation to a recognised charity for the management of care within the new National Care Service.

Boost their egos, and the very rich might donate even more than this.

The key thing, with the very rich, is not to take their money but to make them want to give.

For very rich people will give money away. Look at this headline:

'Scrap metal dealer turned billionaire pledges three quarters of fortune to charity'

His name is Anil Agarwal. He has given away over £2billion.

Lord Sainsbury has given away over £2billion too.

These people will give to charity.

But you have to nudge them.

APPEAL TO VANITY

Another way to inspire rich people to give money to charity is to appeal to their vanity.

We need to develop a programme of 'naming rights' whereby large donors to the new National Care Service can, if they like, have their donations publicly recognised by naming wards, wings and whole care homes after these people.

We need to engage them with local communities and specific causes (cancer etc).

As I demonstrated in my last post, the UK charity sector is highly fragmented.

The whole thing needs to be pulled together, and joined up, so all the time spent by heroic volunteers, and money spent by equally heroic donors, adds up to more than the sum of the parts.

It *can* be done.

Yes it can.

And please don't think donations to the new NCS will be restricted to the very rich. All of us, however poor, will be encouraged to donate money and contribute to the NCS too.

There is a special way we can do this.

Which I will reveal next time.

Yes I will.

5.4 EVERYBODY CARES, EVERY DAY

17 DECEMBER 2014 8:14

This is the last of four posts which provide a new, more creative way of funding the NHS.

So far, I have proposed:

1. That NHS services be more clearly divided into 'treatment' and 'care'
2. That NHS care services be integrated with – and managed by – the charity sector
3. Tax incentives to encourage people to contribute generously to a new National Care Service

Last time, I showed how the very rich could be incentivised by an income tax reduction to 30% subject to that sum being matched by a donation to the National Care Service (NCS). One 'reward' would be the allocation of naming rights to NCS homes, wings and wards.

Now, in this post, I will show how everybody can contribute to the NCS *every day*.

Let me start with an observation I made to the Department of Health several years ago:

As part of a successful professional project, I pointed out how surprising it is that, rather like the 'iron curtain' that isolated the old communist bloc, there is a 'hospital curtain' around the NHS.

What did I mean by this?

From a marketing perspective, there are two things about the NHS that make it different.

For any other business, professional marketing people can identify and profile the 'consumers' of that business. We call it the 'target audience'. When the target audience buy the product, they become 'customers'. When they become customers, we can define when and how they 'consume' the product. This helps define the marketing strategy.

The NHS is different, isn't it?

The NHS does not know who is going to be sick or what treatment they will need or when they will need it. Thus, uniquely, the target audience of the NHS is 'everybody, all of the time'.

Yet, bizarrely for an organisation that employs over 1.7million people – and which all of us are likely to need at some time or another – there is remarkably little activity *about* the NHS *outside* the NHS.

To demonstrate this point to the Department of Health, I walked from Tooting Bec Underground station to St George's Hospital, not much more than a mile away. There were seventeen – yes, *seventeen* – NHS touch points on the way: pharmacies, opticians, GP surgeries, chiropodists etc.

But there was not one NHS sign at not one of these places. As far as the NHS is concerned, you might as well now know they are there – or that there is busy activity going on every day.

How is such an enormous organisation so invisible in the community?

Well, I expect the answer is that, because it is funded by central taxation, the NHS becomes an expectation rather than a want. And when you do not need medical treatment, you do not want to think about when you do, do you?

Let's park this thinking for a moment and talk about the National Lottery.

You may not be a Tory and you might not have voted for John Major. For me, having voted both Labour and Conservative in my time, John Major is one of the few politicians whom I am prepared to concede is 'a good bloke' with his heart in the right place.

And John Major did do one thing that has changed our lives and improved society.

He launched the National Lottery.

Since 1994, National Lottery has raised over £32billion for good causes, including £2.2billion for the Olympics. According to the Guardian – 'give John Major the credit he's due – the National Lottery has transformed British sport'.

How can we learn from the lessons of the Lottery, and the human insights I have provided, to help us transform the 'care' (as opposed to the medical 'treatment') of our citizens?

I have touched on this before but, when I was brought up in Hong Kong, there was a national charity called the Community Chest. Everybody knew about it. Everyone bought into it.

The Community Chest was so heavily advertised I can recall the corny jingle decades later:

Give, give, give to the Community Chest
Give, give, give and they will do the rest
Give, give, give just as much as you can
Give, give, give to help your fellow man.
If you're from the East, if you're from the West,
Help your neighbours with the Community Chest.
Give, give, give to help the sick and the poor
Give, give, give and then just give some more.

Now, today, the time has come for us to launch another National Lottery, along the lines of the Community Chest, which can act as the 'central bank' for the new charity-managed National Care Service.

The National Care Lottery or, if you like, the Community Chest will be different from the National Lottery in that donations can be made straight into the fund without buying a lottery ticket including, for example, the following 'usage occasions':

- if you have been well treated by the NHS, as a gesture of thanks, you will be encouraged to make a donation into the Community Chest at collection points at every NHS touch point, including GP surgeries and on every high street.
- the charities which manage care homes and services under the NCS will be encouraged to organise local fund-raising initiatives and events.
- a Community Chest 'prompt' for every payment at every chip & pin device at every point of sale in the country (this is technologically possible, as I know from a client I have worked with in this area).
- a similarly ubiquitous online marketing campaign, especially on NHS and NCS websites.
- an advertising campaign encouraging, for every bet made between two people, the substitution of "if you do that, I'll give x pounds to charity … " with "if you do that, I'll give x pounds to the Community Chest"?

In contrast to the hospital curtain around the NHS, and alongside the tax breaks that will be developed, this continuous and ongoing engagement with the Community Chest will be something we can *all* buy into, *all* of the time.

This is the only way we will be able to protect the 'free at the point of delivery' NHS principles.

In conclusion, I accept the insights and ideas I have put forward in my last four posts might benefit from development and refinement. But I am convinced, even as a lonely blogger, that a more professional – and more creative – approach is required to resolve the core issues facing the NHS and care in this country.

In the book 'In It Together: The Inside Story of the Coalition Government' (June 2014), the overhaul of the NHS is described as 'an unforced error of epic proportions'.

In the book 'The Blunders of Our Governments' (September 2014), the full extent of the failings in our political system is revealed.

In this lead up to the General Election, how can we allow our political parties, and inadequate career politicians, to blunder onwards as they do?

Yes, they may feel they have their fingers on the pulse of public opinion, but there are professional people in a host of professional marketing services' companies who are better qualified to:

- identify the problems
- define the core issues
- understand the human dynamics
- develop original and creative solutions

There is still time for all the parties to invest in original thinking and creative advice at a more upstream level.

But not much.

6
WELFARE
MATTERS

6.1 DISABILITY LIVING ALLOWANCE (DLA) DISGRACE

5 SEPTEMBER 2011 08:50

"We will extend a hand if you are willing to unclench your fist".

So, famously, said President Barack Obama at his Inaugural Address.

I would like to take this sentiment and apply it to a particular social issue happening in Britain today but, first, here is the full context of what Obama said:

> *"To the Muslim world, we seek a new way forward, based on mutual interest and mutual respect. To those leaders around the globe who seek to sow conflict, or blame their society's ills on the West – know that your people will judge you on what you can build, not what you destroy. To those who cling to power through corruption and deceit and the silencing of dissent, know that you are on the wrong side of history; but that we will extend a hand if you are willing to unclench your fist."*

This was a direct message – a promise – 'to the Muslim world'.

Have we helped Obama keep this promise to Gaddafi? Absolutely not. Gaddafi 'ruled' Libya for decades. For his oil, we greased up to him during this period. We knew what he was like. Let's not pretend we have the moral high-ground here. As I tweeted in February, and have posted since, I am convinced we could have done a face-saving deal if we had acted smartly and quickly. But we didn't.

Another young, gung-ho British Prime Minister clenched his fist, leaving Gaddafi no option but to fight fire with fire – at the cost of thousands of lives.

Who knows where (or when) it will end. What a mess.

Now, as promised, I would like to apply Obama's line *'we will extend a hand if you are willing to unclench your fist'* to something that has been going in your town or borough, at home, today and for the last few months.

Once you have read this, you are no less guilty of turning a blind eye than the Germans to the holocaust under Hitler.

The Coalition Government is clamping down on benefit cheats. Fine, nothing wrong with that. Of course, in a civilised society, we want our taxes to be used to provide benefits and care to those who need it, not those who fiddle the system – and it is a 'Role of Government' to manage this.

One of the benefits being 'cut' is Disability Living Allowance (DLA). This is provided to those who are disabled, sick or in chronic pain, mentally and/or physically. It is a higher level of benefit than the basic Employment Support Allowance (ESA).

I am sure that we agree that we should track down and stop the people who claim DLA fraudulently. We have all seen pictures of them playing golf, taking water-slides on foreign holidays, or engaged in other physical activities. In Wandsworth, a woman was fined heavily for using a Disabled Blue Badge for which her father qualified – except he had died three years earlier.

So, all around you – in this country, today – the Government is testing all the people who are claiming DLA to weed out those who are cheating the system.

I think we all agree with this objective. But what about the strategy that has been developed to deliver it?

In particular, what about the people who are genuinely claiming this benefit? The ones who deserve it, the sick and disabled who it is there for. Those who are not on the make, but in real need.

Have you any idea what they have to go through?

They are sent a letter by an outsourced private company called ATOS acting on behalf of the Department for Work and Pensions (DWP). Recipients are ordered to present themselves at a stated place at a stated time for 'a medical assessment in relation to your benefit claim'. The letter continues:

"it is important you attend. **If you fail to attend, your benefit may be affected**". (That is not me being bold).

Well, of course, for those who are really sick and/or disabled this is not as easy as it sounds. You may have to take two or three buses and/or trains to get there. The journey itself, to said place at said time, may cause you anxiety or panic attacks or worsen your already chronic pain. Immobility is one reason you are on this benefit.

But no matter, our Coalition Government has its fist clenched. *Be there. Or else.*

Now is the time to get really scared. Because, when you get there, things get worse.

This is how it is:

In chronic pain, complete all-engaging agony, so much so that you are in tears and cannot focus on the paperwork you are required to produce, you have dragged yourself to a dark, dank, dreary building and are gestured through the doors by big, burly people in dark, dangerous suits branded ATOS (not, surprisingly, SS).

You approach the desk and your name is marked. You are told to take a seat with the other claimants, many of whom are in the same agony as you.

The chair is of a type in which you just cannot be comfortable, which is one of the reasons you cannot work. Your pain intensifies. You cannot move. You feel trapped.

You hear noises, you raise your head, wipe your eyes and look around the room. There are people squirming, groaning, moaning, crying, painfully waiting their turn.

There is a young man frothing at the mouth, spitting, screaming and banging his clenched fists against the walls. His mother, presumably his mother, is unkempt, frantic and distressed. She urges him to be quiet: *'don't worry darling, it'll soon be over, soon we'll be home, please don't disturb these other nice people'*. So British. He turns and hits her. Hard. Whack. Right in the jaw. She pretends it hasn't happened.

Feeling it would be too painful to get up and knowing, because you are disabled and aware of your own physical and emotional limitations, that you cannot help this poor lady, you look up at one of the guards and gesture him over. You ask why he and his colleagues cannot help her restrain her frothing, foaming, furious, fighting boy.

"Not allowed to," he says "against the rules. Like this everyday. Can't do nothing".

And so the groaning noises of deep physical pain all around the room underscore the louder, more frightening noise of this boy ranting and raving until your turn is called.

You enter a strange, cold room to meet a strange, cold, uniformed person whom you have never seen before and never will again. You are required to answer the most personal, intimate questions about yourself, your health and your domestic life.

You are moved across to a cold, hard horizontal surface (you would not call it a bed) and you are physically examined. Apart from this strange uniformed person, you are alone in the room.

After, you dress yourself, slowly and painfully because there is no one there to help you, you collect your papers and walk back out through Reception.

The young man is still there, louder now, fists still clenched, banging at the walls, still shouting and screaming, frothing and foaming, flailing and fighting as his mother desperately tries to calm him down. The guards look on. Everyone else turns away.

You leave. You struggle home. You crawl into bed. The pain of your experience overwhelms you. You cry like a baby.

You have been to bedlam. No you haven't. You are in Britain. Great Britain. Not Libya or even some dreadful historic time warp. You are here. Now.

You have been hit by the clenched fist of a British Government.

You have helped fulfil their objective of nailing the DLA cheats and, in doing so, you have suffered from their cold, cruel, heartless failure to develop a strategy for the genuinely sick and disabled.

For them, and their outsourced supplier, you are a number on a list – another box ticked. There has been no humanity in this process.

Yet again, the Government have not thought things through. As I have identified countless times before, they just don't care. Are you surprised their clenched fist approach results in outbursts of protest and rebellion?

And you, how do you feel, reading this on your computer, tablet or smartphone?

How would you feel if you were struck down by serious illness or accident?

How would you feel if you were suddenly helpless?

Would you like to be treated this way?

Are you proud to be British?

Is this why you pay your taxes?

Is this the society you want to live in?

Is your fist clenched or are you extending a hand?

Will you reveal your disgust in the box below?

Will you forward this shameful story to your contacts?

Or would you rather turn a blind eye and sit at home watching Celebrity Big Brother?

You decide.

6.2 EMPLOYMENT SUPPORT ALLOWANCE (ESA) DISGRACE

30 MAY 2014 08:58

Writing these blog posts, it is impossible to predict who will read them or where they might lead.

Thus it is a pleasant surprise that my most retweeted and liked post has been 'Disability Living Allowance (DLA) Disgrace' *(see 6.1)* - especially as I would be the first to admit that I am no expert in the murky confusion of the social security market.

I say a 'pleasant surprise' because the interest generated by this post would seem to support my overarching thesis – specifically that the understanding of human behaviour and creativity of our world-beating advertising agencies could be better employed to improve society as a whole.

Please park this thought while I tell you that it is a golden rule of marketing that any money spent on promoting a product or service must, if nothing else, generate more income than the cost of creating and transmitting it.

Frankly, if your advertising has cost more to produce and transmit than the revenue it generates, what is the point of doing it at all?

It seems pretty obvious, doesn't it?

But you would be surprised how often companies have broken this rule – particularly in the first, fated dotcom boom.

Traditionally, in consumer marketing, the UK population is segmented into simple demographic groups – A, B, C1, C2, D and E – where A are the richest people in society and E the poorest.

I have never worked on an advertising campaign where the target audience has been exclusively in demographic groups D and E. Not once. Nor have I ever heard of anyone else targeting a marketing campaign to the poorest people in the land. Never.

These poor people have no money to spend, so why advertise to them? Why would you?

Of course, for the Government, there are a number of areas where a more professional and creative approach would help these people who, because they don't have any money, need more help than anyone else.

So, to revert to my 'DLA Disgrace' post, and the disgraceful inhumanity of the tests people have to endure to qualify for this benefit, I can reveal a further unfairness that lies within the rules of another social security benefit called 'Employment Support Allowance' (ESA).

Please bear with me. If you get lost with the detail of what I am about to reveal, keep the faith. It is the principle of what follows that counts – and it may surprise you, if not provoke you into civil action.

I will keep this as simple as I can. I like simple.

Here goes:

National Insurance is categorised into three 'classes'.

To qualify for ESA, you need to have paid Class One or Class Two NI contributions for two of the last three years.

If you have not done this, it is possible to 'top up' a shortfall in NI payments.

But there is a trap.

You cannot top up your payments if you have paid NI for thirty years or more.

Well, to be specific, you can – but not at the Class One or Class Two rate. You can only top up at the Class Three rate which, to receive ESA, does not count.

Are you with me?

In short, if you are someone who has paid, say, thirty seven years of contributions into the National Insurance system – nothing short of a lifetime of hard work and toil and good citizenship - it is impossible for you to top up payments and you will not qualify for ESA. You will receive no social security benefits at all. Nix. Nothing. Not a penny.

However, if you have paid NI for less than thirty years, you can top up your NI contributions at the crucial Class One and Class Two rate – and you do qualify for ESA.

And, if you are from an EU country, not even a UK citizen, and you pay Class One and Class Two contributions, it is possible that you can qualify for ESA.

How can this be?

Daft, isn't it?

A disgrace.

Now, let's return to the demographic groups D and E we discussed above. You remember. The people who have no money – nix, nothing, not a penny.

There is one thing the Ds and Es do have.

It is something we all have.

It is called a vote.

And, when it comes to votes, there is one thing we would do well to remember:

Every vote has equal 'value'.

The vote of the poorest person in the land is worth exactly the same as the vote of the richest.

But, the UK Government, unforgivably, have developed a social security system whereby good, honest citizens who have paid tax for over thirty years, and do have a vote, are at a disadvantage to citizens of EU countries who are entitled to receive benefits in the UK but not to vote here.

Thus, it is no surprise that millions of UK voters have become moved by a political party that promises to overturn this unfair treatment of people who have fallen on hard times.

This party is called UKIP.

PS – I am not a UKIP supporter. I believe we should be in the EU and that convergence is preferable to divergence, as discussed in my first ever blog post 'Convergence And Divergence'.

6.3 BENEFIT CUTS: A CALL TO MOBILISE THE DISABLED

17 JANUARY 2013 09:01

So, now we are here in another New Year and, in the UK, the savagery of social welfare cuts continues to slice through our society.

We have had:

06 January: *'Soldiers, nurses and teachers hit by benefit curbs'*

07 January: *'Benefit cuts will see more children taken into care'*

09 January: *'Pensioners could face universal benefit cuts after election'*

13 January: *'Benefit cuts threaten women's refuge services'*

14 January: *'Benefit cuts: reforms will leave disabled people ghettoised and excluded'*

Happy New Year from the British Government!

You have to wonder, half way through their term of office, quite why some of these people went into politics in the first place. They don't seem to care about human beings at all.

They continue to use the 'economic deficit we inherited from Labour' as their excuse for all this misery but, as I have posted before, surely there must be a time when cutting becomes the last resort, not the first as seems to be the case now.

Or, are they driven by some other political ideal?

Aristotle defined *kindness* as:

'helpfulness towards someone in need, not in return for anything, nor for the advantage of the helper himself, but for that of the person helped'.

Do you get the impression that our Government, not in return for anything or for the advantage of themselves, have done everything they can to avoid the suffering they cause?

I don't.

Of the list of cuts identified above, let's take the disabled as an example.

Since my post 'Disability Living Allowance Disgrace'*(see 6.1)*, featuring a true story about a person living alongside you in society today,

I have taken a greater interest in disabled people – and, kindly, some of them have shown their support of what I had to say.

So, I have asked myself if there is anything I can do to find a less cruel solution.

In seeking an answer, there are two insights I think I can provide.

The first is to inform you that disabled people are enslaved by their disability. Unless they attend to their disability on a daily basis, they cannot function. Their disability dominates their lives.

If they are lucky, this could be a regime of medication to which they must adhere.

If they are unlucky, they suffer pain or depression or both and their ability to function will fluctuate on a day-to-day basis.

If they are very unlucky, like a paralysed friend of mine, they will need someone else to clean their teeth, wash them and wipe them which makes getting out of bed a two-hour process.

Believe me, although the extent of this varies, disabled people are slaves to their disability.

The other insight is that the 'normal', able-bodied world runs in strict order. We live more structured, less flexible, lives than we like to think.

For example, I know the Liberal Democrats are pushing for more 'flexitime', but flexitime remains the exception rather than the rule.

For small and medium-size enterprises (SMEs), and for most trading companies, 'normal working hours' are still Monday-Friday, 9am-5pm.

Yet, if you are disabled, 'normal working hours' are difficult, if not impossible.

Furthermore, many disabled people are physically incapable of using public transport, or are incapable of getting about easily at all, especially in the rush hour.

For the disabled, mobility is a major issue.

Can we liberate the disabled from these constraints by flipping these two insights – the enslavement of the disabled and the rigid structures of 'normal' working hours – to find a new way forward?

I think we can.

Despite the 'public sector job cull' announced in last year's budget (there they go again!), the total number of public sector employees in the UK sits at around 5.5million people, with the NHS, it says here, employing more than 1.7m people.

Yet when was the last time you saw a disabled person working in the NHS, let alone in any other of the public services?

Put simply, when did a person in a wheelchair last greet you in a hospital?

And how many Chief Executives of hospital trusts, or people holding other senior executive positions, are disabled?

However many it is, it is not enough.

The Disability Discrimination Act 2005 requires public bodies to have 'due regard' to the need to:

- *promote equality of opportunity between disabled persons and other persons*
- *eliminate discrimination that is unlawful under the Act*
- *eliminate harassment of disabled persons that is related to their disabilities*
- *promote positive attitudes towards disabled persons*
- *encourage participation by disabled persons in public life; and*
- *take steps to take account of disabled persons' disabilities, even where that involves treating disabled persons more favourably than other persons (e.g. the provision of an accessible parking bay near a building, where parking is not available for other visitors or employees.)*

What a load of bureaucratic guff.

It doesn't exactly inspire you to take positive, imaginative, innovative action, does it?

Why can't the 'public sector' develop positive methodologies where 'working norms' can be adapted to the needs of disabled people and the daily requirements that enslave them?

Why can't these public bodies, as a default option, be forced to fit the jobs to disabled people rather than fit the people to the jobs?

I am not normally one for positive discrimination, but that is what I am calling for now.

To be clear, in any and all public sector vacancies, priority must be given to disabled applicants – even if it requires two or three of them working for three or four hours a day.

It seems the disabled were more integrated into the London Olympics than they are to British society as a whole. There certainly seemed to be more of them whizzing round the Olympic stadium than I have seen working in the public services.

What we need is a new, bold, nation-changing approach.

I implore the Government to inject some creativity, humanity and leadership into this issue.

6.4 A MORE CREATIVE APPROACH TO WELFARE REFORM COULD HAVE SAVED LIVES

25 SEPTEMBER 2014 2:28

So, while the UK was talking about Scotland, someone has died:

'David Clapson's awful death was the result of grotesque government policies (9 September):

The DWP brags about ending the "something for nothing" culture, but benefit sanctions punish the unemployed, disabled and poor in ways that are utterly inhumane.'

'Family calls for benefit inquiry after David Clapson death:

Diabetic David Clapson, 59, from Stevenage, died from lack of insulin, 18 days after his Jobseeker's Allowance was suspended in July. He was found dead in his flat on 20 July, with £3.44 in his bank account.'

I have posted on this topic before:

DISABILITY LIVING ALLOWANCE (DLA) DISGRACE (SEPTEMBER 2011)

'All around you – in this country, today – the Government is testing all the people who are claiming DLA to weed out those who are cheating the system. I think we all agree with this objective. But what about the strategy that has been developed to deliver it? In particular, what about the people who are genuinely claiming this benefit? The ones who deserve it, the sick and disabled who it is there for. Those who are not on the make, but in real need.'

CAN YOUR DOCTOR BE TRUSTED OR NOT? (APRIL 2013)

'Until the Government started paying ATOS to do the job, they trusted your doctor's evidence that your disability was as you were claiming it to be. Not any more. The Government would rather trust ATOS. Surely, if doctors provide false declarations on behalf of their patients, they should be named and shamed and punished just as severely as those 'disabled' people

who fiddle the system? Wouldn't such an outcome deter rogue doctors from providing false evidence? For some reason, we don't read about these doctors. Yet, they must exist or we would not need this inhuman ATOS technology for the Government to rely on instead.'

In London, we are known to have some of the best creative advertising agencies in the world. They have a greater understanding of human behaviour than government.

To the deepest marrow of my bones, I have had no doubt, whatsoever, that any one of them would have found a better, more humane way of achieving this goal than has been the case.

This would have been the brief:

'How to cut people falsely claiming disability benefit, while protecting the health (and lives) of those who really need it.'

Earlier this week, in the pub, I was asked what the subject of my next blog post would be. I mentioned the David Clapson story. The reply was:

"Cutting down the fakers is all-important and if that costs people their lives, then this is justified in pursuit of the larger goal."

What do I know, eh?

7

EDUCATION MATTERS

7.1 EDUCATION: EVERY CHILD HAS A TALENT AT SOMETHING

14 FEBRUARY 2013 09:30

For how long will we say that our educational system is our country's greatest failing?

It won't surprise you when I say for as long as our inadequate career politicians are in charge:

In the last few weeks, we have had Education Secretary Michael Gove in an embarrassing climbdown in abandoning his flagship plan to scrap GCSEs and replace them with a new English Baccalaureate.

Liberal Democrat leader Nick Clegg has suggested that he and his wife may send their oldest son to a private school, yet in the past he has said: "Right now there is a great rift in our education system between our best schools, most of which are private, and the schools ordinary families rely on. That is corrosive for our society and damaging to our economy."

And this week, helpfully, John Prescott weighed in with: "Public schools are classed as charities and are therefore entitled to tax relief so every single taxpayer pays about £3.30 a year to effectively sponsor a public school boy... let's scrap this Posh Boy Tax!"

Incompetent, hypocritical, chippy. That just about sums up the British career politician.

Our Prime Ministers aren't much better. Here's David Cameron last year: "I went to a great school and I want every child to have a great education. I'm not here to defend privilege, I'm here to spread it."

And Tony Blair, on 23 May 2001: "Our top priority was, is and always will be education, education, education. To overcome decades of neglect and make Britain a learning society, developing the talents and raising the ambitions of all our young people. At a good school children gain the basic tools for life and work. But they ought also to learn the joy of life: the exhilaration of music, the excitement of sport, the beauty of art, the magic of science."

All these people recognise the divisiveness of the British educational system.

What have they done to change it?

We know that, as career politicians, their job is to get their party into power and themselves up the greasy pole. It is depressing that none of them have vision. They don't dream.

Well, I have a dream.

I agree with Tony Blair that children 'ought also to learn the joy of life: the exhilaration of music, the excitement of sport, the beauty of art, the magic of science.'

And I would like to provide an insight which I believe could point to a new way forward.

What are my credentials for doing this?

As I have admitted in previous posts, I went to one of Britain's top public schools.

Yet, through my own children, I have witnessed the 'great rift' that Nick Clegg identified.

My children went to a local primary school in London. I was able to pay for them to graduate to private secondary schools where many of their contemporaries, their friends no less, were forced into a more uncertain, dangerous future.

When one of my children left the local state primary school, my family suffered at the hands of some local children who were not as privileged as mine. Wet paper bombs were thrown at our house. Drinks were poured over my children as they walked down the road. My car was scratched by a coin.

Aged twelve, the perpetrators had been condemned to the wrong side of the rift. My children went to one school. They went to another. Is their behaviour a surprise?

At the last General Election, I stood for Parliament to help force the main parties to agree to the conversion of a disused local hospital into a school rather than 'executive flats'. The Bolingbroke Academy opened in September and, last week, one of the mothers told my wife how happy her child is to be there. Sadly, her older child, at another local school, is reported to have 'gone off the rails'.

How can we heal this great rift in our society for once and for all?

Well, here follows one belief and one insight for you that, I believe, should underpin every aspect of our educational system.

CORE BELIEF:

Every child has a talent at something.

CORE INSIGHT:

Children know the individual talent of every child at school better than any parents or teachers do.

How does the educational system fail to recognise this?

The answer is because, at school, our children are ranked ('streamed') and judged solely by academic ability - especially since the brainless introduction of academic league tables.

But it is ridiculous to rank human beings, of any age, on an academic basis. We all know academic achievement is no guarantee of 'success'. An ex-headmaster of my school reckoned that, in his experience, the bottom 25% would provide employment for the top 25%.

Remember the mantra – *every child has a talent at something.*

How do the sports facilities in state schools compare with those of private schools?

The answer is that they don't. If you want your child to play sport at school, you have to pay. This has been recognised by Ofsted in a report published today. Chief inspector Sir Michael Wilshaw said: 'Our report found that only a minority of schools play competitive sport to a very high level.'

This is unfair.

But what, as a society, are we doing about it?

Surely we could do more?

I fully appreciate that there is no way every state school will ever match the 400 acres of land my old school enjoys, but is the answer to get all chippy and close it down? Of course not.

You can't throw away your dreams just because they are difficult to fulfil.

Did you know that, at the Great British Olympics last year, if the UK Independent Schools were a country, they would have come 12th in the Medal table? Hard to believe, but true.

Surely the answer is for state schools to *compete* with independent schools, not deny success?

As with so much of our state system, a more innovative solution is required.

It does not need money, tax or investment. It just needs vision, creativity and attitude.

How about this:

Within the Education Department, a Minister of Sport in School should be appointed.

Every borough in the country should have a Sport in School Department whose task will be, on behalf of every school, to pinpoint and reach out to every football, rugby, cricket, boxing, squash club and gym in every borough and force a relationship between schools and sports clubs.

Right now, do the people who run our schools engage with the owners of these facilities?

Do they know why they are there, when they are used, who uses them?

Do they engage with these people, many of whom might be unemployed or disabled?

Do they, as a matter of policy, inspire the schoolchildren in the borough to use these facilities – and to do so with the same enthusiasm, commitment and fun these facilities can provide?

The hell they do.

Remember the mantra – *every child has a talent at something*.

What about the Arts?

Are local schools connected with local theatre groups and enthusiastic, often struggling, artists and musicians and dancers?

The hell they are.

I call for a Minister of the Arts in School to be appointed to match the brief of the Minister of Sport in School. And for each local council to have an Arts in School Department to reach out to local enthusiasts (by Arts in the plural, I include all the Arts, including Drama and Music).

These Ministers will be set targets for engagement of the local community with local schools.

Why is our society so compartmentalised?

Here's more:

There are some kids who are not good at any of the above. They are academically average, clumsy at sport and disinterested in the Arts.

And do you know what they do?

They observe the other kids and they become comedians and the funniest people on earth – and they should be nurtured and embraced.

Or, like the Pistols, they should be encouraged to start a band and make a noise even though none of them can pluck a chord.

Or, best of all, they may be motivated, rewarded and respected by becoming part of the community and learning to help others.

This happened to a friend of mine's son after his father died.

Do you know what he did?

He started a club for other children who had lost a parent. He found a place where they could go and share their bereavement and help each other through the unfairness of their fate. For this he was universally admired throughout his school, not least by all the other kids.

How brilliant is that?

As well as Ministers for Sport in School and Art in School, we need a Minster for Schools in the Community too.

Remember the belief: *Every child has a talent at something.*

Remember the insight: *Children know the individual talent of every child at school better than parents or teachers do.*

It is our duty, as a society, to free our children to discover what they are good at, of all the rich options available to them, and fulfil their potential to the extent that they can all admire and respect each other for – and be brought together by – the rich diversity of their talents.

And do you know what?

If we had a Minister for Sport in School, a Minister for Art in School and a Minister for Schools in the Community, they might just become the most important people in our country.

And, if they were career politicians, I might just forgive them.

That would be my dream.

7.2 TUITION FEES: EVIDENCE OF AN UNKIND SYSTEM

30 JANUARY 2013 09:01

It was revealed last week that, following the introduction of tuition fees, there has been a 40% drop in university admissions.

What a surprise.

You don't have to be the world's most sophisticated marketing or behavioural expert to know that if you start charging money for something you used to provide for free, you are going to lose a large percentage of your 'customers'.

You may be expecting a tirade against another flawed UK Government initiative.

But no.

This is the story of just one humble British student at one, not so humble, English University, one of the so called Russell Group.

Here's what happened.

In her first year at University, this young lady failed to attend the required number of seminars and lectures.

A warning email was sent to her, which she acknowledged but, inexplicably, she continued to miss her lectures.

Why she behaved like this we do not know. It could have been slothfulness or sex and drugs and rock and roll or, a relatively new phenomenon, internet addiction.

No matter. She missed her lectures and she admits she missed her lectures. She will not be the first or last student in the world to do this.

But, in England, her punishment was harsh and unforgiving.

She was told she would have to re-sit her first year exams, setting her back a year and meaning, if she were to complete her course, that she would have to attend four, rather than three, years at University.

A confirmation letter was written both to the student and, separately, to her parents.

In response, her parents made the following points to the University:

1. If they were to be a party to the decision by the University to hold their daughter back a year, why was this only after the decision had been made and not when the final warning was given (at which time they could talk to their daughter and do something about it)?
2. Did the University not realise that their decision to hold a student back a year would cost that student approximately £15,000 in fees, accommodation and living expenses?
3. Did the University not realise that, in the big wide world, you have to commit a really very major criminal offence to be fined £15,000?

The University replied recognising the points made but regretting the decision was final.

This has left a young English student with a £15,000 'fine', a sum which is more than she has ever earned and which could take her a lifetime to repay – and all for a really rather harmless first offence.

How competent are the people who have introduced this tuition fee system?

How heartless are the Universities who are implementing the system in this way?

When it comes to human understanding, it seems they have a lot to learn.

7.3 HOW DATE OF BIRTH AFFECTS EXAM RESULTS

24 MARCH 2010 22:51

Following the announcement of Samantha Cameron's pregnancy, anyone of any humanity should only feel happy for her and Dave, especially after the sad loss of their older child last year.

So, I want to make it absolutely clear that I am NOT being cynical in any way, whatsoever, in this post.

But the importance of the announcement that the new baby is due in September will ring bells to all of us whose children are passing, or failing, their way through the British educational system.

In fact, so important is the date of 1 September, that I believe research has shown that there is a statistical skew in our national birth-rate towards pre-Christmas babies.

It is another one of those little things the Government don't advertise. As is the fact that other countries are far more flexible than Britain as to the academic year a child can attend school – a decision which, in these other countries, is based on the level of development of the individual child.

But we aren't that sensible or sensitive here. Our rules are far more rigid.

This is why some parents actually plan the timing of the birth of their child to arrive as soon as possible after 1 September.

Let me explain. The month young Cameron is born will have a huge influence on the level of the child's exam results later in life.

Say these exams are in June 2029. If born in September, the Cameron child will be 18 years and 9 months old. Other children taking the same exams will have been born August 2011, making them 17 years and 10 months old – as near as damn it a year younger than young Cameron.

But they will be in the same academic year at school. This is the system.

If you have only had 18 years or less on the planet, nearly a year is a big

114

slug of your life and having a September, rather than an August, birthday is going to give you a huge advantage at exam time.

So, genuine congratulations to Dave and Sam. Good on you.

But, to the parents who have actually planned the timing of their child's birth to fit with the British educational system, I find that a bit freaky.

In my patch, Battersea, there is a shortage of secondary schools.

This leads to really freaky behaviour. The wealthier parents rent temporary housing in Tooting with the sole objective of getting their children into a particularly good secondary school there – for which they would otherwise not qualify on a 'catchment area' basis.

Then, having achieved this, they move back 'home' to Battersea.

And the next trick is to pay for private tutoring to train your eldest child to deliberately *fail* the entrance exam.

This is because, if the first child is admitted to the school on a catchment area basis, their younger children qualify for 'sibling priority' and the family doesn't have to up sticks and rent in Tooting again – whereas if Child One passes on academic grounds, then there is no sibling priority.

Clever, eh?

So, good luck Dave and Sam. I mean it.

But Dave, if you can do anything to make the date of birth of our children less important to their lives and less worrying for their parents, I do think it would be a good thing.

Thanks.

7.4 WHY DO SCHOOLS (AND PARLIAMENT) HAVE SUCH LONG HOLIDAYS?

23 AUGUST 2011 09:14

Last week, I was invited by Paul McEntee, Associate Director at JCPR Edelman, to contribute to a podcast on 'the silly season'. Edelman use these podcasts to discuss issues of the day and place them on their website to broadcast to clients and staff.

My co-panellists were Jim Grice, who runs the Press Association video operation and John McEntee, Editor of Richard Kay column for the Daily Mail.

For me, I must admit the silly season has not been a subject I had given a great deal of thought to or, frankly, have felt I have had to consider much in my career.

As someone whose speciality has been the optimisation of paid-for, rather than editorial, media space the main issue raised by the silly season has been the media effectiveness and value of space booked. Even then, rates paid have reflected the size and profile of the audience reached during the period. What's the issue?

Clearly, if the silly season really is a serious business dynamic about which I would be required to show some knowledge, I would have to spend some time on research.

I was surprised to find a Wikipedia page dedicated to the subject which shows the silly season to be an international phenomenon and a recognised social dynamic since the 19th Century.

Within the subject, there are important cultural matters to consider:

- in Germany, the silly season is known as the *sommerloch*, the 'summer hole'
- in France, they have *la morte saison*, the 'dead season'
- in Spain, it is the *serpiente de verano*, the 'summer snake'
- in Sweden, the silly season is *rötmånadshistoria* and Finland *mätäkuun juttu* both literally meaning 'rotting month' (because your food goes off more quickly than it does in winter)

- so naturally, in many countries, the silly season references gherkins or pickled cucumbers: *komkommertijd* in Dutch, Danish *agurketid*, Norwegian *agurktid*, Czech *okurková sezóna*, Polish *sezon ogórkowy,* Hungarian *uborkaszezon*, Hebrew *onat ha'melafefonim* and Estonian *hapukurgihooaeg*.

Fascinating, eh?

If ever there were a case for countries within the EU to maintain and protect their individual cultures and identities, surely we have found it. Rotten cucumbers must become more prominent in the political agenda.

What have our politicians been missing? Oh sorry, they are all missing. Gone off.

Thus, it was with some trepidation that I made my way to the smart Edelman offices. How could I provide my uniquely deep and meaningful insights into human behaviour, innovation and 'upstream' consumer thinking to such a silly subject?

In the event, I had nothing to fear. Thanks to the wisdom of my co-panellists, it became clear that the silly season really is a serious issue to those responsible for creating editorial content in both written and visual media.

They are desperate for something to say.

Bereft of movie premieres, glitzy product launches, and celebrity revelations, there is a real need for the newspapers to fill their pages. John McEntee complained he had been invited to only one launch party in the last two weeks – diddums!

So silly has been the season, and so short have they been of news, that such erudite newspapers as The Guardian and The Independent have featured articles on the subject.

And the broadcast media has to travel to such unseen corners of the nation as Norfolk to track down politicians in polo shirts in their desperate search for a story.

But hasn't the internet, on which rolling news editorial material is freely available, changed all this?

Isn't it time to chuck our rotten cucumbers onto the compost heap and re-consider this whole silly silly season concept?

Shouldn't we be asking ourselves why, in this day and age, the silly season exists at all and structure our society accordingly?

Why is Parliament in recess for such a long time?

Why do our schools have such long holidays?

Because, in the real world, the silly season doesn't exist at all – and it never has.

Some of the world's most important events have occurred in rotten cucumber time: the Great Train Robbery in 1963, the murder by the IRA of Earl Mountbatten in 1979, the Hungerford massacre in 1987, the Iraq invasion of Kuwait in 1990, the death of Princess Diana in 1997, flash floods in Cornwall in 2004, Hurricane Katrina in 2005 and, now, riots at home and tumultuous events in Libya – and so it goes on.

In the podcast studio, I tried, rather unsuccessfully, to generate some interest in the insight that babies born in August rather September have to bear an educational disadvantage for life. This will be the case with Florence Rose Endellion Cameron – born prematurely, in case she ever forgets, in Cornwall in August last year.

Since the podcast, I have been thinking of my own birth, which I happen to know was in Hong Kong. At that time, my father had been posted by his London-based business to the Far East and his holiday arrangements were three years on, six-months off.

Roll forward thirty years, I am managing Ogilvy Thailand and my father has retired.

My parents came out to Bangkok and Dad said he would be interested in a visit to my office.

WPP had just taken over O&M and introduced a financial discipline which required us to send our cash-at-bank statement to Farm Street at the end of the day in Bangkok but morning in the UK, so that this cash could be used during the day in London while we were asleep in Thailand.

The same applied to correspondence. If I asked a question of London in the evening my time, I could expect the answer on my desk the next morning. We used these things called fax machines.

My father was horrified!

In his day, from Hong Kong, he would write a letter to London, it would wait for the next ship to arrive, sail to Singapore, Colombo, India, up through the Suez Canal and across the Mediterranean to Southampton from where it would be posted to London. The reply, once written, would take the reverse route in what was no less than a six-month process.

To him, this overnight stuff was unthinkable. But, inevitably, the world had changed.

And, in the few short years since then, the world has changed again. As I posted on 3 December, 10 December and 17 December *(see 16.1)*, the year 2010 represented the coming of age of the digital era.

And the negative social consequences of what has been called the silly season have been shown to be too great.

We have to recognise this and re-arrange our lives accordingly.

The time has come for shorter school holidays, which should be two weeks at a time with a maximum of six a year.

The debts we are loading upon our university students are outrageous. University courses should be two years not three, again with much shorter holidays.

And the same principle must apply to Parliament which, like everyone else, must limit recess, two weeks at a time, with a maximum of four a year.

In business, our special friends in America only get two weeks holiday a year – period.

I am afraid it is time for teachers and politicians to get real.

This silly, silly season must stop right now.

8

HOUSING
MATTERS

8.1 HOW ZERO VAT ON BUILDING TRADE WOULD STIMULATE UK ECONOMY

20 SEPTEMBER 2012 09:08

'Ideas don't make you rich. The correct execution of ideas does'. So said Felix Dennis in his book 'How To Get Rich'. He's worth over £500 million, so I think we can believe him.

As it happens, last week, I got really excited about one of my big ideas: Make the building trade a VAT free zone!

In one swoop this would kick-start the economy, generate hundreds of thousands of jobs and clean up the 'black economy'.

Dreams of a peerage and celebrity status ensued. Sleepy mornings in the House of Lords followed by lunch at a private table in the Savoy Grill and a siesta. Lazy holidays with Felix in Mustique – out of the prying eyes of the snooping paparazzi. Toplessness no problem.

I could barely contain myself as I googled 'building-vat-boost-economy' to research how my idea would make me rich and famous.

Up popped the first result – a site called 'Cut the Vat'.

Drat!

Someone has thought of my idea already. Here's what it says on the Home Page:

Join us in calling on the UK Government to cut VAT on home improvements to 5% to:

- *Boost the UK economy*
- *Create thousands of jobs*
- *Bring thousands of empty properties back into use*
- *Improve the energy efficiency of our housing stock*
- *Reduce the incidence of fuel poverty*
- *Help those who cannot afford vital repairs to their homes*
- *Significantly reduce the competitive advantage of rogue traders*

Drat and double drat!

Not only had someone already thought of my idea but one Professor

123

Michael Benfield has thought the whole thing through. Built the case, if you will.

As a marketing strategist, purveyor of human insights into people's behaviour, I would have made more of the last point myself -'Significantly reduce the competitive advantage of rogue traders.'

We all know 'the cash economy' enables much greater evils than tax evasion itself – protectionism, illegal immigration, sex trafficking, gun crime, drugs, you name it. Surely the best way to stop people fiddling the system is to make it not worth their while?

Well – perhaps because it is not their idea – the Great British Government does not think like this. In fact, they take the opposite view. David Cameron has announced a relaxation of planning laws, so building new foundations for more under-the-counter transactions.

And now they have another great idea: a financial concoction where benefit payments would be linked to average earnings rather than, as now, inflation. This would cut benefits by £5 per week, including people who are sick and disabled, and raise billions of pounds for the Exchequer.

Is it not perverse to cut the life line of the people who need the money rather than the supply line of the people who are getting away without paying the tax to feed them?

There's no accounting for politicians, is there?

They've got no idea.

8.2 HOUSEHOLD ENERGY: WHAT GAS AND ELECTRICITY SUPPLIERS MUST LEARN FROM THE OIL COMPANIES

22 OCTOBER 2013 09:06

Here we are again.

Great Britain, I can report, has descended to the yaboo politics of yesteryear. Inept career politicians, none of whom have ever managed a business, biff-baff each other with naïve and unrealistic 'policies' to the detriment of us all – especially the old and needy.

Biff. Last week the Conservative-led Coalition government privatised the Royal Mail, a move which runs the risk of devastating rural communities and which, with a bit of forethought, was completely unnecessary.

If, over seven years ago, I was able to foresee that the future of the Post Office (and thus Royal Mail) was in parcels not letters, why couldn't they? *(see 12.3)* If they had, they need never have capitalised on the sale of this precious asset or, if they had to, they could have earned a lot more for it.

And could they not have announced this revenue stream earlier in the Parliament and made less savage cuts? Sometimes, you think they want people to suffer.

Baff. Labour Party leader Ed Miliband's laughably naïve announcement that, if elected, he would freeze energy prices for twenty months from the date of his election (oh dear).

Does anyone think these seat-of-the-pants, counter-punch 'policies' have been properly considered or professionally researched and analysed?

Doesn't Mr Miliband realise that, just like the Royal Mail last week, the supply of gas and electricity to UK households has been privatised and, thus, laid open to 'competitive' market forces? Has he no idea what this means?

Here's how it is:

- any commercial business will focus on the customers who can pay their bills

- no commercial business will market their products to people who cannot afford to pay
- gas and electricity are 'commodities' and traded on global commodity markets
- no business will buy a product for more money than they can sell it
- if the energy companies don't buy gas and electricity, they won't have any to sell
- if they don't have any to sell, householders cannot buy any so they will freeze and starve
- or the UK government will have to step in and take over. This is called nationalisation
- if the Labour Party want to nationalise gas and electricity, why don't they say so?

So, is this price freeze feasible?

The answer, of course, is no. Anyone with any business experience at all will tell you the energy companies won't wear it and householders will pay the price (sic).

Sorry, I'm not being very helpful, am I? Rather than rant and rave, do I have any consumer insights or creative thinking I can bring to this issue?

I think I do. Here goes:

Quite often, the best thing in these situations is step away and start again and apply what one London advertising agency would call 'brutal simplicity of thought'.

So, for now, please forget gas and electricity.

Let's take a look at oil.

Oil is a commodity just like gas. Very like gas, in fact.

We need oil to run our cars. In the UK, we call it petrol. In the USA, they call it gas. See?

How do the oil companies sell us petrol (and diesel) for our cars?

How do what they call 'downstream' services work?

And how do we, as consumers, behave?

We drive along the road and we see from the dial on the dashboard that we need more petrol and so, as we spy the various 'petrol stations' owned by various oil company brands, we choose where to stop and fill up our tanks at the rate the petrol station has on display.

My Dad always used to choose Shell or BP, as he felt it was patriotic. For the same reason, he always drove a British car.

Me? I am a much more ruthless consumer than my Dad. My current car is Japanese, my last one was German and I don't care which brand of petrol I put in my car. I always go for the cheapest.

Hang on. Actually, that's not true. I think I go for the cheapest, and this is what I would tell anyone who asked me. In reality, I sometimes go to this petrol station as they sell the best coffee or, oh yes, that one which sells my Mum's favourite biscuits.

Consumers, eh?

But let's own up to it, in many ways the petrol market is competition at its best:

- the oil companies are dealing in a global 'commodity'
- 'upstream' oil prices go up and down with global markets
- 'downstream' prices are fiercely competitive
- consumers are ruthless
- consumer ruthlessness forces oil companies to 'add value' in different ways
- this makes purchasing petrol a much more pleasant experience than it used to be.

Am I right?

Now, let's return to the household energy market.

When, if ever, was the last time you 'switched'?

I switched last year and, I can tell you, whatever the politicians and energy companies say about how *easy* it is and how many attractive tariffs there are, it is not true. You are being conned.

You may not know who Ed Davey is. He is called 'Energy Secretary' and he got rather huffy in the House of Commons last week. He said:

'We are pushing competition and I would urge customers of British Gas who are unhappy, to change their supplier.'

Well, Mr Davey is clearly a very important person but does he know that, in the real world, 'switching' is a very difficult, complex, confusing and distressing experience?

First of all, there is a lot of reading of meters involved.

Unlike the petrol stations – where you put the nozzle in your car and, very quickly, an electronic gauge tells you exactly how much you are using and exactly, to the penny, how much you are spending.

Yet I cannot be alone when I reveal that my gas and electricity meters are old, dirty, decrepit and inconveniently placed in my basement where I cannot stand upright.

When I am forced to locate these meters (having put on dirty clothing for the purpose), I have to admit I don't like 'reading' them, I don't understand them, I can't be bothered to tell one from another and I don't understand what they are telling me.

Here's my gas meter (I think):

It measures 'cubic feet'.
What are 'cubic feet'?
How big are they?
How much do they cost?

By the way, the meter tells me it is 'the property of British Gas' even though I am not a customer of British Gas and that yellow label below the meter says 'in the event of an escape' I am to shut it down and call an out-of-date phone number. This handwritten, scribbled instruction is dated, reassuringly, '21/10/91'. I think.

And this is my electricity meter:

It measures 'kWh'.

What are kWh?

How many do I use?

How much do they cost?

The answer seems to be on dials displaying units of 1,10,100, 1000 and 1000 but, if the dial is right on a number, how do I tell whether to go above or below the number on display? It is all very confusing.

Within the meter is a little sign saying:

'PROPERTY OF LONDON ELECTRICITY BOARD'

Next to it is another sign saying:

'THIS SERVICE AND APPARATUS IS THE PROPERTY OF BATTERSEA BOROUGH COUNCIL. IT MUST NOT BE TAMPERED WITH. PENALTY FIVE POUNDS.'

Blimey, I haven't gone online to switch yet and they're threatening me already.

And guess what? I've just found out that the London Electricity Board was privatised in 1990 and Battersea Borough Council abolished in 1965. I hope none of my gas escapes.

When I drag myself back to the 21st Century, the 'switch' experience continues to be difficult, complex, confusing and distressing:

- you are required to find all your previous bills
- you have to unbundle gas and electricity
- calculate the rate you are being charged by month, by cubic feet and by kWh
- take into account any rate changes there may have been
- get your head around different suppliers and different tariffs called things like 'Blue'
- recombine gas and electricity again
- commit to a long term deal
- agree to 'fixed tariffs' which, as I can testify, aren't fixed at all.

Did I tell you switching is a difficult, complex, confusing and distressing experience?

Still don't believe me? Here are three comments from the British Gas website. You can skip these if you like or you can read 338 more:

"The account took a long time to set up. (approx 3 months) so instantly we had a backlog of debt. They underestimate the amount you should pay so they look good at the start then up the amount you have to pay. The meter readers they use consistently take the wrong readings and upload them so the figures are wrong! The address we are registered at is wrong. I have tried to get them to change it but with no luck. We should be 1F2 or flat 4 but instead we are down as just 1 (they are downstairs from us!) so any mail they send goes to the wrong address! Then, when trying to see a simple breakdown of energy used seems to be hard too!"

"Having just learned of another exorbitant price rise I wanted to find out what tariff I am on in order to review this and hopefully save money. The information on tariffs is confusing, contradictory to my energy bills and horrendously overcomplicated. The website is continually crashing and I cannot even view historical bill information. I was looking for a more competitive tariff with British Gas but I am now going to change out of principle."

"I struggle to get on my knees to read the meters so have to ask my grandsons to do it. I have now been told my next bill will be over 14,000 pounds and on saying there must be a mistake my grandson has told me I have put the readings in the wrong way round. I am unable to change the readings on line and now I am really worried about my next bill as my pension would never pay that large amount unless they give me a couple of years."

Here are various measures which need to happen in the household energy market, for all of which I will compare the customer experience to that of filling your car with petrol:

1. More consumer choice

As you will see below, consumers have much more choice in the purchase of petrol for their car than gas for their home.

How is this? Can the situation be improved?

Would more choice in the market increase competition and drive down prices?

I think it would.

How?

2. Modernise the equipment

The meters in the household energy business are totally inappropriate in the modern era. In fact they are a disgrace. When I put gas in my car, I can see exactly how much I am putting in and exactly how much I am paying. Why not for the gas in my home?

I do not just want better equipment. I expect it. Specifically, I want a digital display, ideally an app on my iPad, telling me exactly how much I am using on a per unit basis and a contemporaneous rolling total of exactly how much I am spending as my house is warmed.

This antiquated equipment makes it harder for customers to monitor how much energy they are using and how much they are paying for it as they go.

'Smart meters' have been invented. Why haven't I got one?

3. No more bundling of products

Why do energy companies encourage me to bundle gas and electricity from one supplier? And why does my new supplier have a bundle which includes phone and broadband?

Is this in my best interests? The hell it is.

By the way, my new supplier is Utility Warehouse, known in our house as Futility Warehouse. If you query your gas bill with them, they put down the phone. Nice.

Much better to have electricity people sell you electricity and gas people gas. This is much more in the consumer interest. Domestic energy suppliers should not be allowed to con you otherwise. Take it from me, Mr Davey, they bundle these things up to make it difficult for you to switch not easy to switch. It is a cynical, deliberate ploy.

Do the petrol stations bundle their products? Do they tempt you with offers of cheaper petrol if you pre-buy your engine oil at the same time? No they don't. Nor should they.

4. No more fixed payments

When you pull in to a petrol station to fuel your car, is there a system where you are trapped into going back to that place? Of course not. The next time you fuel your car, you can go wherever you like. The same should apply to household energy.

You wouldn't forward buy a year's worth of petrol for your car, would you? You have no idea of the exact amount or when you will need it. There are too many variables – just as there are at home (the weather, Billy staying with his girlfriend, Sally's juicy guitar, Granny coming to stay). The same applies to household energy.

Annual deals are a con. They are a way for the suppliers to make their product more complex and confuse their customers. They are not in the best interests of the consumer.

For products as socially important as domestic energy, these fanciful 'lock in' devices should be banned by law.

5. More transparency

As I drive down the road, the prices charged by the petrol companies are broadcast loud and clear on a large digital display on the roadside and, as I continue my journey, I can compare the price offered by one petrol station to that offered by the next.

This is how an open market works. Why can't my household energy supply be like this?

With every bill sent to every customer, there should be a requirement for like-for-like price comparison costs from all the suppliers in the market. This way, customers will be able to see what they would have paid with a competitive supplier and have the choice to switch for next month. Yes, I said switching should be made easy on a monthly basis.

Domestic energy suppliers will say it takes a week or two to switch because they have to send someone round to read your meter. This is another con. If they had up-to-date monitoring equipment, they could take a reading from a central monitoring point. They have the technology to do this, but it is in their interests not to pay for or install it.

6. More integrity

At a petrol station, you help yourself to petrol, you pay and then you leave. You have the power to go where you like next time. In the household energy market, the power is in the hands of the supplier not the customer.

As privatised businesses, owned by shareholders, energy companies have a duty to maximise their profits and they use every trick in the book to do so.

Do they care about the old and the needy? Of course not. Why should they? In the event of any queries, they put down the phone.

It should be as easy for you to cut them off as it is for them to cut you off. This is very important.

7. Easier to switch

Yes, there are costs attached to the modernisation programme I have proposed. And the energy companies will not like it. But, surely transparency is a price they must pay for the licence to provide such important public services?

Price comparison sites, many of which have floated or been bought at vastly inflated valuations, will also complain. Frankly, if switching was made as easy as it could be, there would be no need for these sites at all. And they know it.

Believe me, if the proposals I have outlined above were adopted, particularly if all the prices in the market were wholly transparent, prices would come down.

Conclusion

Mr Miliband may not realise this but one benefit of privatising businesses, that used to be nationalised, is that they have to operate in a competitive world.

In any market, competitive forces are not restricted to just one sector. Once consumers get used to behaving in a certain way, they will demand the same level of service across every aspect of their lives.

Whenever the time comes that buying gas and electricity for your home is as easy as it is to buy petrol for your car, prices will come down, customers will be more satisfied and the world will be a better place.

Phew. This must be my longest post.

I'm gassed out.

8.3 PROPERTY VALUES DIVIDE THE NATION

8 OCTOBER 2012 09:09

Last week, Labour leader Ed Miliband spent over an hour telling us two things: that he wants us to be 'one nation' and that he went to comprehensive school.

I quite like the 'one nation' thing building, as it does, on our Olympic success and burying, as it should, Labour's bigoted tribal heritage.

But isn't there a contradiction in Miliband's exposition of 'one nation' and, in the same speech, his need to remind us of his comprehensive schooling? If we are to be 'one nation' why drive an educational wedge between us? It isn't where you went to school but how much money you will inherit from mummy and daddy that will drive us apart.

To that end, wasn't that an extraordinary story about the TV presenter Nick Owen selling the house he had bought for £950,000 in the 1990s for £35million a couple of weeks ago?

I wonder if the implications of this have been fully understood.

I have met people who are going to inherit millions of pounds worth of property when their parents die. One has an elderly father who owns a house in Notting Hill Gate. He bought it in the 1960s for £20,000 and it is now worth £3million. Recently, the old man was heard to say: 'I wish I had bought two!'

The life that people who are going to inherit these sums lead is very different to those who are not. They have very different priorities. They don't, for example, have to worry about a pension pot. They will inherit the pot.

As revealed last week when discussing Andrew Mitchell *(see 18.2)*, they behave very differently when faced with a problem or a difficult issue. They don't discuss things or think things through. They are used to getting what they want – and, when they don't, very different behaviour emerges. They throw all manner of childish hissy-fits and tantrums.

Another trait I have observed in these people is they cannot judge other people. They haven't had to, which means that when they do have to, they can't. I discussed this in my post *(see 18.1)* 'The Curse of Cameron'.

I am all for 'one nation', from whichever Oxbridge career politician preaches it to me, but is it going to happen?

For we live in a society where, potentially, a totally useless person who has achieved nothing at all in their life, not worked hard or succeeded in anything, done not a jot for their fellow man, and may even have lived on benefits, gets £3million because daddy bought a house in the 1960s.

Isn't this more divisive than 5% tax here or there on income a millionaire has gone out and earned?

It certainly doesn't seem very 'one nation' to me.

9

IMMIGRATION MATTERS

9.1 THE LESSON OF THE HOOVER FREE FLIGHTS FIASCO

24 JANUARY 2014 09:06

Oh dear, I have a feeling this will be my angriest post since 'DLA Disgrace' in September 2011. Hang on to your hats...

As an independent candidate at the last UK general election in 2010, it was only when canvassing started that I realised that, overwhelmingly, *immigration* was the most important issue concerning the voting public.

And, even worse for me, having taken the time and trouble to publish a 27-page 'personal manifesto' covering what I considered to be the most important issues of the day, I realised that I had not addressed the most important of all – immigration.

So it was that, at my first hustings, sitting alongside Labour, Conservative, LibDem, UKIP and other candidates the first, the very first, question the audience asked:

'What do you think about immigration to Britain and what would you do about it?'

Instantly, I was aware of a frantic shuffling of paper under the table as all the other candidates scrambled through the cribsheets supplied by their party HQs to find the relevant tab and spout their party line.

Me? I had to think.

Slowly, but with brain whirring frantically, I rose to my feet and said:

'I don't know how many of you have read or seen Alan Bennett's play "The Lady in the Van". To me, it is a metaphor for immigration. It is one thing to have a lady in a van park in your driveway for three months and stay fifteen years. But you can't have fifty of them, can you?'

So, I argued, immigration is as much to do with management control as strategy:

1.   Define the numbers.
2.   Control the numbers.

How so?

The Hoover Free Flights Fiasco

The Hoover Free Flights Fiasco is recognised as the biggest disaster in the history of the UK sales promotion business.

In 1992, Hoover was losing money and under pressure to sell off the excess stock that had piled up in their warehouses. A sales promotion campaign was developed whereby customers who spent over £100 on any Hoover products would receive two free flights to first, Europe, and then, disastrously, America.

At this time, the days before budget airlines, the value of these flights was estimated to be £600 – far greater than the £100 that Hoover invited customers to spend.

As we know, the UK public are not stupid. They were 'wowed' by the offer – and flocked, in droves, to their nearest Hoover stockist.

Comedy ensued:

Wedding couples were given up to six vacuum cleaners as wedding presents as their generous friends and family gave away the Hoovers and kept the free flights.

A Hoover customer blocked a Hoover service van into his driveway for 13 days – an action worthy of Alan Bennett himself.

'Instead of spending a little sucking new customers in, they spent millions blowing away their good name.' said the BBC.

'A major snafu of EPIC proportions' said the PR man.

'Hoover sucks' said disgruntled customers, as the company tried to worm out of the offer.

Ooh how we laughed.

From comedy comes tragedy:

The Hoover Free Flights Fiasco 'brought one of Britain's most famous brands to its knees'.

The damage to Hoover's reputation was 'incalculable'.

Three Hoover bosses were sacked.

In 1997, five years later, 'court cases threaten to open the floodgates to more claims'.

All of Hoover's UK factories were closed, ending a 50 year history.

Hoover's whole European division was sold to an Italian company called Candy.

Standing back from the comedy and the tragedy of this, what lessons are to be learnt from a more professional, objective analysis?

And what on earth has the Hoover Free Flight Fiasco go to do with immigration?

Well I can tell you.

In the trade, it is called *redemption*.

For, in the sales promotion arm of the marketing business, there are two key steps:

1. Define the numbers.
2. Control the numbers.

Haven't we heard this before?

Redemption is where, having defined the offer, a calculation is made as to how many customers will take up - redeem - the offer. In many cases, redemption is a comparatively low percentage of sales. Many customers don't see the offer as worth bothering about.

Thus, professionally speaking, Hoover's mistake was not only to make an offer that exceeded that value of the sale price of their product but also to miscalculate – disastrously – the level of redemption.

In simple business terms, it is a question of forecast v reality. And, as anyone who has managed a business knows, you get your forecasts wrong and you pay the price.

THE LABOUR GOVERNMENT AND IMMIGRATION

Two months ago, in November 2013, Jack Straw, who was our Home Secretary in 2004, admitted that throwing open Britain's borders to migrants from other new EU states, that year, had been a 'spectacular mistake'.

At the time, Britain was one of only three EU countries to allow free migration for workers from EU accession states including Poland, Hungary and the Czech Republic. Ministers expected up to 13,000 a year to move to Britain but, by 2006, at least 600,000 immigrants from East Europe had been let through our doors. In 2010 alone, the UK's net migration figure was 252,000.

But, immigration is not just a European issue. Sir Andrew Green, head of the Migration Watch think tank, said: "There's been a lot of focus on EU migration. The reality is this – in the Labour years there was net foreign immigration of three and a half million. Only one in five of those was actually from the European Union."

Three and a half million?!

You what?!

THE COALITION GOVERNMENT AND IMMIGRATION

In August 2006, the Conservative shadow immigration minister Damian Green said: "These figures make it all the more urgent that the government takes an early decision and stops ducking and diving on the issue of Bulgaria and Romania entering the EU."

Did you get that?

The Conservative Party identified the problem in 2006.

And now we learn that David Cameron has slammed Labour's decision to permit workers from new EU members states to come to Britain in 2004 as 'a monumental mistake'. He made the comments as he announced plans to ban EU migrants from claiming benefits for the first three months after they arrive in the UK.

This was on 27 November 2013!

It gets worse. This week, in January 2014, we are told that the UK cabinet is split on immigration.

Isn't this all a bit late?

As anyone who has run a business knows, if you let problems fester for over seven years you will pay the price.

THE IMMIGRATION FIASCO

Our politicians – all of them – have made such an appalling mess of immigration that they are 'not fit for purpose', as they themselves like to say.

What is it about immigration that I'm not getting?

As a country, does immigration really divide us on political lines? Is there really a left and right view on this? Capitalism v socialism? White collar v blue collar? Private school v state school? What is all this? Call me naive, but aren't the good people of Great Britain more united on immigration than our Oxbridgian political leaders like to portray?

Do you know anyone – anyone at all – who wants nil migration? Not one immigrant?

I don't.

Don't we all know that millions of our fellow Britons live abroad; that most immigrants are honest, decent people we are happy to live here; that some immigration is fine, as long as the numbers are controlled – and that our political masters have mucked up again?

And why is this all about EU migration? What about our friends in the Commonwealth, whose languages, cultures and histories we share and who fought alongside us for the freedom for people like me to write things like this (against, as it happens, other EU countries)? Don't we owe them a debt of honour?

Have our politicians got a grip on all this?

Or, have they shown that they are the last people who should decide these matters?

For surely, just like the redemption of a sales promotion campaign, immigration is a question of balance:

1. Define the numbers.
2. Manage the numbers.

It can't be that difficult, can it? First, you calculate how many are going to leave our shores in any given year. Then you get an independent economist to forecast the prevailing issues and work out how many immigrants you can admit by social class, by age, by profession, by country of origin. There are experts who do this kind of thing for a living and, if they muck things up, you can fire them.

It is very important that the people who police the numbers are accountable for their performance. Who has been accountable so far? How many people, like the bosses of Hoover, have been sacked?

Surely letting three and a half million people into our country by accident eclipses even the Hoover Free Flights Fiasco in its gross incompetence? Isn't balance the last thing we are going to get from our adversorial, divisive political system?

And surely, like interest rates, where the Governor of the Bank of England heads a committee of non-political experts to i) define the numbers and ii) manage the numbers, it would be better to keep the politicians away from this key issue. All they would have to argue about would be the proportions of immigrants allowed in within an independently calculated annual total.

For, when it comes to immigration, politicians aren't going to solve the problem, are they?

Let's face it, politicians ARE the problem.

9.2 CAMERON WRONG EVEN IF HE'S RIGHT (AGAIN)

11 FEBRUARY 2011 09:01

This is a telephone conversation I did not have with David Cameron last week. I don't know how he found my number. Is there no privacy these days?

DC: 'I've decided to have a go at multiculturalism. What do you reckon?'

Me: 'What with all that's going on in Cairo right now?'

DC: 'Don't worry about Cairo. I'll be in Munich. It's the right time and place.'

Me: 'What are you going to say?'

DC: 'I'm going to say: "We have failed to provide a vision of society [to young Muslims] to which they feel they want to belong. We have even tolerated segregated communities behaving in ways that run counter to our values. All this leaves some young Muslims feeling rootless. And the search for something to belong to and believe in can lead them to extremist ideology".'

Me: 'Don't you think this will upset some people as in these articles?'

'David Cameron's attack on multiculturalism divides coalition'
'More division over multiculturalism'
'Fury as Labour 'smears' David Cameron after he attacks multiculturalism'
'Three problems with David Cameron's speech on multiculturalism'

DC: 'Well, bad luck if it does. It is what I believe and it is what I am going to say.'

Me: 'Have you done any research?'

DC: 'No. Why?'

Me: 'Because if you research the issue, particularly among the ethnic minorities you are referring to, you will have more chance of fulfilling your objective.'

DC: 'How's that?'

Me: 'Because you will be able to reflect back to these people the views that the majority of them have expressed to you. This will show them you are on their side and that you care.'

DC: 'What if the majority don't agree with me?'

Me: 'Keep your mouth shut!'

DC: 'What are you proposing?'

Me: 'Three things. You appoint an independent research company to conduct the biggest quantitative survey among ethnic minorities ever seen in this country. Then you get another independent research company to conduct a significant qualitative study of at least 24 focus groups, with at least four groups in each of six regions...'

DC: 'Blimey, what's that going to cost?'

Me: 'A lot less than this thing rebounding on you.'

DC: 'What am I going to ask them?'

Me: 'You explore their views on all the values you want to espouse: human rights, including for women and people of other faiths; equality of all before the law; democracy and the right of people to elect their own government; integration.'

DC: 'What's the third thing?'

Me: 'You get well-known and respected opinion-formers from various racial and religious groups to support the values you want to reinforce. Their voices will be more influential than yours.' Has Britain lost the values that drew me here?

DC: 'But I'm the Prime Minister'.

Me: 'Exactly. That means you can do all these things. No problem'.

DC: 'But why should I bother?'

Me: 'I have told you. Your message will be more effective.'

DC: 'But politics doesn't work like this. I'm the Prime Minister. I decide these things.'

Me: 'Yes, but you have to *sell* your thinking and your ideas to the people and this is how you do it.'

DC: 'It all seems a bit of a fuss to me. I'll make a speech and see what happens.'

Me: 'Yes, Prime Minister.'

10
MONEY MATTERS

10.1 BANKERS' BONUSES NEED RE-BRANDING AS DIVIDENDS

4 FEBRUARY 2011 09:01

What a difference a word makes.

This week, 'according to American regulatory filings', Michael Sherwood, joint CEO of Goldman Sachs London, was awarded a bonus of £9million.

In the late 1960s, in Hong Kong, my late father was appointed a non-executive director of the Hong Kong & Shanghai Bank.

He told me that, despite numerous other appointments and directorships, he was particularly nervous before his first Board Meeting.

This was because the responsibilities and decisions taken, including lending enormous sums of money to the Governments of other Asian countries, were so daunting. At this first meeting, he determined to do his homework but say nothing.

However, at the last item of the agenda discussing the CEO's remuneration and the issue as to his receiving a clothing allowance, my father piped up and said wasn't he paid enough already and weren't the board too busy to discuss such trivial matters for their most highly paid executive?

I know my father would have thought that it was the CEO's job to make as much money for his employers as possible. That was why he was CEO and why he was the Bank's highest-paid employee. An enormous bonus for doing the job he was paid to do would be unthinkable.

In today's environment, it seems to me that there is a difference between banks that are wholly or part-owned by their employees and those that are publicly owned or even part-nationalised.

I would advise those bankers who are shareholders of the business to re-brand their bonuses as dividends. Of course, dividends have to be allocated proportionately among the shareholders and a way round this would have to be found.

The next level of 'bonus' could be paid as share options (and branded as such) where employees have the option to buy shares, at the current price level, which they would not be allowed to sell for, say, three years. This would provide them with an incentive to stay loyal to their employers as well as encourage them to contribute towards the longer-term success of the business.

It is a fallacy to claim that not paying employees bonuses would encourage them to leave for other companies because very few banks, and we (and Michael Sherwood) know who they are, are part-owned by their employees and earn 'dividends' accordingly.

Cash bonuses should be decided by the shareholders (because they come out of a total dividend pot) and if this is the Government or, more accurately, all of us, with other priorities, then these bankers should take the hit. If they think they can go and work for a bank that will instantly dole out a chunk of shares, then let them.

The truth is they won't all get jobs and we all know it. In this way, the market will dictate fairer levels of reward.

For me, in today's market economy, I far prefer the John Lewis and Co-op model where the employees and customers own the shares. This seems much fairer for all.

By the way, my father returned all his non-executive directorship fees to his full-time employers because that is what he thought he should do – even when the total sum of his non-executive fees added up to more than his full-time salary.

What a different world it was.

10.2 A CREATIVE INSIGHT INTO THE BANKING CRISIS

19 DECEMBER 2011 08:55

If, as discussed last week, the Eurozone is a mish-mash of politics and economics, then the banking crisis is even more of a hot potato.

On the one hand, the word 'bank' comes fraught with vitriol. On the other, we seem prepared to alienate anyone to save our precious 'financial services' industry. How can financial services be good but banks bad? Aren't banks financial services? To make things more complicated, are all banks bad or just some of them?

Again, brutal simplicity of thought is required. Indeed, such is the mess the banks have caused, we need innovation. We must think the unthinkable. We must be creative.

The first thing is to unbundle the good from the bad.

Let's start with the wider area of 'financial services' that is not banking.

For example, insurance is vital to our economy. Insurance spreads the risk of disaster. If x% of cars are likely to crash then we all pay a little bit towards the cost of this eventuality occurring, hopefully not to us. This applies to all manner of things including houses, ships and our lives. Nothing wrong with insurance.

As to the narrower banking sector, certain elements of banking are elementary and harmless. These are the 'High Street Banks' which take lots of little piggy banks of money and lend big bellyfuls to other people at a higher level of interest, thus creating a profit. Capitalism in its purest form.

In both of the above examples, an insurance company or a bank collects little bits of money out of all of us with the aim of making financial gain from the lump sum that is created. Please note the word 'collects'.

For this is not the case in the nasty side of banking.

This is called 'Investment Banking'. We do not like investment banks at all. They have played a significant part in creating the national debt. What is more, the employees of investment banks benefit from salaries and bonuses far out of scale to everyone else in the economy.

Many investment banks have their European, if not worldwide, bases in London. This makes the countries in the Eurozone doubly angry. Lots of people make lots if money over here but then we, pointedly, walk away from them over there.

I know banking is boring to marketing people and those interested in behavioural insights, but please stick with me. I am close to revealing a creative solution to the monetary crisis in which the Western World now finds itself. Well, actually I am afraid I am not. But I can tell you how we can stop getting into this mess again.

First, let me explain the role of the Stock Exchange. The Stock Exchange allows me to make a very important point. Here, 'investors' buy shares in so-called 'quoted' companies, whose share price goes up and down according to their own performance and the general state of the market.

The important point about the Stock Exchange is that the people who buy and sell shares, humble pensioner or gargantuan pension fund, have to pay to buy the shares – and get the cash back if they sell them.

Now we come to the 'traders' in Investment Banking. Here, a new vocabulary ensues. Hedging, derivatives, short selling, put and call options, securitisation, leverage and, most important of all, risk.

This is not the place for me to explain the meaning of all of these terms (even if I could).

But there is one principle I would like to establish.

Do you remember Nick Leeson? Have you heard of Alexis Stenfors, Jérôme Kerviel or the mighty Yasuo Hamanaka? No? Get Googling!

Between them, these people (and many more, some of whom have been kept under wraps) have lost billions. Dollars, pounds or euros, it does not matter – any which way, it is billions.

Do you think their employers owned these billions for these people to lose?

You bet they didn't.

It is like being let loose in a betting shop and told: 'Gamble all you like. If you win, you get a share of the cake. If you lose, um, yes, er, well, hmm, if you lose we'll worry about it later.'

We need a regulatory system and, preferably, legislation to control people who gamble *money they do not have* on the future price of goods, commodities or even money itself.

For this is the problem behind the financial crisis we are in.

At the moment, if they win, these people get very rich but, if they lose, all of us – from Athens to London – lose too. This situation must not be allowed to happen.

In a capitalist state, where 'financial services' are so important to our economy, these people are out of control. But, because the rest of us are paying the price, they must be controlled.

Indeed, as a sophisticated capitalist economy, and as I argued in my last post, because of the importance of our 'leadership' in financial services, we must take the lead: think harder, think better, be more creative - not just walk away from the table.

When I managed Ogilvy Thailand, every single Ogilvy Worldwide office had to send a daily report of its cash-at-bank position back to WPP in London. If Sir Martin Sorrell can make this sort of thing happen, why can't our far less able politicians?

Why shouldn't people who are gambling with money they do not have be compelled to make a daily statement of their exposure to the Bank of England? There may be better executional or more creative ideas, but let's work them out because the key behavioural insight is vital.

People are being allowed to spend money they do not have and, because we pick up the tab if they lose it, we need to know how much it is.

The current position is very wrong, very wrong. We must stop it now.

A prosperous New Year to you all.

10.3 A CREATIVE INSIGHT INTO THE EURO CRISIS

12 DECEMBER 2011 08:34

We are surrounded by news of the Eurozone. But what positive solutions have we offered by way of Big Society neighbourly help? Or have we just covered our own backsides?

I am proud that our country punches above its weight in creative talent. In technology, music, drama, film, television, comedy and, yes, advertising, Great Britain is a creative force.

Have we mobilised this talent? Can we help by finding a creative solution to this crisis? In this spirit, I would like to offer some 'upstream' creative thinking of my own.

Let's be brutally simple.

We start with what Euclid called axioms.

I am asking you to accept the following five points as the truth:

i) The Eurozone is a clumsy mish-mash of politics and economics.
ii) The politics, based on history, is that Europe is better united than divided.
iii) The Euro is an economic problem.
iv) Politicians are attempting to resolve economic, non-political problems.
v) In times of desperate economic crisis, it is necessary to park the politics.

Please bear with me and accept the above as axiomatic, even if you are a politician.

Thanks.

Having accepted these axioms, let's unpick this Euro problem and start again.

What is the Euro?

The answer, again, is brutally simple.

The Euro is an exchange-rate mechanism where a number of countries are 'pegged' to one currency. There is nothing new in this.

INSIGHT ONE

For nearly ten years, I worked with The Bahamas Tourist Office. Lovely people. Lovely place. As part of my job, I had to visit The Bahamas almost every year. Tough client.

The Bahamian dollar is 'pegged' to the US dollar on a one-to-one basis.

Please note this very important sentence.

Do you know what it means?

It means that, when you go to The Bahamas, you will find in your pocket a mish-mash of American and Bahamian dollars.

But relax, don't worry, stay on the beach, have a swim, chill, float – because it doesn't matter which dollars you have. They only look different. Some Bahamian dollars even feature pictures of The Queen. But each Bahamian dollar has the same value as the US dollar.

INSIGHT TWO

I was brought up in Hong Kong where, even since 1997 when, disgracefully in my view, we gave the place and its people back to China, the Hong Kong dollar is 'pegged' to the US dollar.

Do you get that?

In our world, today, a province of China has a currency 'pegged' to the American dollar? Which politician would have made that up let alone happen?

There's more.

"In 1972, the Hong Kong dollar was pegged to the US dollar at 5.65 HK dollar = 1 US dollar. In 1973, this was revised to 5.085 HK dollar = 1 US dollar. Between 1974 and 1983, the HK dollar floated." (Wikipedia).

You may not be an economist or even be privileged enough to work in our financial service industries but please, please read the above sentence very carefully.

For this is the solution to the Eurozone crisis.

What it means is that a currency can be 'pegged' to another currency but, in times of crisis, the exchange rate can be revised.

It can even float.

Now, the Euro is in crisis.

And what follows is what needs to be done.

CREATIVE SOLUTION

Let's move to Greece. I love Greece. For one glorious summer, immediately prior to commencing my career at Ogilvy, I taught water-skiing in Corfu.

The only solution for Greece is, in principle, to stay pegged to the Euro.

But for now, and until this crisis is over, Greece needs to do two things:

i) Re-launch the drachma. At this sad time, this will help the Greek people soar with pride in their wonderful country. All those heroes – Hercules, Achilles, Odysseus, Socrates, Plato, even my friend Euclid – come back and be noted!

ii) Stay pegged to the Euro but float the drachma at a new exchange rate to the Euro (within whose fiscal rules the drachma will remain). (This is not as difficult as you might think. All shopkeepers need is a till that gives you a price in two different currencies. You will find this in airport Duty Free shops. At one time, even, there was discussion of High Street retailers in Britain accepting Euros as well as pounds. In practical terms, it is not a problem. You can even pay tax in Euros).

Do you know why this should happen?

It is because Greece is in crisis and the drachma cannot survive at an exchange rate of less than 1.2 Euro to the pound. It needs to be at least 1.5 and anywhere up to 1.99.

At this rate, the people of Europe will want the drachma!

Governments and banks will buy bonds in drachma!

People will buy things sold in drachma!

People will go on holiday to Greece!

Everyone will be happy!

Greece is not the only country that should do this, of course.

So, the creative solution to the Euro problem is for all the countries in the Eurozone, other than the 'base' currency (Germany or France or both?) to:

i) Relaunch, reprint and redistribute each Eurozone country's national currency (apart from France and/or Germany).

ii) Meet to agree new, more achievable exchange rates in proportion to each country's national debt.

iii) Don't invite David Cameron.

That is the solution.

Mint.

THE FUTURE

If ever we join the Eurozone, unlikely as it may seem today, all we will be doing is 'pegging' the pound to a centralised European currency. It is an economic decision.

Once we have done this, if we are in crisis, we can float if we need to.

Either way, we can even keep the Queen and our British heroes like David Ogilvy on our currency, thus helping – emotionally – to overcome any political fears there may be.

We would not be selling our souls.

And, by retaining our own 'currency', it would be easier to pull out if we had to.

AND FINALLY

As I hope I have shown, when in a crisis, you need to throw everything up in the air.

You need to be creative.

And you need to be brutally simple.

By nature, economists will not want to be brutally simple. The more qualified, more highly regarded and more intelligent the economist, the less simple he or she will want to be.

Their instinct will be to find theorematic complexities to do with balanced budgets, deficit limits, the current value of Greek bonds, the need to submit budgets to Brussels and conformity to an Economic Planning Commission.

But they have to be more open minded than this.

They have to accept that the only way to recover from this brutal crisis is what used to be called devaluation and the facility to float exchange rates to the centralised currency, just like the Hong Kong dollar did to the US dollar between 1974 and 1983.

After agreeing that principle, the economists and eurocrats can work out implementation. But, they must be prepared to make a creative leap.

In this economic crisis, the politics is the problem (Euclid liked problems).

And the problem needs a creative solution (Euclid liked solutions).

As I hope I have shown.

QED.

10.4 NATIONAL DEBT: WHO DO WE OWE?

21 MARCH 2013 09:03

What is it about the national debt that I am not getting?

Please forgive me for not being an economist but, when you owe loads of money, you can't keep up with the repayments and you plunge deeper and deeper into the doo-doo, there comes a time when you go to your creditors and say:

'Hey guys, hard as I try, I can't pay you this money and, if we go on like this, I ain't never going to repay it. Let's work it out.'

Please forgive me for not being an economist but, back in the day, some Third World countries did this and, rightly, the banks who held the debt recognised the reality of the situation and wrote the money off. It was called *'unpayable debt'*.

So who owns our national debt today? And at what point is it 'unpayable'?

The UK national debt is £1.1trillion (Dec. 2012). It is 'owned', it says here, by banks and building societies (9.3%), insurance (23.1%), Bank of England (25.7%) and 'overseas' (30.7%).

Sorry, did I read that right? The Bank of England? You what? Our Bank of England? The Bank of England that we, the people, 'own'? And what about the banks, building societies and insurance companies? Don't we own them too?

Please forgive me for not being an economist but, are you really telling me that we are being punished because we can't pay ourselves back money we already own? Huh?

Get this:

The American national debt, it says here, is $11trillion, of which the 'overseas' portion is 'owned' by China ($727bn), Japan ($629bn) UK ($157bn) Brazil $129bn) Russia ($116bn).

Did I read that right? America owes Britain $157billion. Great! Can we have it back, please?

The only thing that seems clear about this whole situation is that it is confused, illogical and absurd – and, frankly, people who know better could do better.

It seems to be that the size of the global debt mountain is such that the human suffering around the world, from Cyprus to America, is so out of proportion to the size of the problem that a more innovative and creative solution is required.

So, for the last time, please forgive me for not being an economist but, can someone please stop and think about the lack of humanity in all this and, ideally, wipe the slate clean and start again with a zero balance?

At the very least, surely a worldwide financial readjustment could be achieved?

And, if nothing else, I believe we are owed an explanation of who we owe all this money to and why whoever it is will not take a more humane approach to overcoming this problem?

More transparency, more creative thinking and more leadership please.

11
WORLD MATTERS

11.1 Man's inhumanity to man

18 March 2010 12:36

A seminal moment in my life came when I was one of the first European business managers to visit Vietnam.

At the time, I was the General Manager of Ogilvy & Mather in Thailand. Our US clients were embargoed from engaging with Vietnam and our European and Thai clients wanted to explore potential business opportunities in the Vietnamese population of 70 million 'consumers' before their American competitors were allowed in.

I was told I would have a 'guide' but that really he was a Government employee who would report back on all of my movements. A spy.

At the War Museum in Saigon, in rows of glass jars, were the deformed embryos who had been conceived by Vietnamese mothers whose homes had been blanket-bombed by napalm dropped by American airplanes.

During this trip, I was constantly urging my guide that I was European, not American.

He told me I did not need to do this. The Vietnamese held nothing against Americans.

After all "we won the war" he claimed "but what we couldn't understand was that the Americans were bombing us in South Vietnam when our leaders told us they were on our side".

Of course, the Americans could not tell the difference between a North Vietnamese enemy citizen from a South Vietnamese friendly citizen – so they decided to bomb the lot of them.

And I fear this rather ruthless military strategy may have caused the appalling, and unforgivable, suffering of the children of Fallajuh in Iraq.

We are told that we are in Iraq and Afghanistan to win over the 'hearts and minds of the people'.

Yet when President Obama, who inherited this mess, wanted to win over the hearts and minds of Republican voters to win the US election, did he do it by sending in the troops, by shooting people or by dropping bombs?

Of course he didn't. He used sophisticated 'new media' techniques.

Do we, here in cosy Britain, with a General Election looming, know who votes Conservative and who votes Labour? No, of course we don't.

And I don't think even our ruthless and unprincipled politicians will be blanket bombing us all in the hope that they will mop up the other side.

And now consider what happened when it emerged that thousands of Iranians felt that their election in Iran had been fixed. What did they do?

They used new media channels, especially Twitter, to protest at what was happening. In June 2009, the BBC reported: 'Although there are signs that the Iranian government is trying to cut some communications with the outside world, citizen journalism appears to be thriving on the web.'

Yet when it comes to *us* communicating to *them*, we send in the tanks.

Where is the media strategy that we could develop, and media intelligence we could apply, to work alongside our brave Army soldiers?

In Iraq or Afghanistan, how on earth can these brave servicemen and women tell the Al Qaeda or the Taliban from the rest of the population?

Recently, I heard a radio report that an issue facing our brave servicemen and women in Afghanistan is that The Taliban disguise themselves as local people, enter a village, lay a few bombs, blow up some soldiers and then disappear back into the hills.

What if we provided the villagers (who presumably know who all the Taliban insurgents are but are too scared to say) with the media technology such as laptops and mobile phones to keep our soldiers, or select 'middle men', informed as to the presence of our real enemies within?

And how differently would our Army be perceived if, instead of firing guns and parading around in tanks and dropping bombs as well, of course, as dying for the cause themselves, they handed out laptops and mobile phones and urged the people to listen to the reasons we are there?

Wouldn't it help these poor people in these poor countries if we told them more clearly and more often what we are doing there and what we are fighting for – human rights, the difference between right and wrong, the rule of law, the importance of education, respect for others, 'do as you would be done by', tolerance, freedom of speech, liberty, democracy?

Quite apart from the lives lost, the BBC have reported that the ultimate size of the bill for the wars in Iraq and Afghanistan could reach $3 trillion ($3,000bn). That is a lot of second-hand laptops and mobile phones.

So, my proposal is to allocate just a small percentage of these vast costs to develop a media strategy to communicate what we are up to.

If millions of Americans and Europeans cannot understand why we are in Iraq and Afghanistan, how on earth can we expect the indigenous people to have a clue what we are doing there either?

I believe passionately that, as one of the great 'creative' countries of the world, we should be developing a more sophisticated approach. We have the expertise to persuade people to change the way they behave. It is called Behavioural Economics.

But I do not believe we use our skills in this area to help overcome the really important things in our society or in the wider world.

Instead, we have our creative, media and communications experts using meerkats to sell insurance and a gorilla to sell chocolate.

Come on, we can do better than this.

11.2 GADDAFI, IMRAN KHAN AND BEHAVIOURAL INSIGHTS

21 MARCH 2011 09:15

Behavioural Insights apply to evil dictators as much as consumers or the electorate.

Why shouldn't they? We are all human.

So, what has been the role of the Government's new Behavioural Insight Team (BIT) in the Libya/Gaddafi debacle?

David Cameron is lauded for being the earliest 'statesman' to propose a no-fly zone.

This was when the brave anti-Gaddafi protesters had come together to call for his downfall on the streets of Tripoli (let alone Benghazi).

As I have Tweeted repeatedly, then was the time to do a deal with Gaddafi:

★★

From: @TheSalmonAgency
Sent: Feb 27, 2011 11:28p

Is now a good time to block #Gaddafi UK financial assets? Won't it force him to entrench position against protesters?

sent via Twitter for BlackBerry®
On Twitter: http://twitter.com/TheSalmonAgency/status/
42003184050241536
★★

We should have sent in the peacemakers to tell Gaddafi:

- where he would and would not be welcome to live
- that he must never return to Libya again
- he can have his Swiss bank accounts
- we will let bygones be bygones (i.e. give him an amnesty)
- and, frankly, tell him to f-off into oblivion (Terms & Conditions apply)

166

Unsavoury, I know, and certainly not 'justice'.

But, as we must admit, only a short time ago we were cuddling up to him. Certainly, our PM Tony Blair was (doesn't he owe us a phone call to his old mucker Muammar?)

And has Martin McGuinness faced 'justice'? Of course not (he's an MP!). In Ireland, people were killed over a much longer period – making the deal more difficult to negotiate in the end.

Which is why we should have acted more quickly with Gaddafi.

As it is, we have:

- frozen his financial assets
- seized his properties around the world
- let him make a fool of himself on TV
- opened a war crimes investigation at The International Criminal Court in The Hague
- threatened the military action which is now a reality
- bombed his house

What would anyone with any human behavioural insight expect Gaddafi to do next?

Wave a white flag and face a lifetime in prison or feel Saddam Hussain's rope round his neck?

In the 1992 cricket World Cup, Pakistan's captain Imran Khan urged his losing team to 'fight like caged tigers'.

This is what we have forced Gaddafi into doing.

Rather than leave the cage door open, our Governments have forced him into this corner – and, hence, are responsible for the innocent Libyans who are being bombed and killed as you read this. They have blood on their hands.

They hoped Gaddafi would do a Mubarak but they were not dealing with the same animal – as they should have known. We are all human.

Now the Arab League have threatened to pull out – . They "did not want military strikes by Western powers that hit civilians". They are human too.

No doubt, events will overtake this post.

Whatever happens, what a shambles.

11.3 DAVID CAMERON, ETON AND GEORGE ORWELL

28 MARCH 2011 08:16

I do feel gloating, common amongst footballers and politicians, to be most unseemly behaviour. The words 'I told you so' are rather distasteful too, so sorry about this....

In my blog post dated 29 October 2010 'The Conservatives may be doing the right thing, but in the wrong way'*(see 3.2)*, I predicted that the proposed spending cuts would lead to 'social chaos'. This was proved to be true by the student riots on 10 November 2010 and then again with the anti-cut protestors on Saturday (26 March 2011).

Yet, when I posted that prediction back in October last year, there had not been riots in the streets of London for several years. For this reason, I had thought very deeply about my forecast because the opposite of 'I told you so' – being shown to be wrong – can make you a fool.

As to my post on Libya last week, I stand by every word I said.

More bombs have been dropped and more people killed – yet still the 'protesters' (whom, to placate the UN and Arab League, we are now to call 'civilians', despite their being somehow armed) have not 'reoccupied' Green Square in Tripoli, where they were on 22 February. As of today, they – or, now, we – are still not back at base.

I felt that when the protesters were there on 22 February, this was the time when a deal with Gaddafi should have been cut. As posted last week, I tweeted this view on 27 February – the day before David Cameron hawkishly proposed the no-fly zone.

He also said there would be "further isolation of the regime by expelling it from international organisations and further use of asset freezes and travel bans to encourage those on the fringes of the regime that now is the time to desert it... we do not, in any way, rule out the use of military assets".

I believe history will show that David Cameron missed his moment.

This week, a new Conservative voice on Libya has been ubiquitous in the media. His name is Rory Stewart. Although touted as an expert on

Middle Eastern affairs, he has been an MP for less than a year and shown to be completely out of his depth. When asked repeatedly by Andrew Neil on the BBC 'what is our strategy in Libya?' our Rory gave four different answers in four minutes. He was completely flummoxed.

Still, we can forgive him. He went to Eton. And David Cameron has a penchant for Etonians. On 6 March, he made school friend Tim Luke a business policy adviser:

'David Cameron's Eton chum to be No 10 adviser" trumpeted The Sunday Mirror.

Talking of Etonians, I wonder if it might be beneficial for the Prime Minister to read these words by another Etonian, George Orwell – however contrary their views on humanity might be. In fact, in my view, David Cameron – and all political leaders – should have this peerless writing copied, mounted and framed on the wall by the mirror in their bedrooms so they can read them every day.

It is from an essay called 'The Hanging':

> 'It was about forty yards to the gallows.
>
> I watched the bare brown back of the prisoner marching in front of me. He walked clumsily with his bound arms, but quite steadily, with that bobbing gait of the Indian who never straightens his knees.
>
> At each step his muscles slid neatly into place, the lock of hair on his scalp danced up and down, his feet printed themselves on the wet gravel. And once, in spite of the men who gripped him by each shoulder, he stepped slightly aside to avoid a puddle on the path. When I saw the prisoner step aside to avoid the puddle, I saw the mystery, the unspeakable wrongness, of cutting a life short when it is in full tide.
>
> It is curious but until that moment I had never realised what it means to destroy a healthy, conscious man.
>
> This man was not dying. He was alive just as we were alive.
>
> All the organs of his body were working – bowels digesting food, skin renewing itself, nails growing, tissues forming – all toiling away in solemn foolery. His nails would still be growing when he stood on the drop, when he was falling through the air with a tenth of a second to live. His eyes saw the yellow gravel and the grey walls, and his brain still remembered, foresaw, reasoned – reasoned even about puddles.
>
> He and we were a party of men walking together, seeing, hearing,

feeling, understanding the same world; and in two minutes, with a sudden snap, one of us would be gone – one mind less, one world less.'

Prime Minister, in God's name, what have you done?

11.4 Barack Obama makes Martin Luther King's dream come true

9 November 2012 08:58

I am sure we all admired the rolling brilliance of Barack Obama's oration when, in his Presidential acceptance speech, he said:

> *"If you are willing to work hard, it doesn't matter who you are, or where you come from, or what you look like, or who you love. It doesn't matter whether you are black or white or Hispanic or Asian or Native American or young or old or rich or poor, abled, disabled, gay or straight you can make it here in America if you are willing to try."*

Please read them carefully because these words represent a defining moment in the history of America – just as I felt the Olympics were for Great Britain *(see 2.3)*:

> *"The London 2012 Olympics could mark the moment when the British people accepted, at last, what it means to be British and became comfortable with the cultural diversity we embrace – a diversity which is not defined by our place of birth or the colour of our skin but by the way we have behaved over the last two weeks."*

So significant is the juxtaposition of these two events, less than four months apart, that it takes time to consider just how momentous they are. I suspect the older you are, the more time you will need – particularly if you were alive on 28 August 1963.

For a new world order has been defined, in which the American people, and possibly all God's children, are *free at last*.

How so?

Because Americans voted for individual freedom over corporate finance. They recognised the economy was the most important issue facing their country – but however superior Mitt Romney's track record in financial management, when it came to issues like abortion and gay marriage, the American people simply did not want to live in his world.

Thus, by his re-election, the US President is the living embodiment of his own message. He is his own mandate for the next four years.

In Barack Obama, Martin Luther King's dream has come true.

And the world, surely, is a better place.

At last.

11.5 WHEN A HUMAN RIGHT IS A HUMAN WRONG

24 JULY 2012 23:49

Sitting, lounging, reading books – as I am now – by a swimming pool overlooking the Mediterranean Sea, it is natural to absorb more sunshine than news. But the full horror of the Denver Dark Knight killings has penetrated this tranquil state and destroyed the lives of hundreds of innocent people oceans away from here.

No doubt thousands of commentators have written millions of pages about this crime (not many of which, frankly, have I read).

But how many people were reading – as I was last week – the seminal American novel 'Freedom', by Jonathan Franzen, on the very day the news from Denver came through? In the book, Franzen writes this:

'It's all circling round the same problem of personal liberties ... even if your kids are getting shot down by maniacs with assault rifles ... Bill Clinton figured out that we can't win elections by running against personal liberties. Especially not against guns.'

Creepy, huh?

I am sure much comment has been made in defence of America's gun laws but I would like to contribute one small thought – and I am sorry if you have read this elsewhere.

What about the protection that the victims of these Denver killings were entitled to?

Is *protection* not a role of government, a civil liberty, a human right?

Over the Olympic period, and in this Presidential election year, I wonder if, every time the American national anthem celebrates 'The Land of the Free', there will be hundreds of victims in Denver and billions of people around the world thinking 'oh no, you are not'.

11.6 US GUN LAWS: COULD TWITTER AND FACEBOOK BE FORCES FOR GOOD?

20 DECEMBER 2012 09:03

What a world.

Twenty-six children have been slaughtered.

To protect them, teachers have thrown their bodies into hails of gunfire.

'Carnage', as President Obama said:

'It comes as a shock at a certain point where you realise no matter how much you love these kids, you can't do it by yourself, that this job of keeping our children safe and teaching them well is something we can only do together, with the help of friends and neighbours, the help of a community and the help of a nation.

And in that way we come to realise that we bear responsibility for every child, because we're counting on everybody else to help look after ours, that we're all parents, that they are all our children.'

Why did President Obama stop at 'nation'? Surely, this is a world issue? As Obama said, our children 'are all our children'. If 'all', why not all of us? The world. He went on to say this:

'Can we truly say, as a nation, that we're meeting our obligations?

Can we honestly say that we're doing enough to keep our children, all of them, safe from harm?

Can we claim, as a nation, that we're all together there, letting them know they are loved and teaching them to love in return?

Can we say that we're truly doing enough to give all the children of this country the chance they deserve to live out their lives in happiness and with purpose?'

I invite you to re-read these words and substitute 'nation' and 'country' with 'world'.

For, in my experience, the level of response to this horror has been unprecedented. 'The day after the shooting... photographs of Victoria Soto began to go viral on Facebook' (International Business Times).

Many of my own friends and contacts on Facebook and Twitter were part of this movement. I have never known anything like it. Unanimously, they agreed with Obama:

'We can't tolerate this anymore. These tragedies must end. And to end them, we must change.'

Yes, America, it is you who must change. You must change your gun laws in line with the rest of the civilised world. You must collect up your murderous weapons, throw them onto the fire and destroy them.

The over-riding sentiment on social media has been revulsion and anger at the US gun laws. How can the US – the US of all places – have such uncivilised gun laws and not connect them with the barbaric behaviour of its people?

There is a very fine line between going viral and direct action. Could the following happen?

We, the world, will not let you, America, slaughter children in this way.

We will rise up against you.

We won't shoot you.

We won't kill you.

We will isolate you.

Smell the coffee, America, 'cos we ain't drinking it. Ask Starbucks.

We will spit out your hamburgers and your ice cream and your fizzy drinks.

We will stop buying your shampoos and your washing powder and your denim.

We will shred your credit cards and withdraw investment in your financial markets.

We will boycott your computers and your software and your e-commerce platforms.

Will we, use your social media channels to do this?

Can Twitter and Facebook be a force for good?

Could it happen?

You bet.

Will it happen?

Hope so.

12
BUSINESS MATTERS

12.1 WHY CAN'T COMPANIES HAVE 'SOCIAL' AS WELL AS 'LIMITED' LIABILITY?

5 MARCH 2012 20:04

It does get lonely, this blogging business.

My career has been in the much more collaborative world of marketing and advertising, where I am used to researching opinion, sharing knowledge, knocking around ideas, listening to other people's thoughts and making innovative judgements based on the team view.

The over-arching theme of all my posts is that the talent and creativity in marketing and advertising could be better used for the benefit of society as a whole, rather than restricted to gorillas selling chocolate and meerkats insurance.

Thus it is frustrating, by definition of the medium, to be forced to progress, all on one's own, from 'insight' to 'strategy' to 'execution' – and then find one is judged at the executional rather than strategic level (often by people who are even more sad and lonely than you are).

It is a frustration that not all of the most worthy strategic insights I have provided have been taken as seriously as I would like. So, I am, with apologies, going to return once more to the point I was trying to make in 4.3 (*How the banks can save the NHS*).

This was that 'privatisation' (aka 'competition') and 'nationalisation' used to be seen as conflicting ideals.

But the banks have shown that the state can have a stake in the ownership of a company (and an influence of the salaries of the directors) but not be accountable for its day-to-day performance. I used my bank, the NatWest, a subsidiary of the Royal Bank of Scotland, as an example.

As 'competition' is the hot topic in the NHS (and, now, rather surprisingly, the police) I proposed that 'the state' could invite private companies to tender for public service contracts in return for, say, a 30% stake in the business. Given that we own 84% of RBS, I thought this was a rather innocent suggestion. It was also what I would call an 'executional' interpretation of a much more 'strategic' insight. I really don't care what the percentages are.

I am more interested in principles. So let's get back to them.

On the one hand, it is commonly accepted that civil servants are not the best people to provide the most efficient management and the highest standards of customer service in the public sector – especially health, education, security and transport.

On the other hand, there is a deep-rooted fear of private companies encroaching on this territory and, horror of horrors, making money out of us, the people.

The current debate shows 'competition' and 'public ownership' as polar opposites. No one is right. No one is wrong. Politicians go round in never-ending circles stuck in the mud of out-dated dogma and the self-justification of views they formed as students over twenty years ago.

Someone has to break through this.

My own contribution is that the banks have shown that private and/or public companies can survive and, hopefully, thrive with 'the state' (us) as shareholders.

I am not into corporate finance, and I really don't care how the corporate structures, memorandi of association, and shareholder controls are defined. I am happy to leave this detail to someone else.

But I do insist that, in today's free market economy, there has to be a Role of Government whereby the principles of competition and improved customer delivery, particularly in the public services, are defined and refined for the greater good of society as a whole – and that part-owned private companies can be structured to be liable to perform to this greater good.

In this way, it might just be that 'our' position as shareholders in, but not managers of, the banks might just – out of distress, debt and default – have shown us a new way forward.

That is my position and I am sticking to it.

12.2 HOW A FORMULA ONE RACING CAR DESIGNER COULD HELP REPEL THE FLOODS

25 FEBRUARY 2014 09:08

The overarching theme of this blog is to show that better use of the skills and creativity of the UK advertising and communications sector would benefit society as a whole as well as business.

But even I admit that, with all the creativity in the world, none of us could stop the floods which have dominated our media landscape – even if, as our austere Prime Minister said, 'money is no object'.

However, one doesn't get the impression that the relevant parties were communicating very effectively with each other:

- David Cameron, the Prime Minister, was criticised for getting involved when it was too late and events were escalating out of control.
- Eric Pickles, Secretary of State for Communities and Local Government, was accused of shabby and brutish conduct and making an 'epic blunder'.
- Chris Smith, chairman of the Environment Agency, said his staff know '100 times more about flood risk management than any politician'.
- Owen Paterson, Environment Secretary, complained to Number 10 about Mr Pickles' criticism of the Environment Agency and said he was 'grandstanding'.
- Downing Street rejected suggestions that the Cabinet was at war over the Government's response to the floods.
- Ed Davey, Liberal Democrat energy and climate change secretary, attacked 'the ignorant, head in the sand, nimbyist Conservatives who question climate change'.
- Ian Liddell-Grainger, Conservative MP for Bridgwater and West Somerset, called Lord Smith a 'little git' and said 'if I have to stick his head down the loo and flush, I will.'

You do not get the impression that these people could run a bath, let alone quell the tide of our wettest winter month since 1767, do you?

I think we can take it that the people in charge of the response to this crisis were not communicating very effectively with each other, if at all. Their rather pitiful performance certainly antagonised the unfortunate people whose houses were flooded and who felt stranded, abandoned and afraid.

Let's hope that, should floods such as this return, our governing bodies will have a prepared communications plan to improve the effectiveness of their response.

I do have one thought which might help:

Would it be feasible to identify all the houses in Britain which are vulnerable to flooding, draw up a list of of their occupants and develop a communications campaign informing them, on a regular basis, of all the actions and innovations that are being drawn up on their behalf should the apocalypse reoccur?

After all, over the last few weeks, one of the most common complaints of these unfortunate people has been their complete ignorance of anything, if anything, was being done to help them.

Even better, perhaps such a campaign could include input from these people to reassure them they are being looked after and help them feel they have a say in their own recovery process.

I don't see why such a brief could not be issued. After all, if we are to have a quango called the Environment Agency, surely we are entitled to know what keeps them busy? And, as with all quangos, do any of us really know what they do all day? The EA should be pushed and challenged and, above all, be accountable for their actions.

Me? Fortunately, I live in London and my local river The Wandle which, I am told runs below my local High Street, has not burst its banks.

Last week, I found myself watching a TV documentary about the fascinating and extraordinary career of Gordon Murray, the 'renowned' Formula One car designer.

Not only was he responsible for some of the most iconically innovative ideas in motor racing but he designed the fastest and most sophisticated road car ever built – the McLaren F1.

Nowadays, Murray is at the cutting edge of more ecologically efficient and affordable road car design and development – the T.25 and T.27.

Some of Gordon Murray's thoughts are well worth considering on a wider level:

INNOVATION

'In the 70s, I got to design the monocoque, the engine installation, the gearbox, the suspension geometry, the aerodynamics, the cooling systems, the fuel system. Everything on the car. Nowadays, you'll find someone doing front suspension. And that's what they do. They sit in an office and draw front suspension for eight or ten years. That culture stops innovation.'

COMMUNICATION

'I've followed my own mantra all the way through and that's communication. You have to communicate with people if you want the team to work properly and you can see in an instant the teams who have communication and the teams that don't.'

INSPIRATION

'I definitely could not have done this without F1 experience. You think differently. We have worked with a lot of the large manufacturers. It's not that they are not bright enough. Its just the constraints of the large corporate structure that tends to suffocate the innovation. And stops it coming to the surface and stops people taking a chance.'

CONCLUSION

Frankly, if you want to attach the word 'innovation' to any human being on the planet, Gordon Murray would have to be on your shortlist.

I wish I could force every one of the political goons listed above to read and heed his words.

Not one of them is qualified to polish his boots.

12.3 THE POST OFFICE – PUTTING THINGS IN BOXES

A few years ago, in a moment of visionary genius, I realised that, over time, more and more products were going to be sold over the internet. Amazon's business was growing at an extraordinary rate.

At the time, Amazon had made its name as the website of choice for books. Now, of course, Amazon sells virtually everything. But I remember thinking that books were a great place to start because, especially if you bought one at a time, they fitted conveniently through your average domestic letter-box.

Generally speaking, though, if you bought more than one book, or anything larger than the size of your letter-box, you had to be at home or a little card was popped through your door telling you that the Post Office had tried delivering a package but that, in order to retrieve it, and most annoyingly, you would have to pick it up yourself – back at the Post Office.

Well, I didn't know much about the Post Office other than posting letters in nice, warm-red pillar boxes and receiving them through my letter-box. But I did know that sometime, somehow, somewhere, a box containing my online order arrived at the Post Office, was loaded into a nice red van and driven to my house. Then, if I was out, the driver would drive my box back to the Post Office it came from – with my order still undelivered.

In this new-age world, with more and more people buying more and more products online, this all seemed a rather inefficient, and decidedly non-eco-friendly, delivery system.

Now, please put all of the above in a little box in your head because while I realised this was happening, I became aware of another market trend.

More and more, at a rate similar to the growth in online purchasing, I read that Post Offices were being closed all over the country. In fact, the deeper into the country you lived, the more likely would it be that your

Post Office would be closed. This meant that if you jumped onto the bandwagon of buying products online, but were not at home for them to be delivered, the wagon with your box in it would drive even further to find you were out and even further back to where it had come from.

Surely, if there was a system where you asked for your products to be delivered to your Post Office and that the card saying it had arrived was delivered by lunchtime with the rest of your morning mail, then you could go and collect your order at your convenience?

And, surely this would save time and petrol and carbon for the Post Office as well as provide an exciting new reason for your local branch to survive?

Online retailers would offer their customers two options:

1. Would you like your order delivered to your home?
2. Would you like your order delivered to your local Post Office for you to "collect at your convenience (you will be notified when it arrives)"?

By saving all the inefficiencies outlined above, Option 2 might even be cheaper, creating a win-win-win situation. No need to close Post Offices (and perhaps the opportunity to open bigger and better branches); online retailers offering a choice of delivery options (and possibly cost savings); consumers in more control of their purchasing decisions (and supporting the survival of their local Post Office, especially in rural areas).

Perhaps, even, the Post Office could develop an expansion strategy? Maybe they have a wider product offering than they think? Maybe, because they have to store all these undelivered boxes, the Post Office has become a *storage*, as well as a *delivery*, service?

Why not invest in those storage places that have sprung up all over the place (especially those revolting, ugly, intrusive, big yellow ones which you can paint in your nice, warm, royal, pillar-box red)? There's lots of boxes in those and they make lots of money. And yes, PO, you can charge money for storage.

Even if only pennies a day, there'll be lots of them.

So come on PO – please don't GO, we want you to GROW!

What a great idea. I dreamt of my destiny as a dotcom millionaire and, on 2 November 2005, I wrote to the Post Office. I told them what their problem was.

What happened? Well, I know my letter arrived, because a person describing himself as 'Managing Director' of a branch of the Post Office called me. He asked me to tell him my idea over the phone. I replied that if I did that, the Post Office could nick my idea (and my millions). He told me the Post Office had loads of new ideas and if I wouldn't tell him mine over the phone, then he wasn't interested. He put me back in my box.

Much more recently, Adam Crozier has been on the box. On the Andrew Marr Show (BBC Sun 27 Oct 09) he said: "Our market in the letters side is shrinking all the time whilst, at the same time, we are growing massively in terms of packets and parcels".

There you go. Even the Post Office agrees with what I told them would happen four years ago. So now we have more and more products being sold online, more and more boxes being driven around in more and more vans to more and more empty houses and more and more Post Offices being closed – apparently, since 1997, the number of post office branches has fallen from 19,000 to 11,000.

Can this be right?

And, where did I go wrong?

*For seven other 'random consumer insights', please see chapter 13 of my book 'Thoughts on Life and Advertising'.

13
RULE OF LAW MATTERS

13.1 CUSTOMER RELATIONSHIP MANAGEMENT (CRM)

28 JUNE 2013 09:07

More and more companies are spending more and more time and money on Customer Relationship Management (CRM).

This is based on the theory that happy customers will buy more products more often (repeat purchasers) and, because they are happy customers, they will advocate these products to other people (word of mouth).

Thus, it seems strange that companies are willing to sacrifice their CRM investment in their after sales methods.

I have a little domestic experience of my own to share…

Well over a year ago, I received an invoice from a 'utility' supplier. As it was over 50% more than the previous period, I queried the sum stated on the invoice.

None of us like to complain of course, especially when it involves the telephone experience we all hate – twenty minutes listening to a recorded message "please hold on, your call is valuable to us" etc. followed by a futile conversation with an operator who, is unauthorised to explain or agree to anything at all.

In this experience of mine, after several minutes of going round in circles, I asked the call centre person to make a note of my query and pass it on to whoever could explain the unexplained increase in my bill.

Later, out of the blue as it were, I received a letter threatening me that, unless I paid up within seven days, my case would be passed on to a 'Debt Recovery Agency'.

No attempt, whatsoever, was made to respond to my query.

I was told that, unless I settled by bill within 14 days, I was at risk of the following:

- Registration of a County Court Judgement which could affect your credit rating for six years
- Registration of a charge against any property you own

- Instructing Enforcement Agents to visit your property and remove goods
- Contacting your employer to deduct your debt directly from your salary
- Ordering your Bank or Building Society to pay your debt directly to us.

You what?!

All I am doing is querying a bill and I face the possibility of 'Enforcement Agents' bashing through my front door and nicking my possessions from my house?

What sort of system is it that big business can override genuine customer queries with scare tactics and bully boy behaviour, such as this?

For scare tactics and bully boy behaviour this certainly is. The threatening letter from which I have quoted above was dated over six months ago in 2012. Yet, despite the seven day deadline, none of these threats have been carried out. So ...

Who are these 'Debt Recovery' people?

Who and what are 'Enforcement Agents'?

What right do they have to force their way into my house?

How many people are being treated like this?

How can they be allowed to frighten people in this way?

To what extent would this terrify vulnerable customers such as the elderly?

How many of them have the resources to resist such aggression?

Is this behaviour legal?

What happened to the judicial process?

What happened to the rule of law?

13.2 SECURITY

Recently, I was invited to meet a television production company at well-known studios just outside London. Having supplied its colour, make and registration number in advance, I was directed to park my car just outside the studios.

After the meeting, I began to take my leave and was asked to wait for 'security'.

Wondering what this meant, I shut down my tablet and packed my bag. Then, much to my surprise, a big burly man in a black uniform entered the room and, holding it open, stood by the door.

My hosts, very politely, said their goodbyes and informed me that this big fella would escort me back to Reception and out of the building.

Well, I may be a sensitive soul but, as I walked down the corridor to leave the studios, I felt very un-nerved by this unknown character walking behind me.

Why was he there?

Was I in danger?

What was this danger?

From where would it come?

In what form would it be?

As my heart beat faster, my imagination ran wild.

And then it struck me.

Perhaps I was not in danger at all. Perhaps I was the threat. Perhaps this man was not protecting me from someone but was protecting someone from me.

What had I done?

What had I said?

To paraphrase Butch Cassidy and the Sundance Kid: 'Who was this guy?'

It was all very worrying.

Luckily I found my way out of the building without being beaten or stabbed, or having beaten or stabbed anyone else, made my way to my car and, with some relief, drove home.

Since this incident, I have carried a picture of this man in my head.

Suddenly, people like him appear all over the place: outside pubs and clubs, at train stations and on the streets. Everywhere I look.

Who are these people?

How qualified are they?

What powers do they have?

How are they allowed to behave?

Who are these guys?

I know, in Britain, the police have been revealed to be a devious, untrustworthy bunch but give me a suitably qualified, legally endowed British copper any day.

These puffed up cowboys with puffed up muscles in puffed up jackets give me the creeps.

13.3 DEBT COLLECTION

In free market economies, providers of products and services need customers.

In marketing, without customers, none of us are anything. Or, if that is too tortuous a double negative, without customers we are nothing.

Customers are the name of the game. They need to be identified, understood, targeted, persuaded, looked after, nurtured, *retained*.

Customer retention – sorry for the marketing jargon – differs from product to product, service to service. In simple terms, the more expensive the product, the less important the retention.

These are called high value, low volume products where even the wealthiest customers buy a limited number of yachts or swimming pools. You get my drift.

Other products, to maximise their profit potential, depend on customer retention.

These are the 'repeat purchasers' who buy the same product several times a week and sometimes every day. This is the low value, high volume end of the market. Food is the most obvious example. Daily bread.

Down here things get interesting – and, sometimes, nasty. Very nasty.

For there are 'products' which all of us buy every day without realising we are doing it, some of which we 'buy' before we turned the lights on in the morning or wash.

When we wash, we buy water. As it gushes out of the tap, so the meter ticks over and so do the 'units' for which we are charged by our water supplier.

If the water is hot, another meter, often tucked away in a cupboard or a basement, ticks over.

And, as these meters tick over, the money we owe our utility suppliers builds up until, sometime later, and as part of a faceless and, in this sense, timeless process we are sent a bill.

To some people, especially if they have children or are part of an 'extended household', the size of this bill comes as a shock. As they are spending money on their household utilities, and every time they wash their face, they have no idea how much money their household is spending.

The shock comes when the bill arrives.

And the reason it is a shock is because, when the bill arrives, when they have to pay, these customers, especially if they are old or sick, simply do not have the money.

Nor are they given room to query the amount they are being charged.

This is when things can get nasty.

For when a customer cannot pay his or her utility bill, the utility companies put the squeeze on. Threatening letters arrive in the post:

- If you don't pay, we are going to cut off your supply.
- If you don't pay, we will add your name to a 'credit blacklist'. You may never get hot water again.
- If you don't pay, we will pass your name to a 'debt collection' agency.
- If you don't pay, we will apply for a 'warrant of entry'. We will turn up at your front door, invade your house and take your belongings. 'We will arrange for a locksmith to be present and, if necessary, a Police Officer, so that we can access the meter'.
- If you don't pay, we will take you to Court. You will pay the 'extra costs' of this legal action. 'These extra costs can be substantial: up to £350 per meter'.
- If you don't pay, you will have a criminal record. You could go to prison.

Retention becomes detention.

And, during this process, do you know what these companies do? They distance themselves from their aggressive, bullying behaviour by sending you letters from 'debt recovery companies' who you have never heard of. Certainly, you have never agreed to a contract, a working relationship, with them.

Don't you believe me?

There is a utility company called Utility Warehouse. They have a nom de plume, as it were, called 'BCW Group'. In small letters at the bottom of the letter heading it says 'BCW Group is a trading style of Utility Management Services (BCW Group) Limited.'

'Trading style'?

You what?

What is a 'trading style'?

Over the course of a long and successful career, I have come to know the difference between a 'limited' company and an 'unlimited' company, a 'public' company and a 'private' company but I have never – ever – heard of a 'trading style'.

You may not have heard of a 'trading style' either.

For you have a bigger problem.

You still cannot afford to pay your bill.

You are terrified things have got so out of hand and the threats that have been made to you.

The bully boys have stepped in.

And things have become really scary.

So scared are you that you make one of the worst decisions of your life. You decide to go and borrow the money to get your utility company off your back.

To get rid of one debt, you commit yourself to a company who will provide you with another, even bigger debt.

These are the 'payday lenders'.

What do they do?

They say: 'Bills to pay? No money? No worries! We will lend you the money! No problem.'

Except, of course, there is a problem.

A massive problem.

The interest rates are so punitive, the 'customers' of these companies are never going to be able to repay their debts. They are in a nasty, vicious spiral to desperation and destitution and fear.

Because these 'short-term credit' providers are not actually providing anything, are they? All they do is move their 'customers' from one level of debt to another.

Here is last week's news about Wonga.

"Wonga could face a criminal investigation after it emerged that the payday loans giant had sent 'thuggish' legal letters from fake law firms to threaten customers behind on repaying their loans, and charged them for the letters.....
City of London Police have confirmed they are to look again at whether they think a criminal investigation into Britain's biggest payday lender would be appropriate after the firm agreed to pay out £2.6 million in compensation to

45,000 customers who had received the bogus letters after being named and shamed by the Financial Conduct Authority (FCA) watchdog."

Let me tell you, this is the merest tip of a very large iceberg.

I am deeply suspicious of the 'reviews' and 'public enquiries' and kangaroo courts called 'parliamentary select committees' that have crept into our society, but I do believe that the whole subject of debt collection and legalised gangsterism needs to be properly examined and redesigned in a more humane way.

I would go so far as to say that, with the 800th Anniversary of the signing of the Magna Carta coming up next year, never has the 'rule of law' been so threatened as it is today by these disgraceful debt collectors.

The Magna Carta decreed that the rule of law was all powerful. It superceded the monarchy, the barons, the landowners, everyone.

Until now, in 21st Century Britain, where debt collectors, like celebrities, think they can operate above the law.

Where is the justice in this?

14
MEDIA MATTERS

14.1 THE PERVERSE CULT OF CELEBRITY

16 OCTOBER 2012 09:01

When I was at school, we had a visiting preacher in Chapel who told us there were three things in his sermon that we would never forget. And I haven't. They were:

Don't poison Socrates.

Don't crucify Christ.

Stand up and be counted.

At times in my life, I have thought of these three mantras, particularly the last one in which I have my own little track record.

I have thought about it while watching and listening to pious celebrities pontificating about the perverted behaviour of that famous celebrity Jimmy Savile.

Not only was Jimmy Savile a celebrity, he was a BBC celebrity.

Once, at a Ball in an expensively famous London hotel, the seating plan had me sitting next to a BBC celebrity. I had never seen or heard of her. Apparently she read the news.

When it came to sit down, this famous person I had never heard of moved her place up one so her husband was sitting next to me. Next to her, another famous BBC news reader I had never heard of did the same thing which meant they sat next to each other flanked, guarded, by their husbands, one of whom told me they always do this. It protects them from 'the public' (like me).

Who on earth do these people think they are?

Apparently a lot of them heard about what Jimmy Savile was up to. Some of them say they knew what he was up to. But none of them did anything about it. 'It wouldn't have been worth it', they say. 'No one would have done anything.'

Shouldn't they have reported it anyway?

As it happens, I do not believe they did not report him because they thought no one would do anything. I think they kept quiet because they see themselves as 'celebrities'. And there is an 'honour amongst thieves' rule among celebrities that they don't tread on each others turf. They

199

don't have to behave in the same way as lesser mortals like us.

I admit, occasionally, a celebrity will slag off another celebrity. When they do, it makes headlines. When you think about it, it is surprising how little it does happen, given the way they behave.

And who are they, these 'celebrities'?

Some people segment them into 'A Listers' and 'B Listers'. The A Listers have a rare and wonderful talent like great actors or musicians or writers or record-breaking Olympic athletes (who, ironically, do not feel too superior to engage with the plebs in the crowd).

The B Listers are what you might call 'media' celebrities. These people are talentless nonentities who, in my view, have done nothing at all to warrant the 'celebrity' title. They either have a famous mummy or daddy or they do something which millions of other people could do too such as appear on reality shows or they read the news (couldn't a monkey be trained to do this?).

In this context, Jimmy Savile – Sir Jimmy Savile no less – was surely a B Lister. Apparently not. It emerges that people at the BBC and other media channels worshipped the ground he walked on to the extent that he was above the law.

Really?

A bloke who, on TV, looks at an autocue and says 'Now for the gorgeous Pan's People' followed by some inane donkey-like noise and a cloud of cigar-smoke? The guy who, on radio, puts a record on a turntable and tells you the name of the band? Or who tells his next victim that he will 'Fix It' for something to happen while his hand gently, creepily caresses its way up and down the poor child's back?

This guy – this pervert – was above the law.

Who says he was above the law?

Well these other 'celebrities' do. With their 'celebrity' attitude and behaviour towards each other, they were part of the cover up. They did not report him.

Why didn't these B List people 'stand up and be counted'?

Didn't they think of the poor under-aged children who were the victims?

Where do these celebrities put their morality, their human conscience, their social responsibility?

It is up their own backsides, that's where it is. And there is nothing I would like more than for someone to find evidence on these self-serving, gutless 'celebrities' and have them locked up for perverting the course of justice.

That's what I said:

Perverting the course of justice.

14.2 GAGGING CLAUSES: WHAT EVERY BUSINESS MUST LEARN FROM THE BBC

8 AUGUST 2013 09:01

Last week Stuart Hall, a BBC broadcaster, 'admitted 14 charges of indecently assaulting girls, one aged nine'.

It emerged in what the BBC call a 'Respect At Work' review, that 'some behaviour appeared to go unchallenged by senior managers, with certain individuals seen as being "untouchable" due to their perceived value to the BBC'.

Appallingly, especially if you are or have been a parent to a nine year old child, 'the BBC turned a blind eye to Hall'.

I suspected as much in my post 'The Perverse Cult of Celebrity' last October *(see 14.1)*.

Political writer Linda McDougall, who worked with Hall at BBC Manchester in the late 1960s and 70s, says she was sexually harassed almost every day during the four years she worked with Hall ... but was told by watching staff 'not to make such a fuss'.

McDougall insists that the BBC bosses must have known what was going on, recalling how Hall occupied a private room in the building where he would entertain female visitors. 'It would have been impossible not to know,' she said. 'If I knew, if others knew, I cannot imagine our bosses did not know'.

Indeed, and worse, 'fellow BBC staff may have helped Hall gain access to victims'.

Who are these BBC staff who 'helped' this monstrous child molester?

Surely they should be named and shamed and prosecuted?

As you may never have worked at the BBC, or never will, you may think all this media coverage at the BBC is not relevant to you.

Well, let me tell you it is.

As a publicly owned and funded institution, not least whose business is journalism, the BBC's duty of truth and integrity is under greater spotlight than other businesses. For example, the management has to endure such things as Select Committees in Parliament.

It is because of this scrutiny that all companies should be forced to behave like the BBC and these BBC initiatives should apply to all employment contracts drawn up by all companies.

The BBC director of human resources Lucy Adams has said: 'What needs to be fixed is that we have let bullying behaviour go unchallenged.' A confidential hotline will be set up to report abuse ... and 'gagging clauses' will be ditched, although confidentiality clauses will be used where appropriate, such as to protect business interests.

Surely, as I have said, all this should apply to all companies?

A national 'abuse hotline' needs to be established.

And, if gagging clauses are to be ditched by the BBC, this should apply across the board.

Furthermore, if the intent of gagging clauses is to cover up criminal behaviour such as theft, clinical negligence and child abuse, surely these devices should be made illegal and their perpetrators, including their lawyers, prosecuted?

Finally, I would like to call for an amnesty for all whistleblowers, including me, to be allowed to reveal the criminal behaviour that gagging clauses have blackmailed them from concealing.

Far from being bribed into signing gagging orders, often by the threat of otherwise withholding payment they are contractually entitled to receive, employees should be actively encouraged to report wrongdoing and rewarded, not penalised, for doing so.

I think this is very important, as my posts on whistleblowing have shown (*see Appendix II*):

These posts took five years of my life to write.

14.3 How the Beeb blew it

4 December 2009 14:37

Don't any of these highly paid BBC executives or flipping MPs understand just how much £142.50 means to people in the real world out there?

Actually, I mean the real Britain, not the real world. In fact, that's my point.

When CNN was launched in 1980, it had had almost zero content. Now it is a massive worldwide media powerhouse. And, in those far off days of 1980, do you know what content viewers were prepared to sign up to?

Well, I can tell you. In some parts of the world, such was CNN's dearth of content, and so desperate was CNN to expand globally, that viewers in say, Asia, were prepared to sign up and pay for the CNN weather forecast for yesterday in Florida from the day before yesterday.

Get that? On a Wednesday in Asia, people would watch the weather forecast from the previous Monday for what the weather would be in Florida on Tuesday, the day before they were viewing this 'forecast'. Why would people, sweating in Hong Kong or freezing on Mount Fuji, pay for that? But they did.

And, more importantly, how *on earth* did the BBC ever allow this to happen? How did the BBC even allow CNN to take off at all, let alone for Ted Turner to laugh all the way to the bank and into Jane Fonda's arms?

I'll tell you why. It was because of the licence fee.

The BBC management never had to worry about revenue, never had to bother about the sheer hunger for news and entertainment from billions of people with billions of televisions and radios, never had to think about the explosion in world markets with worldwide corporations and worldwide brands and certainly never saw that, one day, there might be a worldwide web of people with a world vision.

They just sat their – myopically – in Regent Street or Shepherd's Bush and 'earned' their fat salaries based on their entirely forecastable revenue that was being provided by taxing the relatively small number of Brits who were forced to pay for these short-sighted people.

And, all this time, which of the BBC and CNN had a worldwide reputation, largely through the World Service, for editorial integrity, expert journalism and *trust*?

And which of the BBC and CNN had a catalogue of content of such outstanding creative quality that they are still repeating it to this day?

The answer, of course, is the BBC.

Remember, we are talking about *all* of the programming *ever* produced by the BBC up to 1980 versus CNN with virtually *no content* at all.

Because of this, CNN's very existence is a national disgrace to the British people. We should be ashamed of ourselves.

So what can we do about it?

Well, there is only one answer. Punish these BBC wasters by setting them a commercial challenge that – if they cannot fulfil – will force them to take their fat pensions and fast forward themselves off somewhere else. They should be ashamed to show their faces in the High Streets of Britain.

Right now, they have a strategy to save money and be more politically correct by moving a chunk of their business to Manchester. What do their potential audience in India and China and the whole wide world care about that? We are talking about an audience of *billions* here.

It gets worse.

According to Campaign last week, "The BBC is considering floating a portion of BBC Worldwide, its commercial arm, following increased pressure from the government and commercial rivals to reduce its media market power....the company is reported to be holding talks with City advisers regarding the issue as part of a strategic review of its worldwide entity, which is estimated to have a total equity value of £2 billion."

Billions of people – and now *billions* of pounds?!

And, in all this, the BBC *still* wants a few million Brits, many of whom are struggling like never before, to cough up £142.50 a year to fund this madness. Get this – £142.50 is *double* the dole of increasing numbers of our people – and, to some, over *a month* of their disability allowance.

What *on Earth* is going on?

Here is one solution. The UK taxpayer should set the BBC a limit of five years to reduce the licence fee to nothing by that time. As a sop, they should be allowed to sell advertising on a commercial basis except on BBC 2, BBC Radio and BBC World Service. After that, they should be set a target of paying corporation tax on profits at competitive market levels so that some of this £2 billion can be returned to the hands that have fed this antiquated and myopic anachronism for so long.

I don't care about the execution but it must be right that the strategic objective must be to force the BBC to face the commercial realities of the big, wide world out there and stop bleeding the poor people in the UK to enrich yet another bunch of 'City advisers' and entertain audiences around the globe.

It is the UK taxpayer who deserves – at last – to receive the BBC for free.

It is the time for the rest of the world to pay us for that privilege.

And it is the human responsibility of the BBC's management to make this happen.

14.4 OPEN LETTER TO RUPERT MURDOCH CONCERNING THE TIMES PAYWALL

12 AUGUST 2010

Dear Rupert Murdoch,

Last week, on 4 August, this website reported that you 'gave the first hint' that subscriber levels to The Times pay wall are 'strong'.

Good on you.

But what you have done has really hacked me off. You may not care about this. After all, who am I?

Well, I am one of your customers.

I have been reading The Sunday Times for all my adult life and I still pay £2 a week for the privilege. My kids think this is heathen behaviour and a complete waste of paper – especially as I don't read half of it.

The 'Money', 'In Gear' and 'Home' sections go straight in the orange bag.

In 'Travel', I read that naughty little article 'Confessions of a Tourist' and then chuck that out too. Such a waste of paper.

As I'm a cultured kind of guy, I read 'Culture', especially the book section, but I'll come back to that.

By the way, I used to keep 'Culture' for a week to refer to the TV and Radio listings (sometimes returning to book reviews and other articles I glossed over on Sunday) but now I chuck it on the Sunday with the rest.

Ironically, this is thanks to you. Because not only do I buy The Sunday Times every week but I subscribe to Sky for TV, phone and broadband.

And on my Sky HD+ box, it is much easier to see what programmes are coming up than it is in your Sunday Times 'Culture' section. So I bin it.

The sections I do read are the newspaper, 'Review', 'Business' and 'Sport' (even there, the 'Cowes Week' supplement went straight overboard).

So, for years, I have paid for your products and been a loyal customer.

But, last week there was an article in The Sunday Times about a medical condition in which I have a particular interest. I wanted to 'save' it on my computer in the special computer file I keep for this subject.

I looked the article up on your website to see if I could save it electronically.

No doubt, you will say this is illegal. But I feel I have paid for the article and, having paid up, the format in which I want to file it is my business.

Then I hit the pay wall.

Well, I am sorry. I have already paid for this content in your paper.

And I deeply resent the fact that you are trying to extract even more money out of me for something I have already paid for. So what did I do?

I could have scanned in the article and saved it electronically but, before bothering to do this, I found the same subject on one of your competitor's websites. They covered it quite well, actually, and they didn't charge me to access it (so I'm thinking of transferring to their newspaper too).

Anyway, I think I have a better idea (or rather, on this site, an insight) which, on a one-off basis only, I am prepared to share with you for free.

First, I have to declare an interest. I am a the founder of two websites www.Lovereading.co.uk and www.Lovewriting.co.uk.

Lovereading reviews and recommends books and charges publishers to email this content to readers who have opted in to receive this service for the genres of books they have told us they are interested in.

Lovewriting doesn't review and recommend books, but is a media channel where self-published authors pay us to promote their books on the site.

To help these independent authors, we urge our 200,000+ Lovereading users to browse books on Lovewriting.

All Featured Books on both these websites have free Opening Extracts.

Admittedly, compared to your empire, these are tiny businesses.

However, because of what I have learnt, I can accuse you of being lazy.

Why don't you use your Sunday Times website to find out from me the 'sections' of content that I am interested in and pay for on a weekly basis?

Why don't you unbundle your customers into their areas of interest rather than by media channel (newspaper, TV, digital etc)?

Why don't you ask us if we would be interested in receiving digital content from your media channels in our individual areas of interest (e.g. books)?

Then you could charge advertisers to reach clearly defined audiences who you know, because they have told you, are interested in certain activities (books, cars, sport etc) and likely to buy the products that apply thereto.

Perhaps you could do this across all your media channels and point your customers to 'destination sites', such as Lovereading, which would offer them more in-depth coverage of their areas of interest.

This way, you can avoid hacking off previously loyal customers like me by asking us to pay twice for the same content.

Yours sincerely,

Hugh Salmon

14.5 HOW CREATIVITY CAN
SAVE YOU MONEY

23 JUNE 2010 06:59

Bonjour to the great and the good sunning themselves in Cannes, while we all celebrate last week's IPA report 'proving' (no less) the connection between 'creativity' and 'business success' – although I think these two findings contradict each other, more of which later.

'Creativity' is hard to define. It is intangible and subjective. Sometimes, even the creators of award-winning advertising themselves fail to recognise the creative essence of their own work. For example, for me, the Cadbury 'Trucks' execution missed the core insight behind the success of the earlier, breakthrough, award-winning 'Gorilla' commercial which is that eating chocolate is pure self-indulgence. That naughty confection can only pleasure the mouth in which it melts.

That (male?) gorilla ain't banging them drums for anyone but himself. Just watch him preparing to savour his personal moment. He's not there to offer 'joy' to anyone else as, it seemed, 'Trucks' set out to do.

Nor can I agree that 'Surfer' is the greatest commercial of all time. Do we really connect that undeniably brilliant film with the experience of waiting for a Guinness to be pulled in the pub? I do a lot of this and find the two experiences – watching the ad and drinking the beer – strangely separate.

Lastly, on this personal – and purely subjective – executional journey, at Kirkwoods in the 80s, I was privileged to work on the 'Toys in Front of the Fire' commercial for British Coal.

When the account moved on, 'Dog kisses Cat kisses Mouse' won shedloads of awards. But who made the real creative leap? I know what I think. So you see, 'creativity' is subjective. What do I know? Who am I?

That is what makes awards so important. They recognise work that has been commonly, albeit subjectively, agreed to be 'creative' by a number of people.

Creative awards are also important to those who have created the work.

Individually, there is the opportunity for a pay rise or a new, better job.

Corporately, awards can win new business from clients who are impressed in this way – because clients, with their own careers, love the glory too.

But surely, from a business, rather than entertainment, point of view awards should be a means to an end, rather than an end in themselves?

Years ago, back here in London (Knightsbridge actually) I was up for a job at Lowe Howard-Spink. These were the glory days when the agency was independent and Sir Frank was on fire.

There I waited, all suited and booted, awkward and lonely, in the strange Reception (all Receptions are strange if you have never been there).

Of the reading material on offer, I went for the agency brochure which, in pre-Google days, was a key, if rather last-minute, piece of learning.

Frankly, I couldn't believe it. Not only did the brochure gloat over all the creative awards the agency had won but it claimed that winning these awards was the agency's prime objective.

'Hold on!' I said to myself, fidgeting nervously in my suit. If I work here, my job will be to persuade 'my' clients that our aim is to win awards, over and above 'business success' (IPA term not mentioned in Lowe brochure).

As an account man, would this philosophy suit me? Would I fit?

Then it hit me.

What do creative awards mean? What is 'creativity'? Original, unexpected, impactful, memorable, award-winning? All of these? Whatever. And what is the benefit of 'creativity' to the clients who pay for it?

Surely, if 'creativity' includes impactful and memorable then, de facto, the client won't need to spend as much in the media to
 i) become noticed by customers,
ii) help them remember the message
iii) persuade them to do what we want them to do? The more 'creative' the message, the less it costs for consumers to notice it, remember it and act on it. Simples.

Throughout my career, I have stuck by this argument and been amazed that creative agencies haven't made more of it.

So, back to the two findings of last week's IPA research:

1. "Pound for pound, creativity makes ad campaigns more efficient; on average, creatively awarded campaigns (i.e. in major awards competitions recognised by The Gunn Report) are at least 11 times more efficient."

There you go. I've been right all along. QED. Phew!

2. "Creatively awarded campaigns that invest strongly in Excess Share of Voice (ESOV) perform particularly well, suggesting that many creative campaigns could further improve ROMI [Return On Marketing Investment] by investing more in Share of Voice (SOV)."

Hang on. Doesn't this second finding contradict the first one?

If 'creatively awarded campaigns' are at least 11 times more efficient, why would you need to chuck in more SOV to improve your ROMI? Isn't there a mathematical non sequitur here (quite apart from acronym overload)?

Of course, 'investing strongly in ESOV' is likely to improve performance, but why does this 'suggest' that more investment, rather than less, could further improve ROMI for 'creative campaigns'? Why would you need to?

Remember, 'E' in ESOV stands for 'Excess'. Exactly.

So I am sticking with my position.

I am confident, in Finding One of this research and thus the full backing of the IPA, that the more creative your advertising, the less you need to spend in the media for consumers to notice and remember your message.

In fact, in this digital age, you may not need to buy any media at all.

But Creativity? Innovation? Upstream thinking? Absolutement.

15
SOCIAL MEDIA MATTERS

15.1 TWITTER WARS

Last week, my 26 April post on 'Super-injunctions' *(see 'Thoughts on Life and Advertising' 10.1)* attracted a surge of interest on a spectacular scale, partly through the national news agenda but also on Twitter.

I guess one follows the other but, these days, I am confused as to which is which.

Does Twitter set the news agenda or does the news agenda follow Twitter?

Today, as I write this, Twitter is on the front page of all the national newspapers, so I really cannot do anything but return to this topic – hopefully in such a way that it will not be out of date by the time you read it.

And, please don't worry, I won't name names or break the law. I am an identifiable human being posting these views on a reputable business website.

First, I have a small confession to make. I sneakily changed the title of my earlier post from 'Contra Mundums etc' to include the word 'Super-injunctions' because a month ago 'super-injunction' had not entered our language as it has now.

And I still think 'Contra Mundum' is a really cool term. What a great name for a book, film or rock band (speaking of which, there is a legal term called a 'Motley Fool Order' which may enter your vocabulary soon).

Anyway, whatever the language, my earlier post was about:

i)   the enforceability of super-injunctions
ii) the role our marketing and advertising industries could play in achieving this.

Today, a month later, we all know the name of one of the footballers involved.

In fact it wasn't difficult to find out as long ago as 9 May (as I did).

There is another footballer, a TV presenter and an actor – I think I know who all of them are.

So where are we now?

On enforceability, the first issue was whether British (European?) law can apply to a company 'registered' in California. Lawyer Mark Stephens said: "If you want to sue Twitter, you have to go to San Francisco. Any attempt to enforce English privacy or libel law will not be accepted in the US."

Well, legally, that may be the case, but surely if advertisers in the UK and Europe offer (or are forced) to refuse to use Twitter in their marketing campaigns, then wouldn't Twitter have to sit up and take notice?

And this is the core development we have reached. A polarisation has emerged between what Twitter, Facebook and LinkedIn might call 'mainstream' online media on the one hand and the small, independent, often anonymous private sites who like to slag people off left right and centre.

These 'mainstream' sites have achieved massive financial valuations which will be justified by their attaining significant advertising revenues.

And herein lies the issue. Why would any reputable company advertise to an audience of demographically 'strange' (sometimes very strange) people?

Surely it is in the best interests of Twitter and other social networking sites to ensure their users are identifiable human beings, not anonymous weirdos in internet cafes?

I am no expert on capital markets but I gather Twitter is valued at around ten billion dollars (Facebook $100 billion). If they don't achieve their worldwide advertising revenue forecasts, their valuations will plummet and they may even go bust.

The brands won't disappear of course – just the companies and people that own them.

The second issue is the sheer number of Twitterati worldwide who are said to have ignored the law (ignorance is no defence). How can they all be traced and punished?

Well, maybe they can't – but we live in a 'new media' world and perhaps new legal principles need to be established. For example, what if Twitter was punished in proportion to the number of their users who had used Twitter to break the law?

Then, for sure, they would know who their users are. They are not difficult to 'verify'.

And I don't believe Twitter will never be accountable to the laws in the countries they operate. Yes, they are worldwide websites, which is part of their attraction but, as argued above, what about the countries from whom they want to attract revenue?

Will Twitter really never have a UK or European office who can be forced to reveal details of UK and European users?

Of course not. As we speak, according to Brand Republic and the Financial Times, Mr Tony Wang has moved from San Francisco to the UK to open a Twitter office.

This must be true because he has tweeted the news himself.

Indeed, there is a 'verified' @TwitterUK account. And Facebook have an office near Regent Street.

These 'mainstream sites' absolutely must open offices in the UK and Europe. If not, how will they justify these huge valuations?

That's where we come in.

As per my previous post, we need a Code of Practice (the 'Contra Mundum Code'?) whereby 'mainstream' advertisers using 'mainstream' agencies to communicate to customers via 'mainstream' media channels must insist that these 'new media' channels can identify the users who make comments on their sites.

Do you think the 'readers letters' published in national newspapers haven't been double-checked as real people whom the publishers cannot identify if they need to?

For the umpteenth time, our politicians (who, unlike judges, make laws) need to engage more fully with the marketing and advertising industry.

By doing so, we can help them force these sites more accountable and, if required by law, reveal the personal details of users who have broken the law on 'mainstream' online media channels.

Oh dear, I've chosen to make this point in the very week it has been revealed that 10 Downing Street has been sending letters to the people of this country using fake computer-generated names like 'Mrs E Adams'.

Oh me of little faith.

15.2 THE SPONTANEITY OF TWITTER

4 AUGUST 2011 07:59

In my post of 23 May, I wrote 'Does Twitter set the news agenda or does the news agenda follow Twitter?' This question is even more apposite today.

As I have discovered myself as @_HughSalmon, Twitter crosses the absolute extremes from the most serious to the extremely silly. This is what makes Twitter both important and fun.

This week, right across the media, in all the newspapers, on TV and the radio has been the story of Charlie Gilmour whose mum, novelist Polly Samson 'has taken to Twitter to reveal details of her son's incarceration'. I have some sympathy with her position, about which she feels very strongly and to which she has given much thought (and feeling).

There is also the kidnap threat to Duncan Bannatyne's daughter which is clearly very serious indeed. It will be interesting to see if they track the Tweeter down. Some people, who think they have been tweeting anonymously, will be worried if they do.

On the other hand, the media has amused us by the much more spontaneous little spats between Piers Morgan and Jon Snow, Lord Sugar and Kirsty Allsopp, George Michael and Jeremy Clarkson, Rory McIlroy and BBC golf commentator Jay Townsend – all of which have hit the headlines.

I started wondering if these 'celebrities' (a sub-species who, in my experience, are trained to flatter each other and, strangely, invite each other to their weddings when they have never met) would have allowed these lively tiffs to have occurred if they had given their tweets a second thought.

Put this together with the more serious issues raised in my more serious earlier post, and I began thinking of the benefit of Twitter introducing a pop-up before every tweet along the lines of:

- are you sure you want to send this tweet?
- do you mean what you have said?

- is it offensive?
- is it defamatory?
- are you aware you could be breaking the law?

This thought was drifting round my head as I started reading One Day by David Nicholls (good book). It is about the developing relationship of two characters, Emma and Dexter (bad name).

In Chapter Two, Em is writing a letter to Dexter (this is 1989). She asks herself:

> *"how to sign off? 'All the best' was too formal, 'tout mon amour' too affected, 'all my love' too corny... and (so) quickly, before she could change her mind, she wrote –*
> *God I miss you, Dex*
> *– then her signature and a single kiss scratched deep into the pale blue air mail paper".*

So spontaneity can be exciting, erotic even.
Spontaneity is refreshingly unplanned.
But be careful.
Spontaneity could get you into trouble.
One day.

15.3 THE EVIL OF SOCIAL MEDIA

29 JULY 2011 07:47

At last year's General Election, I argued for the more intelligent use of social media in modern warfare.

With the application of a greater depth of human understanding in Libya, I have no doubt that a more successful outcome would have been achieved. It is now nearly August and the protesters are not back in Tripoli where they were on 27 February (as I Tweeted on the day).

Our leaders have blood on their hands.

At Super-injunction time (remember then?), I argued for the media, marketing and advertising industries to pull together to help control the explosion, and valuations, of social media sites especially Facebook and Twitter.

Since then, the admirable withdrawal of advertising from the News of the World was a key driver in its downfall.

Why don't the same principles apply online?

For we have reached an even darker phase.

The atrocities of mad Norwegian Anders Behring Breivik were fed by his rantings on Facebook and Twitter plus other more obscure sites:

"Lars Buehler, a Norwegian scholar and terrorism expert, said he had debated with Breivik on an extremist website frequented by xenophobes and Islamaphobes all over Europe."

What site can this have been? I don't know and don't really want to know.

But I do know that:

- social media gave Breivik his voice.
- social media connected him to other like-minded nutters.
- social media, arguably, gave him the confidence to do what he did.

So, while recognising the inevitability of the growth and development of social media – and respecting the principle of freedom of speech – what can we do to detract evil monsters like Breivik?

After all, the hacking scandal has led to public statements, debates in Parliament, Select Committees and all manner of enquiries – not to mention resignations, arrests and criminal charges.

How can there be one law offline and another online?

It seems to me there are two things we can do straight away:

i) As I have argued before, advertisers (who acted individually, rather than as a group, in withdrawing from the News of the World) should agree a Code of Practice for 'mass-market' sites like Facebook, Twitter, Google and others. Such a Code would include these sites being able to identify the human beings who use them so they can be chased down and prosecuted if they break the law.

ii) I believe it is a Role of Government to introduce procedures to police the web far more efficiently than anyone does now.

If Esther Rantzen can inspire the launch of Childline, then why can't we – as an industry – engage with the Government to set up some kind of 'Online Helpline' whereby people can report abusive, defamatory or illegal behaviour on the net?

Of course, there are always the abominable no-men with reasons why this cannot be done – deluge of messages, too many monitors required, cost etc.

But what other option is there?

At the moment, if you came across a blog or webpage where you were worried that some fruitcake was about to mow down 76 people, what would you do to report it?

Dial 999?

There must be a better way.

15.4 COULD TWITTER BE DELIBERATELY EXPLOITED TO PROMOTE EVIL?

28 NOVEMBER 2012 09:03

"Was last week a watershed week in terms of unsubstantiated online gossip?" Andrew Neil asked radio presenter Richard Bacon on the BBC current affairs programme 'This Week' last week.

On Twitter, as @richardpbacon, Bacon describes himself as a 'minor celebrity' (and we all know how much I admire celebrity) but, following his brave battle against internet trolls, Bacon needs to be taken seriously on this issue.

"Yes" said Bacon. "From people with only a small number of followers, Lord McAlpine is asking for an apology and a token £5 to Children in Need and … it has turned it into a watershed moment. People's attitudes about tweeting and, more crucially, re-tweeting libellous comments will change as a result of this."

"In the Twittersphere, and social media in general, will we see a pulling back from the nastiness?" asked Neil.

"I hope so" replied Bacon "One of the solutions would be if providers of social media compelled users to see their real photo and their real name, a lot of that nastiness would dissipate because people are emboldened by anonymity."

AC Grayling made this point in 2007: "Let us get rid of anonymity of posts on The Guardian blog and agree or disagree, support or lock horns vigorously, in the open – with common courtesy as the only system of governance we need."

Having made the point about anonymity myself, I wonder if we don't face a greater danger from Twitter than we might think.

With my advertising and marketing hat on, I know that, from a commercial point of view, anonymous users are of no value, whatsoever, to Twitter. Free-to-use sites can only survive with advertising revenue. And advertisers need to know precisely who they are promoting to. 'If its free, you are the product' goes the mantra. If Twitter doesn't know who you are, and at least one of your contact details, how can they sell you to anyone else?

Yes, Twitter can be harmless fun. But to what extent is 'harmless fun' outweighed by the 'nastiness' of Twitter to which Richard Bacon referred?

Lord McAlpines' lawyers reckon they can identify no less than 10,000 Twitter users (1,000 original tweets and 9,000 retweets) who made 'untrue pervert accusations' against him.

Now 10,000 is a heck of a lot of people to have been provoked into a physical act, even as simple as a retweet, to malign an innocent person. Talk about the Wisdom of Crowds (not).

But were these 10,000 tweeters nasty? They were wrong and they were malicious, but were they nasty? And, if deliberately plotted, how much nastiness could Twitter provoke from its gullible users?

On the same TV programme, the former Cabinet Minister Michael Portillo compared human behaviour on Twitter to road rage: "You see it even with people in a car (where) people make gestures and yell obscenities at people. Somehow that little bubble of a car protects them from normal human behaviour."

What does it take to turn people from normal to abnormal behaviour, from nastiness to evil?

After all, in road rage, stepping out of the bubble of a car can lead to physical assault and even murder.

Is there an online equivalent of this behaviour?

Could we see, one day, the anonymity of Twitter being cold-heartedly exploited in a planned and calculated way by an evil person? Could Twitter be used to incite physical violence and murder?

I think it could. I believe there is a scenario where, say, religious or political zealots could plan and develop Twitter campaigns to provoke an instant, mass-market, evil response.

So, we need to be careful. And, as non-politicians, we should stop it happening before rather than after it happens.

In the McAlpine case, not only should Twitter be forced to publish the identities of its gullible users but made jointly liable with a fine, not of a fiver, but at least £5million for enabling 10,000 human beings to falsely accuse an innocent man of being a paedophile.

That should do it.

15.5 BEWARE, IN THIS DIGITAL AGE, OF THE WRATH OF THE PEOPLE

9 MAY 2014 09:01

WRATH:
i) strong, stern, or fierce anger; deeply resentful indignation; ire.
ii) vengeance or punishment as the consequence of anger.

Snatching some early summer sun in Greece, I have been reading John Steinbeck's seminal American novel, The Grapes of Wrath.

For those who do not know, it is the story of an agricultural 1930s American family – the Joads – who are driven from Oklahoma to California in search of work. As the Joads strive to survive, the book tracks their lives, and their world, disintegrating into chaos and despair.

Published in 1939, the people and the scenes in The Grapes of Wrath are, in every way, a world apart from modern Britain.

Or are they?

It is impossible to read The Grapes of Wrath without thinking of where we are in the market economy we have created – and in which, we hoped, especially after the fall of the Berlin Wall in 1990, the world might be, safer, better place.

1. Get this:

> *'Once California belonged to Mexico and its land to Mexicans; and a horde of tattered feverish Americans poured in. And such was their hunger for land that they took the land.... They put up houses and barns, they turned the earth and they planted the crops. And these things were possession, and possession was ownership....No matter how clever, how loving a man might be with earth and growing things, he could not survive if he were not also a good shopkeeper...And all the time the farms grew larger and the owners fewer.... it came about that owners no longer worked on their farms. They farmed on paper; and they forgot the land, the smell, the feel of it, and remembered only that they owned it, remembered only what they gained and lost by it.....'*
> *(Chapter 19).*

Ring a bell?

Tesco anyone?

Here you go: *'Tesco milk price cut sparks farmer anger' (link)*

See the comments below the article. Wrath. Or what?

2. Get this:

'And now the great owners and companies invented a new method. A great owner bought a cannery. And as cannery owner he paid himself a low price for the fruit and kept the price of the canned goods up and made his profit. And the little owners who owned no canneries lost their farms, and they were taken by the great owners, the banks, and the companies who also owned the canneries...The great companies did not know that the line between hunger and anger is a thin line. And the anger began to ferment.' (Chapter 21).

How are your local shopkeepers faring?

Small independents being forced out?

Anger fermenting?

Here you go: *'The familiar face of Marlborough High Street changes again as independent shops close' (link)*

3. Get this:

'This little orchard will be a part of a great holding next year, for the debt will have choked the owner....This vineyard will belong to the bank. Only the great owners can survive, for they own the canneries too....The works of the roots of the vines, of the trees, must be destroyed to keep up the price, and this is the saddest bitterest thing of all...And the smell of rot fills the country...

In the souls of the people the grapes of wrath are filling and growing heavy...' (Chapter 25).

Banks? Business? Brands? Backlash?

Here you go: *'Three famous Instances of Consumer Backlash' (link)*

4. Get this:

'And gradually the greatest terror of all came along... They ain't gonna be no kind of work for three months... In the barns, the people sat huddled together; and the terror came over them, and their faces were gray with terror. The children cried with hunger, and there was no food... Then the sickness

came, pneumonia and measles... Then from the tents, from the crowded barns, groups of sodden men went out, their clothes slopping rags, their shoes muddy pulp. They splashed out through the water, to the towns, to the country stores, to the relief offices, to beg for food, to beg for relief, to try to steal, to lie. And under the begging, and under the cringing, a hopeless anger began to smolder...' (Chapter 29).

Been to your local unemployment office recently?

Wandered around any big cities?

Have you?

Here you go: 'Nearly half of all children in Britain's most deprived urban areas are living below the poverty line,' new report reveals.

So.

What to do?

On the admirable BBC Radio 4 programme 'Great Lives'- a must for anyone who is interested in human beings and human behaviour – Matthew Parris described The Grapes of Wrath as 'a novel of passion and compassion'.

In today's world, it is encouraging that digital technology provides communication channels whereby people can direct their wrath at commercial and political targets – albeit, admittedly, and frustratingly, hidden amongst giant inboxfuls of drivel and junk.

And, of course, we have a General Election next year.

However, I do believe that, over time, online campaigning and complaining will become more and more sophisticated – and, as a result, more effective.

When this happens, it might just be that the idea of voting on a five-year basis for increasingly untrustworthy and inept career politicians - who have imposed welfare cuts with such a disgraceful lack of compassion – will become an irrelevant business model.

If this happens, I have no doubt that The Grapes of Wrath will have played its part.

16
SOCIAL MEDIA LEGACY 2010

16.1 CONNECTIVITY AND ISOLATION

So, it is December 2010. Christmas is coming. And, as a load of snow is dumped on us, I have been reflecting on how the world has changed in 2010.

For I do think that, although 1984 and 2001 were going to be world-changing years, 2010 actually was. The likes of Amazon, Google, Facebook, Twitter, smart phones and MP3 players have come of age – and tablets will become increasingly accepted as competition drives down price. I know some of these businesses started in the last decade, the last century even, but I do believe the year 2010 has defined them – and they have defined 2010.

No doubt, countless print and online articles are being written right now as we move into 2011. I am not the best person to add to the mass of information that will hit us as we approach the New Year. But I am sure technology will be a recurring theme.

I now realise my opening sentence is wrong already. I haven't been reflecting on how the world has changed. I have been reflecting on how my world has changed.

Why should this be of any interest to anyone else?

Well, professionally, for various reasons and circumstances that I did not foresee (or want) my career has not developed in the way many would have predicted.

This has opened my eyes to a real world out there that I would not have experienced had my career path been more conventional. I think I can claim a unique perspective on our society from top to bottom and from good to bad.

How can I say this?

Well, since the beginning of my career at Ogilvy & Mather in 1979, a close friend of mine was made a peer this year and others have made millions, some hundreds of millions, of pounds. One has three aeroplanes, two of which take-off and land in his back garden. However, another friend broke his neck in a motor racing accident and has been paralysed from the neck down for 30 years. Without extraordinary medical technology, he would not be with us now. How and why do the dice fall this way?

More recently, earlier this week, I found myself with a poor old lady who was clearly severely disabled and in chronic pain. We were both awaiting a medical examination and told, after two hours in uncomfortable and unforgiving chairs, that the clinic had run out of time. We would have to re-arrange our appointments – and go home.

This was Tuesday, the first day of this week's frozen weather. This lady, who could barely walk, had taken a train from Coulsdon to Purley, changed to Clapham Junction and then taken a bus to the clinic. Now she had to undergo the reverse procedure having not been seen by a doctor. And all to be repeated in two weeks for her re-arranged appointment.

Of course, I had driven there in my fancy car and parked less than 100 yards away. Concerned about her slipping on the ice, I offered her an umbrella from my car as a walking stick but her pride forced her to refuse. She shuffled and slid into the dark. I hope she's ok. It has worried me all week. Should I have offered her a lift? Oh dear. (*This is the same experience as described in 6.1*)

Who is looking after people like this lady? I couldn't. Politicians and policies won't. What humanity was shown by the Government-employed medics, for whom we had waited so needlessly not to see? The answer is none. They just wanted to get home. It's cold outside.

I accept this small experience could have happened to any of us. I don't know why but, in my life, it has happened to me more than most of us with 'business careers'.

Perhaps because of this, the thought struck me that while my day had been spent online, on email and Facebook and LinkedIn and Twitter, connecting with people, this lady may not have connected with anyone at all, all day. She was alone. Ok, we were alone together in an inhospitable waiting room – but we are a world apart.

I said I have seen good and bad and, again, I think I can claim mine to have been a unique journey – certainly in our line of business.

I have been exposed to corporate corruption, financial fiddling and nasty little cheats who have got away with it – unpunished. I have seen the human effect of their cheap scams and met people whose careers, and lives, have been broken by these crooks. I tried to stand up to it, but where has that got me? A lot of money, yes, but I have never worked for a big agency again – not for the want of trying.

At the other end of the moral scale, I have met good people and seen great work, not just business and creative work, but good work and good works in charities and in the community where the depth of human kindness has truly touched me.

This week, I watched two TV programmes that support the case I am about to argue.

'The Secret Millionaire' features the exposure of rich people to the real lives of people living among us in a completely different world from that which we enjoy. Every time I see it, I cannot believe that these filthy rich people are so ignorant of the filthy, scary, violent world that pervades so much of our society.

'Age of Do-Gooders', presented by Ian Hislop, showed the likes of William Wilberforce refusing to accept the lives of the 'underclass' and forcing through real social change on a scale that reveals how the shallow, and totally uncreative, slogans of 'change' thrown out by today's politicians are part of the game of deception they live by.

William Wilberforce? The Slave Trade Act was passed through Parliament in 1807.

Two hundred years later, who matches him? Mandela, for sure. Who else? I hope, in the next decade, Bill Gates, Warren Buffet and the billion-dollar-boys will join him. They are our only hope. It won't be our second-rate politicians, that's for sure.

So, as A Different Hat, I have been trying to carve this space where the commercial media and marketing worlds meet the real world outside and where, somehow, the skills employed within our industries can be used to a wider, social benefit – and not just the relatively trivial commercial products we promote for our livings.

And, it seems to me, that – despite all the talk of quantitative easing and benefit cuts and our young students facing a lifetime of the debt that today's politicians are so keen to denounce yet, hypocritically, foist upon them – there must be hope.

And my hope is this. It is very simple. The connectivity which those of us who work in marketing and the media find relatively easy to adopt becomes increasingly available to those who *need* it – rather than just those of us who *enjoy* it.

This is the first of three 2010 legacy posts and I will return to this theme.

In the meantime, this quote by Mark Read, WPP Digital's chief executive, supports my retrospective view of 2010:

"As Facebook has surpassed the half-billion-users milestone, and is effectively the third largest country in the world, it is no longer a matter of if brands should have a presence on Facebook, but how they can be successful."

As a society, the next challenge is to make this technology work for the benefit of everybody – and not just because Bill Gates has made so much money out of it.

In 2010, a neat number, the world has turned.

16.2 Privacy and Transparency

I already had Transparency and Privacy down as a discussion point but the recent torrent of media comment about Wikileaks has left me completely out of my depth.

The implications are just so immense.

After all, how can the following Wikileak, plucked at random from the 'Enemy Action' file of 130,781 documents out of the total 466,743 documents in 'Iran & Afghan War Logs Explorer', make any sense to a simple soul like me?

> "KAF-1BDE -S3 REPORTS: SUMMIT 09 B CO ELEMENT SALUTE REPORT AS FOLLOWS: S- 3-4 PAX, A- SMALL ARMS FIRE, L-IVO 42 SWB 3910 1617, U-UNK, T-0415Z, E-AK-47. 0448Z ENEMY ELEMENTS BROKEN CONTACT. 0442Z AIR QRF PREPOSITIONED TO ORGUN-E. 0550Z UPDATE SUMMIT 09 B CO ELEMENT HAS REGAINED CONTACT. SALUTE REPORT AS FOLLOWS: S-3-4 PAX, A-SMALL ARMS FIRE, L-IVO 42 SWB 3902 1627, U-UNK, T-0540Z, E-AK-47. 0620Z UNIT IS NO LONGER IN CONTACT. REPORTING INDICATES POSSIBLY 3X SUSPECTED ACM''S WERE KIA."

Clicking 'Expand Acronyms' ('Take care; definitions may be wrong') would seem to make more sense, but doesn't really – not to me, anyway:

> "Kandahar Air Field-1BDE -S3 REPORTS: SUMMIT 09 B Commanding Officer ELEMENT Size/Activity/Location/Unit/ Time/Equipment REPORT AS FOLLOWS: Size: 3-4 Passengers/ People, Activity: SMALL ARMS FIRE, Location: In the vicinity of 42 SWB 3910 1617, Unit: Unknown, Time: 04:15 GMT, Equipment: Assault rifle. 04:48 GMT ENEMY ELEMENTS BROKEN CONTACT. 04:42 GMT AIR Quick Response Force

PREPOSITIONED TO ORGUN-E. 05:50 GMT UPDATE SUMMIT 09 B Commanding Officer ELEMENT HAS REGAINED CONTACT. Size/Activity/Location/Unit/Time/ Equipment REPORT AS FOLLOWS: Size: 3-4 Passengers/People, Activity: SMALL ARMS FIRE, Location: In the vicinity of 42 SWB 3902 1627, Unit: Unknown, Time: 05:40 GMT, Equipment: Assault rifle. 06:20 GMT UNIT IS NO LONGER IN CONTACT. REPORTING INDICATES POSSIBLY 3X SUSPECTED Anti-Coalition Militia''S WERE Killed in Action."

The criminal allegations against Julian Assange, and what he has been doing or not doing to, or with, women in Sweden, are a 'no comment' from me, but it must be the case that this guy and his Wikileaks concept will affect all our lives in some way.

Again, as with my last post, all I can offer is a personal perspective.

I believe our political lords and masters should be held to account for their actions – especially retrospectively, when their deeds have been done and decisions made. In principle, I am all for transparency.

As for military matters, there is a concern that our operational methodology is something that it would be in our interests to keep private from our enemies.

But these are massive issues, way above my pay grade. I guess the only Insight I can contribute – which is pretty obvious really – is that Wikileaks, and all the copy-cats that will follow, are not going to go away. In fact there can only be more.

We are going to have to deal with them somehow. And they support my thesis that 2010 has been a world-changing year in terms of what has happened online and its effect on all our day-to-day lives. In 2010, the world has turned. The Big Brother society George Orwell envisaged in 1984 is now upon us. Ok, Orwell wrote 1984 in 1949 and, in a fictional novel, showed astonishing foresight and imagination, but this is *real* and *now*.

Get this. It was reported in the Sunday Times this week (5 December 2010) that:

> *"Insurers are preparing to use people's Facebook profiles and online spending habits as a way of setting premiums....data detailing their food purchases, activities and social groups can be as good an indicator of their*

life expectancy as conventional medical examinations......Facebook (is) potentially valuable because profiles could reveal who the customer socialises with, where they go, whether they drink too much or exercise a lot and what groups and fan pages they 'like'."

They call it 'predictive modelling'. I say Big Brother is watching you. Twitter ye not.

Get this too. There is a boarding school where the Deputy Head Teachers created a fake Facebook Group under a Facebook Profile. They knew this Group would be irresistible to the students and, once the students had joined it, this meant the staff could access the students' own Profiles and monitor their behaviour. Did your teachers do this?

So, individuals like us may not feature in the millions of Wikileak files but, in our day-to-day lives, we are being watched and monitored in ways that we could never have conceived even last year.

In my successful legal action for malicious falsehood against Lintas in the 1990s, which arose from my reporting a financial fraud at the agency, my lawyer warned me of 'the other side' behaving 'in the modern manner' – to assume my phone was tapped, my car followed and that personal checks would be made on me. Perhaps they were. Certainly, an anonymous caller telephoned my old school to check my 'A' Levels were as claimed on my CV. I have learnt in life that unsavoury people tend to judge other people's behaviour by their own low moral and behavioural standards.

These things were frightening to me then, not that many years ago. Now all of us are in the frame. We are all being tracked and followed.

And what if you manage a business? What if every transaction, every expenses claim, every internal email was opened to the public? This would include publicising opinions and comments about your agencies or clients. Would that worry you?

Finally, back to Wikileaks, I cannot resist making a couple of points in relation to this world-changing development:

i) As stated above, Wikileaks will not go away. It is a benchmark of the year 2010.

ii) The 'interception evidence' debate, a major issue in recent politics, has been turned on its head. Now, it seems, there is no option but to pro-actively intercept anything we can from terrorists, and use this evidence against them – especially as we are intercepting ourselves from within. Human rights be damned. Through online technology, they know everything about us. We need to know what they are up to – otherwise they will blow us up.

iii) I did say at the General Election that the use of new media had a part to play in modern warfare. If you read my past posts, I did not claim to have the executional solutions to this point but it seems, only a few months later, that there may have been some truth in my hypothesis.

That's my story – and I'm sticking to it.

16.3 WORK AND PLAY

17 DECEMBER 2010 08:37

Two weeks ago, I argued that 2010 has been a world-changing year.

Now, by 'crowning' Mark Zuckerberg Person of the Year, I am pleased to report that Time magazine appears to agree with me. How opinion forming is that? "This honour is awarded to the figure deemed to have had the most influence on world events that year – not necessarily in a positive way. Both Hitler and Stalin have won in the past".

Bizarrely, if you read my last post, Mark Zuckerberg was born in 1984. In this post, I brought your attention to the George Orwell novel and, earlier to this quote by Mark Read, WPP Digital's chief executive quoted on Brand Republic:

"As Facebook has surpassed the half-billion-users milestone, and is effectively the third largest country in the world, it is no longer a matter of if brands should have a presence on Facebook, but how they can be successful."

Now, on 15 December, Time magazine has said:

"This year, Facebook ..... added its 550 millionth member. One out of every dozen people on the planet has a Facebook account. They speak 75 languages and collectively lavish more than 700 billion minutes on Facebook every month. Last month the site accounted for 1 out of 4 American page views. Its membership is currently growing at a rate of about 700,000 people a day."

Only a year ago, if you had forecast that Facebook would grow at 700,000 members a *day*, people would have said that you were mad.

What does all this activity mean?

I have discussed some aspects of this in my previous two posts. This week, as my last post (sic) of 2010, I will discuss one aspect of modern life that online connectivity, including Facebook, has challenged and this is the muddy water that we used to call Work and Play.

In the old days, in true Mad Men style, advertising people like me put on our smart clothes and went to work. Life was clear. When we were in the office, certainly in office hours, we were working.

Some office workers knew the trick of leaving their jackets draped haphazardly behind their chairs, implying they were in the office somewhere – in another department, talking to a senior person behind closed doors or in the lav. They were 'in'. They were working.

If they weren't 'in', unless they were at a meeting outside the office (which would be clearly noted in the diary on their desk), they were not working. They were 'out'. The difference between being in and out of the office was clearly delineated.

In reality, a lot of the time we were getting pissed in the pub. Forgive me for being chippy but, without Facebook et al, did this mean we spent more time meeting people face-to-face, talking to them and getting to know them?

These days, all this has changed. Are Facebook friends really friends? Do they all really know each other? Is Facebook a serious social connection – or is it a game? The old definitions of work and play no longer exist.

At work, companies can play Big Brother and monitor your 'working' day on Facebook or not – but they cannot do this to all of us all of the time. And they don't really know if you are there anymore (and if in working hours, unless you actually are in the office, you leave your 'location finder' on, you must be mad). No one knows where they are. Of course, we know where we ourselves are – but not where anyone else is. They are not 'in' anymore.

Anyway, with the emergence of tablets and wifi et al, you don't have to be using company equipment anymore. Who is to know if you are sending a work-related or social message – or researching an important topic online?

By the same token, at the week-end, how are you to get away from your boss? What possible excuse could you have for not being connected to the office? "Great news, we've got a meeting in Seoul on Monday. We're flying out this evening. Be there".

Of course, not everybody has a job. In fact, during 2011, fewer and fewer of us will have jobs. In this case, the opposite dynamic applies. You don't work, which means you don't have any money. You don't have any money, so you can't play either.

You might as well get pissed in the pub. At least you will meet people face-to-face.

I believe in 2010, in some part because of the ubiquity of Facebook, the delineations of work and play have disappeared.

So, if you are working and are given some nice toys this Christmas, enjoy them while you can. You won't have many days off in 2011.

If you are not working, please make the most of life, with or without nice toys.

Either way, I hope you have a mad 2011 when the world will change even more.

Merry New Year!

17
PARTY POLITICS MATTER (NOT)

17.1 Coalition Government? They're all over the place!

14 January 2011 08:58

Last September, we learned about 'a secretive department set up in Downing Street' call the Behavioural Insight Team (BIT) – aka David Cameron's 'Nudge Unit'.

The Sunday Times picked up on the story:

> 'The BIT has been disseminating its ideas to government departments which are now implementing nudgy policies. Francis Maude, the minister for the Cabinet Office, says that "evidence from across the world suggests that behavioural insights can deliver considerable benefits and save money". In the past 10 days a number of new policies have been announced that owe their genesis to these theories .....
>
> Critics complain that "behavioural insights" are little more than snake oil gimmicks dressed up as policy wonkery. Advertising agencies have been hooking our sensibilities with clever words, they say'.

I'm not sure what that last paragraph means but let's read on because the exciting bit is about to come. Yes, Rory Sutherland gets his say. I think Rory has been one of the best Presidents of the IPA we have ever had, but here he is described as 'the vice-chairman of Ogilvy, a marketing agency'.

I am delighted that Rory's proposition (if not the vital role he has performed for our business) has, at last, been recognised at Government level. Indeed:

> 'Cameron is such a fan of behavioural insights that he has appointed his cabinet secretary, Gus O'Donnell, chairman of the BIT. It is part of his drive for a big society in which people are given more freedom and responsibility over their lives, with government providing nudges for guidance'.

I wonder how many creative people are in this BIT?

Surely Rory Sutherland must get the credit for nudging the government into nudging – arise, Sir Rory! – so there must be creative people in there. But who are they?

In these posts, I try to avoid discussing creative work or issues. But surely it follows there is a creative role here? Behavioural Insight – Nudge – Innovation – Creativity.

Before the creative input, how much disciplined and objective strategic planning is going on? Where is the 'upstream' consumer insight?

This is where I can contribute.

And my view is that before the Government starts nudging the common people, it needs to look at itself.

There are nudges and insights that could be applied to the Role of Government, and the way it is structured, that precede what the Conservatives can do to nudge the plebs into Big Society behaviour.

For example, what are the roles that are important to good government and that the common people in the Big Society cannot manage?

1. Defence

In Prime Minister's Questions this week, David Cameron said:

'We have an enormous terrorist threat'.

What a surprise.
But, as I wrote in March 2010:

'Why is it that the responsibility of countering terrorism within Britain is the responsibility of The Home Office (i.e. the Police), but outside Britain is the responsibility of the Ministry of Defence (i.e. the Military)? …. Surely terrorism is an international problem that, like the internet, transcends national borders? …. In my experience, expecting two units within one Government Department to communicate with each other is a recipe for disaster, let alone two completely different Departments with different hierarchies and different Ministers…. I reckon this muddled management structure makes us sitting ducks.'

I also urged a more sophisticated use of new media in the war against terrorism.
Perhaps the 07/07 inquest that is currently taking place will nudge

the Secretary of State for Defence, The Right Honourable Liam Fox MP, towards a more united and innovative resistance to this 'enormous threat'.

Mind you, he isn't responsible for Police. That's the Home Office.

2. Home Office

As well as counter-acting terrorism and stopping drivers from speeding, on Thursday 9 December last year, one arm of the Police were on duty not controlling the student rioters when the other arm was not protecting Prince Charles and Camilla on their night out to The Royal Variety Performance at the London Palladium.

As the Daily Telegraph reported on 11 December 2010:

> *'Officers guarding the royal couple were using radios on a different channel from those patrolling Thursday's student riots, meaning they received no warning that protesters were blocking their route.'*

Of course, whereas the police were all over the place, the students were connected to Twitter and knew exactly what was happening in real time.

If the police don't know what is going on in one side of Central London from another, it doesn't give you much confidence in their sniffing out the terrorists in our midst, does it?

Perhaps a nudge in the direction of the Right Honourable Theresa May MP, our Home Secretary, might result in a more intelligent use of new media by the police in future.

Ah, Media. Sorry, we've got another department for that.

3. Department of Culture, Media and Sport (DCMS)

The Right Honourable Jeremy Hunt MP is the Secretary of State for Culture, Media and Sport. He was formerly Shadow Culture Secretary (2007-2010) and Shadow Minister for Disabled People (2005 – 2007).

Perhaps someone could nudge the DCMS towards a more innovative, joined-up use of new media to deliver the vital Government responsibilities of defence and security more effectively.

Did I say 'innovative'? Sorry, that's another Department.

4. Department for Business, Innovation and Skills (BIS)

According to its own website the BIS (as opposed to BIT) "has an important role at the heart of government as the 'department for growth'."

The Secretary of State for Business, Innovation and Skills and President of the Board of Trade is the Right Honourable Dr Vince Cable MP.

Oh dear, 'Growth' and Vince Cable. We're getting quite a long way from defence, protection and anti-terrorism, aren't we?

Do you think someone could nudge Fox to May and May to Hunt (yes, there's Fox Hunt in the Tory Cabinet!) and then Hunt to Cable? Is this happening? After all, as a Liberal Democrat, Cable isn't even in the same Party as the other three, who are all Conservatives.

But Nick Clegg's got the answer!

5. Alarm Clock Britain

This is from the Independent this week (12 January):

> *'David Laws, who was forced to quit the Cabinet in May over his expenses claims, has been put in charge of a drive by Nick Clegg to support the citizens of "Alarm Clock Britain"..... Liberal Democrat strategists have alighted on the phrase to describe the low and middle-income families that the Deputy Prime Minister views as the backbone of the country..... It was devised at a recent brain-storming session with senior Liberal Democrats, including Mr Laws, at the Deputy Prime Minister's grace-and-favour mansion at Chevening.'*

No mention of BIT or Nudge or Behavioural Economics here. Do the LibDems know about them?

Do the Conservatives know about Alarm Clock Britain?

Do any of them know what the other is doing?

Or are they, like the Police, all on a different wavelength?

I promised an upstream consumer insight and a disciplined and objective strategic recommendation:

My Insight is that people in the Big Society, especially terrorists, do not live their lives by Government Department.

Strategically, the UK Coalition Government should get its own act together before it nudges the electorate towards looking after itself in what is called the 'Big Society' (although a re-branding and clearer communication of this concept should also be considered).

17.2 'YES TO AV' FIASCO

10 MAY 2011 08:03

The purpose of my 'A Different Hat' blog is to connect our skills in marketing and communications (in all its forms) to a wider world than commercial products and services.

So, I was going to spend the week-end writing a hugely insightful discourse into the brilliance of the 'Yes to AV' campaign.

Based on my own experience as an Independent (cross-bench) Candidate MP last year, I know there are very good reasons why AV would have been good news – for Independent Candidates as well as our country as a whole. I was a strong supporter.

Mind you, I didn't do much about transmitting my views. I am not a member of a political party, I was aware that the Electoral Reform Society had been gearing up for this campaign for over a year and, frankly, no one asked me. Why would they?

And after all, as only the second referendum we have ever had – and the backbone to the LibDem membership of the Coalition – I was confident London's top marketing and communications brains and talent would have been thrown into this vital cause?

Well, I am afraid it was all hugely under-whelming. A complete waste of time.

And what is frustrating to supporters of AV like me, is that I am left with rather a sick feeling that the campaign flopped – not because of the merits of the case but because the 'YES to AV' completely failed to communicate its positive benefits.

Surely 'Yes to AV' was crying out for a simple explanation of how Alternative Vote works and why it is better than First Past The Post?

In the event, I don't think people got it at all.

We were reduced to confused hypothetical analogies culminating in truly pathetic footage from the 1970s TV series 'When The Boat Comes In' where some builders vote to paint a wall yellow even though yellow was the second choice for all of them.

Something like that. I think.

Don't worry about it – like the 'Yes to AV' campaign, you'll just get lost.

From a personal point of view, all I can say is that I do not understand how the LibDems can continue in this Coalition. They have no democratic mandate at all.

Nor do the Conservatives, for that matter.

The LibDems can carry on under, apparently, a 'newly drafted' Coalition Agreement (for which read LibDem jobsworths and Tory brinkmanship).

Or they could call it a day with dignity intact, saying that at least they gave it a go until the Referendum. From a much smaller base, they can pick themselves up, learn the lessons and define a credible positioning based on honesty and integrity – perhaps from principled lessons learnt from the Scottish National Party?

Don't hold your breath, though. They are politicians.

17.3 LIBERAL DEMOCRATS A COMPROMISED BRAND

22 SEPTEMBER 2011 08:48

It is Party Conference time, which really is a silly season *(see 7.4)*.

I have never been to one and cannot imagine doing so. The tone of voice seems so false and obsequious, I think I would shrivel into a little cringy ball.

They are all over the media – to the extent that you can read the Party Leaders' speeches in the newspaper before they orate them. I am not a PR man but the idea of making the speech yesterday's, rather than today's, news has always seemed a rather bizarre tactic to me.

What is the status of our three main parties as brands?

And, as brands, do they have any integrity?

This week, the Liberal Democrats and Nick Clegg have taken to the floor. He said quite a lot of what I have been saying on this site for the last couple of years, not least that we are 'a nation divided' – the subject of my very first post. And I feel I ought to be nice as they have taken up the cause of my last post - even against the particular company I mentioned *(see 6.1)*.

Their history is so confused and their current status so, well, accidental that the Liberal Democrat brand is difficult to pin down.

Of course, one can understand the words 'liberal' and 'democrat' but what is the underlying truth behind putting them together to add some meaning? It is all a bit of a fudge, isn't it? When you see the people at the Conference, they are so diverse and even rather bizarre that you wonder how they have all got together at all.

Perhaps, this – their sheer individuality – is the Lib Dems virtue. It seems there is an inclusiveness which overrides the bigoted tribalism of Conservative and Labour.

It could even be their opportunity. I can think of a number of areas where the Lib Dems could offer society more individual freedom (for which read 'liberal' and 'democrat') – but they cannot do this because they are fatally flawed.

'We are in nobody's pocket', said Clegg 'we are free to tell it like it really is'.

He claimed this is because the Lib Dems have no vested interests by which he meant they are free from Labour's ties to the unions and the Tories ties to the banks – and both their ties to the Murdochs.

But is this true?

I am afraid not.

By definition, as part of a Coalition Government, the Lib Dems do have a vested interest – and their vested interest is the Conservative Party.

We all know Nick Clegg is only Deputy Prime Minister as a result of expediency and tactical game-playing after the General Election last year – a position, disgracefully in my view, reinforced after the fiasco of the AV referendum in May.

'The brave decision was to go into Government and not sit on Opposition benches throwing rocks at the Government. We put aside party differences for the sake of the national interest. People before politics. Nation before party'.

Sorry, Nick, but that is complete rollocks and you know it. You took an opportunistic punt, you held out for the AV referendum, you lost it and now, by your continued subservience to the Conservatives, you have given away the freedom of your 'liberal' party which, by your own admission, is all you have left.

I can prove this by what you yourself said in your Conference speech.

You were very soft about the rioters about whom you said:

'In terms of opportunity, we are a nation divided …. odds stacked against too many of our children …. a deep injustice where birth means destiny …. So many of those who joined the riots seemed to have nothing to lose. It was about what they could get here and now, as if their future had little value …. offenders must become ex-offenders …. an end to the corrosive cycle of crime ….Effective justice. Restorative justice. Liberal justice. Reason not prejudice. Compassion not greed. Hope not fear.'

But did you say this at the time? No – you did not.

Were you compassionate to this rebellious minority? No – you were not.

Did you stand up to the clenched fist of our Prime Minister? No – you could not.

In today's society, I believe there is room for a political brand that supports the individual, that can help build a society of plurality and, at the same time, cohesiveness, but I am afraid the Lib Dems are not being true to those values now.

They can't be. Their vested interest (the Tories) is too overpowering. This is their fatal flaw and why, despite all Clegg's pleading, they have lost all their integrity.

And why the Lib Dems are a compromised brand – and a waste of time.

17.4 LABOUR A CONFUSED BRAND

28 SEPTEMBER 2011 08:46

This week it is Labour's turn to make us cringe.

At 'Conference' (cringe), did Ed Miliband clarify his own position and his party's positioning, for surely the two are intertwined?

The answer, as with all these interchangeable career politicians, is that it is very difficult to pin down what they stand for. You have to go by what they say. But how much of what they say can you believe?

Are they people of conviction and integrity – or do they put their own careers first (even before family (*see 18.6*)? I think we know the answer.

What makes it worse, and again we all know this, is that since the old ideological battles of socialism and capitalism were fought and won (we thought), the individual personalities of all three Party Leaders are more important than ever.

And no more so than this week.

For, as you may have noticed, the 'New' in the Labour brand name has disappeared.

In his Conference speech Miliband said:

'You know, I am not Tony Blair. I am not Gordon Brown either. Great men who, in their own ways, achieved great things.'

But, in saying this, what he actually meant was that New Labour is not 'New Labour' any more. That was 'Blair Labour'.

And both of them – Blair and New Labour – have, very quietly and deliberately, been put to one side. In praising Blair, Miliband has ditched him. This is politics. After all, he did it to his own brother.

Strategically, ditching 'New Labour' is undoubtedly a wise move. All of us in marketing know that you can only be 'new' for a certain length of time. This is why it is even more dumb to attach the word 'new' to your brand name. But that is an old issue now.

So, apart from Blair the man and Blair the brand, which of the principles of 'New Labour' have been retained and which have been discarded?

For, since the launch of New Labour, in fact since the demise of New

Labour, new problems have emerged. In other words, what was new in 1997 is not new now and what was new last year is not new now either. Oh dear, this is all very confusing.

Where does Labour stand now – today?

Ed Miliband is free to redefine the Labour brand in his own image and set himself against these challenges. But has he achieved this?

The answer is that he sort of has and sort of hasn't.

He took some textbooks on leadership on his summer holidays to help him define himself and his party. This is what he tried to do in his Conference speech, in which he said:

> 'My top demand of my Shadow Cabinet, my party, my team is this:
> Ambition. Ambition to change our country.
> It's why we were founded.
> It's in our souls'.

Which book did that load of balls come from?

Actually, it is even more confusing than you might think because although this is what it says in this script here, I am not sure if he actually said it because, in the Liverpool of whose council Miliband is so proud, the lights went out and my TV turned blue.

Whatever.

I don't know whether 'ambition in their souls' will win Labour an election.

Nor is it my job to dissect and analyse each of the 'policies' Miliband announced, but I have observed consistently in these blogs how strange it is that politicians do not take decisions in the simple, effective way we do in marketing: 1. Objective. 2. Strategy. 3. Execution.

Politicians just leap blindly, and amateurishly, into things called 'policies'.

At this stage, what Miliband needs is *principles* not policies.

He went some way to achieving this by saying 'we need a New Bargain in our economy'. At the time, I thought there might be something meaningful here, that the 'New Bargain' might just be a Big Idea for old Labour.

But then we went down a blind alley and back up Miliband's septum.

We had the complicated introduction of different tax systems for 'producers' and 'predators', good companies and bad companies.

Then we endured, as we had to, a stab at Murdoch and the Coalition cuts, including the subtraction of the value of public shareholding in the banks off the national deficit figure, which I proposed at the end of my post in October last year *(see 3.2)*.

And then there were cheap (or should I say expensive) pops at Fred Goodwin which surely only reflect badly on Labour and their as-yet-unredeemed Shadow Chancellor. They do not move the Labour brand forward at all.

Plus an obscure comparison between Fred the Shred and the Chairman of Rolls Royce, whose name would not have been known in many a pub quiz.

If you want to launch the New Bargain party, with ambition in your soul, it is much better to leave Goodwin behind with Brown and Blair Labour. A simple apology for past disasters and undeserved knighthoods is quite enough.

Muddling all this up with predators and producers only detracted from the bigger, over-arching brand challenge.

So Ed, for now, why not stick with a 'bottom up' approach and focus on developing direct strategies to help overcome the needs of the low-paid, unemployed and disabled which are closer to the blue-collar heritage of your Labour brand?

Leave the 'top-down' issues such as the banks and complicated private finance controls in the NHS for later. Labour's execrable failure in these areas is too recent, and the tangible benefits to your core following too remote from their day-to-day needs, to matter at this stage.

You have opened the door for Cameron to bite back at you next week (just wait).

Stick to what you can do for the people who need you. There are plenty of innovative ways you can achieve this.

Focus on what you can give to the poor (and be a producer) not take from the rich (like a predator).

If you have a New Bargain between the Citizen and the State, and this really is a Big Idea, please explain – in a way that we can understand – exactly what you mean.

Otherwise, all you will do is confuse.

Just keep it simple - for the easier you are to understand, the stronger will be your brand.

You will find this simple human insight well worth remembering.

17.5 CONSERVATIVES A CARELESS BRAND

6 OCTOBER 2011 08:56

Last week, I dutifully recorded Ed Miliband's speech at the Labour Conference.

I watched it in the evening and stayed up late writing my post only to find that, apart from the unique human insights to which you are accustomed, most of my views were reflected across the mass media.

"Get a life", said the wife. So less to read this week, you will be pleased to hear.

In 2007, I advised the Conservatives how to win the last election (*see 3.2*). '*The Conservatives may be doing the right thing, but in the wrong way*'. In the same post, months before the riots, I told them the human effect of their savage cuts would be social chaos. Alienating people is not good leadership.

I showed the Tories what life is like on the receiving end of these cuts (*see 6.1*): '*Disability Living Allowance (DLA) Disgrace*'.

In a most unleaderly way, our Prime Minister has had to apologise to women (yes, all of you!) for his patronising approach. I have explained his behaviour in 18.2: '*The Curse of David Cameron*'.

I will leave it to the rest of the media to report his Conference Speech, but I would like to report his response to a question from Nick Robinson, the Political Editor of the BBC.

Robinson challenged Cameron on the social effects of the cuts to the poor, sick and needy amongst us.

Do you know what Cameron replied?

He said petrol costs had been kept down and Council Tax had been frozen.

Is that it?!

Dave, don't you understand that loads of people don't pay Council Tax or have cars? They are called the underclass, the majority of whom are things called women.

You don't believe me? Read this:

"The government's spending cuts have hit women hardest: two-thirds of the 140,000 public-sector jobs that have been cut were held by women. There's been a 72 per cent rise in redundancies among women over the last quarter – redundancies among men, instead, are up only 21 per cent. Women face a big increase in childcare costs at the same time as child benefit has been frozen.... Women are also more likely to be caring for a relative, and more likely to need social housing than men. Finally, female unemployment has hit a 23-year-high with 1.05 million women on the dole – the highest figure since 1988. No wonder Cameron's advisers have warned him that his popularity has dropped 10 per cent among women since he came to Downing Street."

So this is how he *should* have replied to the BBC:

"Well, for example, we have kept petrol costs down and frozen Council Tax, but we know too many people, particularly women, fall below these initiatives. And, to show we are aware of them and care about them, these are the strategies we have developed to help the sick, poor and needy in our society......".

But he can't say this. He is not a natural leader. He does not understand people. He has no 'common touch'. No empathy. No humanity. I wrote about this in 11.3: '*David Cameron, Eton and George Orwell*'.

George Orwell wrote about human behaviour. He understood *people*. That is what made him such a great writer.

As this Conference has shown, to millions of people up and down our country, the biggest negative of the Conservative brand is as relevant today as it has always been.

It is that, if 'the people' are their 'customers', the Conservatives just don't *care* about them.

Worse, in these times of economic woe, they don't care that they don't care.

Happy days!

17.6 CAN 'CONSERVATIVE' BE 'RADICAL'

1 MARCH 2010 22:29

So the Tory slogan is 'Year for Change'.

Well, how creative and inspiring can you get?! Really modern. Really radical.

It is, in fact, a phrase that is so obvious, unimaginative and lacking in meaning that the only merit it can claim is that it is impossible to say anything about it.

So you have to dig deeper, perhaps to an email David Cameron sent to his followers last week:

The Subject Line read: "We are a modern and radical party".

The title read: "We are a modern and radical party".

The body copy read:

> *"Four years ago, when the Conservative Party elected me as Leader, we made a choice about the way our Party should be. We made a choice to be modern and radical – not to play it safe or retreat into the old comfort zone. Today, the Conservative Party is modern and radical – and that's the way it's going to stay. Britain is crying out for a modern and radical alternative to this failed Labour Government……*
>
> *Our plans for our country are not timid, and the truth is they cannot be. The Conservative Party is a modern and radical party – and our modern and radical values are what this country urgently needs."*

I think Cameron is trying to claim the Conservatives are modern and radical.

He follows in the footsteps of Winston Churchill, a master of the English language.

Here are the definitions of three words from my Concise Oxford Dictionary:

Conservative:
"averse to change or innovation and holding traditional values".

Modern:

"of or relating to the present or recent times, characterised by using the most up-to-date techniques, equipment etc.".

Radical:

"innovative or progressive….an advocate of radical political or social reform".

What a moron (oxy).

17.7 TOMORROW NEVER COMES
(UNLESS YOU'RE GREEN)

15 MAY 2012 08:41

That 'capable, most extraordinary politician' Caroline Lucas has announced she is stepping down as leader of the Green Party. It says here this is 'part of a strategy centred on challenging the Liberal Democrats at the next election.'

I wonder if the Greens will succeed in this objective or, indeed, if they are aware of the strategic opportunity that is staring them in the face?

In the recent London Mayor elections Jenny Jones, the Green candidate, did beat the Lib Dems. But will her party overcome their prevailing image as a bunch of environmental dreamers as out of touch with the needs of today's world as a Woodstock hippy stick-in-the-mud awaiting the resurrection of Jimi Hendrix?

After all, Ms Jones spent ten years of her life as an paleobotanist in the Middle East 'studying carbonised plant remains' which does rather summarise the Green image. How can they unhinge themselves from the environmental shackles which bind them?

My instinct is that there is a strategically viable, more relevant positioning the Greens could exploit where:

i)   the Greens, and only the Greens, can build on the integrity, conviction and long-term commitment they have shown to their cause
ii) differentiate themselves from the more established parties
iii) appeal to a wider electorate than those engrossed by environmental issues.

My insight is that Green is the only political party in Britain with the foresight to think about how we live today will affect our children tomorrow.

After all, as Ken Livingstone pointed out in his pitiful losing Mayoral speech, ours is the first generation in the history of man to leave a worse world behind us than generations before.

Surely this is what the Greens have been banging on about all along?

If they can position themselves as the only 'long-term thinking' (LTT) party and apply this positioning to issues beyond the environment including the long-term effects of austerity and the shambles the Coalition are making of welfare, the NHS, police, education, child benefits, divided Britain et al, you kind of think more people might go Green.

The Greens simply need to recruit acknowledged experts in each Department of State and for these people to work between now and the next General Election to develop credible and practical policies that meet both the short and long-term needs of the country. In this way, a credible Shadow Cabinet may emerge from the hills, valleys, icecaps, oceans and out-of-space places where these Green people currently reside.

No doubt some of these experts might be disaffected Lib Dems whose parliamentary party have shown themselves to be a bunch of unprincipled chancers with no democratic right, whatsoever, to hold the Government positions onto which they cling (or, in the case of David Laws and Chris Huhne, not).

As I said last year, if they had any integrity at all, the Lib Dems should have split from the Coalition straight after the AV fiasco. By not doing so, they lost any shred of integrity and conviction they might have held – and are themselves guilty of the opportunistic short-term thinking they have dumped on the rest of us. They are destined to be hoisted by their own petard (and were at the recent local elections).

By emphasising their established long-term commitment to a better world for future generations, and widening their sphere of interest, the Greens may have a brighter future than they think.

18
POLITICIANS MATTER (NOT)

18.1 THE CURSE OF DAVID CAMERON

21 JULY 2011 00:13

Never before has 'the establishment' – as defined by Politicians, Police and Press – been so derided, discredited, and utterly disgraced as they are today.

After his 'performance' in Parliament yesterday, those of us interested in current affairs – and human behaviour within that sphere – are entitled to review the position, and character, of the man at the top.

Let's face it, our country is now in a worse state than David Cameron himself can ever have imagined when he became Prime Minister just over a year ago.

Frankly, his 'reign' has been a complete disaster.

On 7 July, even The Daily Telegraph screamed: 'Cameron is in the sewer'.

Why is this? How has he let this happen?

Napoleon said 'give me lucky generals'.

Is Cameron unlucky?

Is he incompetent?

Or is he fatally flawed?

He is undoubtedly able, as testified by his first class degree from Oxford – and the fact that he seems to have achieved his position without resorting to any particularly devious, underhand or hypocritical tactics.

As a human being, he seems balanced and well mannered. His peers (sic) appear to like him. I know of no stories of bad-temperedness, bullying or throwing phones at people.

Yet, from every perspective, can he ever have imagined a worse year than his last?

Is David Cameron cursed?

While he has been Prime Minister, his father and a son have died. It would be tasteless to refer to these personal sadnesses other than as facts – and, from a human perspective, of course we sympathise – but they must have affected him.

The rest is in the public domain.

On 26 June, Christopher Shale, Cameron's local Conservative Party Chairman, was found dead in the public toilets at the Glastonbury Festival. What was all that about? Perhaps it was all perfectly natural, but it is a kind of weird way (and place) to go.

And it must have freaked out Cameron, which is what we are discussing here.

Politically, despite his apparent personal charm, Cameron has had a nightmare year.

Every Conservative Party member knows he should have strolled through the last Election with an overall majority. But the positive discrimination inflicted on the local parties left them with the selection of some pathetically weak candidates, way short of electable standards, leading to the loss of constituencies that all Conservatives know should have been won.

This led to the Coalition (which, in principle, I rather like). But, again, how weird has the Coalition been? 'Bad luck' has been a recurring theme.

David Laws resigned in disgrace after being caught fiddling his expenses and Chris Huhne can't agree with his ex-wife over who drove the car home from Stansted Airport – so his son's phone has been seized by the police and Huhne faces a possible charge of perjury.

These are very strange events, dear reader, very strange events.

Cameron's own Ministers have behaved equally strangely with u-turns and cock-ups right across the board in the NHS, welfare reforms and even forests.

And the cuts. Ahh, the heartless cuts. Riots in the streets for the first time in years. Humble teachers on strike for the first time ever. Royal cars attacked outside the Palladium. Even the Archbishop of Canterbury is revolting!

All this as a result of the cruel axe being wielded by George Osborne. You know, he who holidays off Corfu on a Rothschild yacht with Peter Mandelson. That's the chap.

And then there's Cameron himself. He personally led the charge into the 'no-fly-zone' against Libya. What on earth was he doing? (*see 11.2 and 11.3*). It's like there's a bloke in your local pub who is a known nutter, beats people up and smashes the place to bits – so you nick his wallet and kill his kids. Why do that? What would you expect him to do in return?

Are we getting close to the truth now?

Is the inner David Cameron being revealed?

Could it be that he simply does not understand *people* – human beings?

This brings us back to the beginning and the state our country is in. Cameron has stated – very firmly – 'I take full responsibility for everyone I employ, for everyone I appoint and for everything this Government does'.

So here goes.

According to Wikipedia, Steve Hilton met Cameron at Conservative Central Office, was praised by Maurice Saatchi and 'came up with' the infamous 'demon eyes' poster. Later, one of the most execrable pieces of communications material I have ever seen emerged through my front door - something to do with connecting the phrase 'Broken Society' to a motor car engine. What else has he done?

In 2008, after a 'dispute' at a railway station, Hilton was arrested and issued with a penalty notice for disorder which, I am led to believe by Wikipedia, may mean he has a criminal record.

As we know, Rebekah Brooks (known as Wade before she married her Etonian Charlie) was arrested last week-end. She was also arrested in 2005 after an alleged assault on her ex-husband Ross Kemp. Charges were dropped but what on earth was Cameron doing socialising with her? I am not the only one to ask this so I won't go on about it here.

Andy Coulson has been arrested too. 'Hi, Andy, did you know about that hacking business'. 'No'. Sure?' Yes'. 'Fine – fancy 275 grand a year?'. 'That would be nice'.

Is this 'leadership'? Isn't leadership something to do with *people*?

It seems that Cameron simply cannot put the right people in the right place. He has no nous. He can't smell a rat (and he seems to know a few).

I think I know the reason for this. I know some Etonians. And I know people who have been in the Bullingdon Club at Oxford. I know what some of them are like.

Years ago, a Bullingdon Club member asked me what I thought of one of the other chaps (an Etonian), and I said I felt his friend was a bit 'plummy'. My friend replied: 'he can't help how he was brought up'.

These people have an arrogant smugness, a patrician manner, a sense of superiority. They don't understand people from outside their 'set' because they don't have to. They never meet them.

Thus, Cameron is oblivious to the vast swathes of our community who detest him and everything he stands for. Each of them have a vote and will one day cause his downfall.

Just look at the way he behaves.

He is constantly reminding us of his role: 'Since I became Prime Minister' etc. How does he think this makes Nick Clegg feel? A more humble 'since we came to power' would be beneficial, but he would not get this. He was not brought up this way.

At PMQs last week, he received a reasonably positive press report. But did you see how he treated Rushanara Ali? Take it from me, it was a disgrace – arrogant, rude and unbelievably patronising.

In your office, there is no way you could treat anyone like that. It would be an unforgiveable, perhaps even instantly dismissable, offence. For most people watching, those outside the Wesminster Village to whom Rushanara Ali means nothing, this would have been the stand-out moment.

But, again, if you pointed this out to him, Cameron would not understand this.

And, where you work, is your CEO surrounded by quite so many people who have been arrested, face criminal charges or have criminal records? Laws, Huhne, Hilton, Brooks, Coulson et al – *this is not norma*l.

So, where does all this leave us? How do we evaluate 'brand Cameron'.

First of all, please let me emphasise that I am not a party political animal. I am not a member of a political party. As I can demonstrate, I am politically 'independent'.

But, having worked in the field of human behaviour all my career, and experienced more of 'life' than Cameron can dream of, I conclude that David Cameron is a snob.

He cannot help this. It does not make him evil.

Simply, he is in the wrong place at the wrong time. He is cursed by his birth.

Because he has not lived in the 'real world', he simply does not understand *people*, and this is why most of the problems outlined above are his fault.

Great novelists do understand people. This is what makes them great novelists.

In his recent TV series 'Faulks on Fiction', Sebastian Faulks divided the entire canon of British literary novels into four characteristics: Heroes, Lovers, Snobs and Villains.

Under 'The Snob', this is what Faulks said about 'Emma' by Jane Austen:

> 'The thing about Emma is that, despite her intelligence and genuine desire to do good, she almost always gets it wrong.
>
> And that is because the perspective of a snob is, by definition, skewed.
>
> Like all snobs, she suffers from a vision defect – her failure to see the world clearly.
>
> It is a question of focus.
>
> The snob can't see the wood from the trees, the individual for the group.
>
> And, if it is not corrected, this defect can be dangerous.'

Ring a bell?

18.2 WHAT MAKES A SNOB?

26 SEPTEMBER 2012 09:10

In Britain, the question is did Andrew Mitchell call the Downing Street police 'plebs'?

Elsewhere it is 'who on earth is Andrew Mitchell?' I suspect, at the time of the incident, the police did not know who he was either: which may be why they asked him to exit Downing Street by the little gate at the side rather than the big gate in the middle.

Andrew Mitchell is the Conservative MP for Sutton Coldfield. In the recent Cabinet reshuffle, he was appointed government Chief Whip and Parliamentary Secretary to the Treasury. Not for long methinks.

The police record of the incident is revealing:

> *"Mr Mitchell was speaking to Pc ★★★★★★★★ demanding exit through the main vehicle gate into Whitehall. Pc ★★★★★★★★ explained to Mr Mitchell that the policy was for pedal cycles to use the side pedestrian exit. Mr Mitchell refused, stating he was the chief whip and he always used the main gates....*
>
> *After several refusals Mr Mitchell got off his bike and walked to the pedestrian gate with me after I again offered to open that for him.*
>
> *There were several members of public present as is the norm opposite the pedestrian gate and as we neared it, Mr Mitchell said: "Best you learn your f★★★★★★★ place... you don't run this f★★★★★★ government... You're f★★★★★★ plebs." ...*

Here is the media line:

Did Mitchell call the police plebs?

As a public schoolboy, is he a snob?

Are all public schoolboys snobs?

In a post last year 'The Curse of Cameron' *(see 18.1)* I suggested that David Cameron is a snob which is why he simply does not understand *people*. Quite simply, he has never had to live in the real world.

Since that post, we have hosted the Olympics and witnessed the extraordinarily positive response given to Boris Johnson and the real affection in which he is held. Like Cameron, Boris went to Eton. How can two Etonians be perceived so differently?

Having been to public school myself, I have observed a behavioural difference in those of us who have to work for a living and those with a private income: who do not have to work for a living.

When faced with pressure or adversity, such as not being allowed to leave Downing Street through the important gate, the people of independent means – spoilt brats you might call them – are more prone to hissy fits like Mitchell.

I do not know their individual circumstances, but this might explain the contrasting ways in which David Cameron and Boris Johnson relate to the rest of us. Apart from his likeable personality, natural sense of humour and willingness to admit mistakes, is a reason why Boris has more 'common touch' than Cameron that Boris has to work for a living?

And what about disrespectful, self-important, jumped-up, cry-baby Mitchell?

Apparently, he made a lot of money as a merchant banker.

What a superior chap he must be.

Not.

18.3 Tony Blair – no more excuses on Iraq

1 February 2010 22:06

Until last Friday, I was prepared to give Blair the benefit of the doubt. Once, I even gave him my vote. It was all I could do.

If nothing else, as a brand, our Tone has always intrigued me. In the commercial world, the most successful products deliver to their consumers what the consumer wants to buy. Otherwise they don't buy the product any more.

Because of this, many brands like, say, Marmite stand the test of time and their consumers stay loyal to that brand because they know what they are going to get (and some of them, like me, love it!). These brands have an essential *truth*, which occasionally needs refreshment to stay relevant, but the product delivers what you know it says it will deliver – it does what it says on the tin. But maybe, in politics, particularly in career politicians, the truth doesn't matter.

Maybe this is why they have things called 'policies' rather than what we in marketing and advertising call objectives and strategies and executions.

Maybe 'policies' are like 'principles' or 'promises' which, to unprincipled career politicians, can be dumped and broken and spun into bare-faced lies.

And maybe this is why they prefer to be advised by former tabloid journalists rather than strategic marketers. I think this is a pity. Stuff the strategy. Stuff the brand values. Stuff the truth.

SPIN?

You're IN!

And this, to me, is why Blair is an interesting brand because he got where he got to by ditching his early socialist political beliefs (his brand heritage), stole the opposition's 'policies' and then somehow made them his own. Alongside a couple of rather tasteless and untrustworthy cronies, he spun his way to the top.

And some mugs - like me – believed in him.

Now, I have always felt it important to deliver on my promises so when

I believe in someone else I find it very difficult to throw that belief away.

And so, until Friday, I was clinging onto my belief in Blair because there was one scenario in which I felt that I could understand that he had to lie to us, he just *had* to – for our own good, and even for the good of the big wide world.

On Friday I thought our Tone, with a new US President in the White House, had the chance to tell us the truth.

Here's how it goes. Your career has peaked. You are Prime Minister. You've spun your way to the top of the greasy pole. You've ditched your youthful ideologies. You've seen off the loony extremists. You've stabbed some backs and dropped a clause here and there. So what? Just smile, that's what you are good at. It's what got you there. You're at the peak of your career. You've got the job.

But this job ain't no poker game. It's hard. And it's hard because sometimes, whatever you do, whatever the spin, you just can't win.

You are a Tone in the Hole. And, in this hole, you simply *cannot* tell the truth.

This is why:

You know that George Bush is going to invade Iraq. You can't change his mind. Whatever you say, whatever you do, he's going in. Decision made. Done deal.

You also know that the two big moving forces in Europe are not going to move against Iraq. They just won't. Non. Nein. Never.

So this is one tough call. You stick with Europe: "Yo Bush! Sorry, man, we're just not with you on this one".

But you know that if you stick with Europe, all hell will break loose. You give the terrorists one target. The USA split from Europe. Manna from Heaven. Can you just smile and wave and wish them well from over the pond? The hell you can.

So you back Bush. And you do what you've always done. You smile and you spin. You play for time. Charm the UN. Smarm Europe. Smile. Spin. Play for time. And then someone says "WMD".

OMG WMD! He's used them before. We know he's got them. Hell we sold them to him. Let's find them. Play for time. Keep smiling. Spin. Keep spinning.

But Europe aren't playing and Bush ain't waiting. Yo, he's gonna go!

So you decide that the lesser of two evils is to back Bush. But, although this is the reason for going in, it is the only reason, politically, you cannot give.

Speech:

"I do not agree with the Bush invasion of Iraq but I have decided to support it because, in my judgement, the consequences of not supporting this invasion are more dangerous than doing so."

Even with your spinning toadies behind you, you can't say this because, by the very act of telling the truth, you undermine the special relationship and the worldwide stability you are trying to protect. This is Tone in the Hole.

So, until Friday, I was about the last person left to offer Tone the benefit of the doubt. I was prepared to believe that Blair believed that the lesser of two evils was to back Bush rather than let the USA go it alone and, by so doing, isolate the rest of the Western world (and Russia).

I hoped this might be the truth and that he honestly believed this to be the right decision and that I could forgive him.

But it wasn't.

And I don't.

Career politicians?

You are all rotten. The whole flipping lot of you.

And that's because, unlike Marmite, what you see is *not* what you get.

You just can't be trusted.

18.4 Unfair Gordon Brown

28 February 2010 23:26

The Labour Party's new slogan is "a future fair for all". Well I'm sorry, Gordon, this just isn't true.

It is not fair that you lost an eye playing rugby.

It is not fair that you and your wife lost a young child.

It is not fair that David Cameron was born with a silver spoon in his mouth.

It is not fair that Tony Blair didn't play fair with you.

It is not fair that the guy who lives opposite me drives a Porsche.

It is not fair that he and his kids went skiing at half-term.

Life is not fair.

And you know it.

As anyone in marketing and advertising will tell you, if you don't tell the truth about your product, then it won't sell.

Your product is The Labour Party. And what a fun fair your party has been.

But if fair is the best you can offer, then I'm afraid things ain't looking good.

18.5 Iain Duncan Smith The brand

12 November 2010 08:19

To return to the views I expressed two weeks ago in my longest and most read post – *The Conservatives may be doing the right thing, but in the wrong way (3.2)* – I can report that yesterday (11 Nov) the Conservatives made a major PR error which may lose them the next General Election.

They wheeled out IDS to announce the new uncaring 'claimant contract'.

From a figure of fun as Leader of his Party, IDS has spent years trawling the country and re-positioning himself as a champion for the poor and needy in a 'Broken Society' (now ineptly re-branded 'Big Society'). Two weeks ago, I said I believed IDS to be an innately good man who has made personal sacrifices to help the underclass in our country of which we should be so ashamed.

Now, in one day, the re-branding of IDS has been cut to shreds. What sort of PR strategy is that?

As a brand, IDS should have been wrapped in cotton wool and used to balance out the cruel cuts with his caring message. As a political party, the Conservatives have never convinced their doubters that, as long as the money is rolling in, they give a damn about 'common' people. Now, they have played into the hands of their opponents by fielding their one potential Mr Nice Guy as the voice of the devil.

Just wait until half of Manchester or Newcastle or Nottingham have to move to Bracknell or face three years without benefits.

After all that work in the slums, IDS will carry the can.

Poor guy.

18.6 IF YOU HAVE A POLITICIAN IN YOUR FAMILY, BE CAREFUL!

10 APRIL 2014 09:08

One of the nicest things anyone has ever said to me was a teacher at my children's school. On discussing their potential careers, he told me:

'Your children don't have to worry about their career choices, Hugh. They'll be fine. They've got your values.'

I replied that, while I appreciated him telling me this, the difficulty my children would face would be how to identify the contrasting values of the other people they might come across in the big, wide world.

In my career, as described in Appendix I, I have been unfortunate enough to encounter people with rather a warped view, shall we say, of the difference between right and wrong.

I have found that, working with these people, it is relatively simple to move on and, with a grateful sigh, eliminate them from one's life.

But what about their families?

How will their children emerge?

With what values are they imbued?

Or their partners by whom they might have expected to be 'deeply loved' until the day they die?

For over a week, the British media has been dominated by the behavioural shortcomings that have been revealed by our Culture Secretary, Maria Miller.

How on earth can Ms Miller, a Cabinet Minister no less, have let things get this far:

'In 2012...The Daily Telegraph, which broke the original expenses scandal, began investigating Miller ... after a tip-off that her parents had been living with her in taxpayer-subsidised accommodation. A reporter visited the Wimbledon home and this was confirmed by the culture secretary's elderly father.'

You what?!

Her elderly father?

What was Maria Miller thinking?

The behaviour of three more politicians comes to mind:

One is Jeffrey Archer, formerly deputy chairman of the Conservative Party, about whom the BBC said this:

'In October 1986 a sensational story hit the tabloid headlines. The deputy chairman of the Conservative Party, Jeffrey Archer, was accused of paying money to a prostitute. During the 1987 libel trial Mary Archer famously took the stand to support her husband.'

You what?!

His wife? In court?

What was Jeffrey Archer thinking?

Then we had Jonathan Aitken, an MP and Privy Councillor. On sentencing him to prison, the judge said:

"The fall from grace has been complete, his marriage has broken down, he has lost his home, he is one of only three people this century forced to resign from the Privy Council, he is bankrupt and his health has suffered. His public humiliation has been absolute. These are real and considerable punishments. Sir John said Aitken now felt 'profound remorse and shame', particularly for drawing up a false witness statement for his daughter, Victoria, to sign."

You what?!

His own daughter?

What was Jonathan Aitken thinking?

In March last year, former MP and Cabinet Minister Chris Huhne was sentenced to eight months in prison. During the trial it emerged that his son had sent him texts saying:

'You're a pathetic loser .... You are the most ghastly man I have ever known'.

You what?!

His own son?

What was Chris Huhne thinking?

Do you see what I mean?

How is it that some people refuse to accept the implications of their own behaviour to the extent that they risk the destruction not only of their own lives but also the people who are closest to them?

Maria Miller seems to be one such person.

All I can do is warn you that, next time your other half says to you... :

"Darling, can you do me a favour please?"

... be very careful.

Especially if you are married to a politician! :)

18.7 Caroline Spelman a metaphor for tumbling Coalition

18 February 2011 09:16

I wonder if the people of our country know what a seminal week this has been?

The Government have been forced into an embarrassing climbdown (sic) from the sale of forests and woodland.

The Right Honourable Caroline Spelman, Secretary of State for Environment, Food and Rural Affairs, told the House of Commons: *"I am sorry. We got this one wrong, but we have listened to people's concerns."*

Now they might have listened to people's concerns. But why didn't they ask *first*?

Regular readers of this post will be all-too-familiar with my thesis that a better use of the professional marketing and communications skills would make for better Government of our country.

I railed against the haste and confusion of NHS reforms *(see 4.2)*:

I showed how David Cameron would have benefitted from professional market research before rushing out with his multiculturalism speech in Munich *(see 9.2)*:

And now, in 'the mother of all Parliaments' of which we are so proud (even though, historically, Iceland beat us to it), we have a Tory Cabinet Minister – a Cabinet Minister – standing at the despatch box in our House of Commons and apologising for rushing into a policy without 'listening to the people'.

No quantitative research. No qualitative research. No engagement with community experts or opinion formers. No thought. No strategic thinking. No judgement.

All of us – yes, all of us – should all be ashamed of the state we are in.

What is the reason for all these rushed-through policies and bad government?

Ah well, let's calm down for a moment.

The answer to this question also emerged this week – and it is much more quietly tucked away than in our disgraced corridors of power than the humble Ms Spelman.

The House of Lords 'caved in' on voting reform.

Why has this caused all these rushed-through policies and bad government?

Well, I can tell you.

The Conservatives know that a 'no' vote to AV could be the end of the Coalition.

This is because the anti-Coalition (or, more accurately, anti-Tory) Liberal Democrats will feel their one main sticking point has not been achieved. Nick Clegg will find it impossible to hold his party together and this may lead to another General Election.

Labour have been most desperate of all to postpone this referendum, requiring tired old peers to camp down for all-night sittings in Westminster. They know that, under Ed Miliband, they are nowhere near ready for another Election.

If there is a 'yes' vote in the referendum, a General Election is even more likely.

Disaffected Liberal Democrat MPs will withdraw from the Coalition and go to the country in the hope that, under the new voting system, they are likely to win significantly more seats.

The Conservatives are unlikely to enjoy an overall majority ever again. Ditto Labour.

The Liberals will have achieved a massive breakthrough.

Even though the Alternative Vote (AV) is not their preferred system, it will be a step up the ladder to the Single Transferable Vote (STV) for which the Liberal-inspired Electoral Reform Society have been campaigning since 1884.

As I know from personal experience, politicians never know what is going to happen in an election – the latest being a case in point where the exit polls were not believed early in the evening but, by morning, were found to be almost spot on (what did I say about research?).

So now, with this AV referendum looming, our politicians are all engaged in this party political game playing, scheming and wheeling and dealing and what do they care about the rest of us?

What about the people who need the NHS – both as patients and employees, hundreds of whom are losing their jobs as I write this post?

What about Muslims who feel estranged and unwelcome – and who have to listen to ignorant and uncaring claptrap from our allegedly intelligent Prime Minister?

Or, people who love their trees and their forests – and anywhere else they can find to escape from all this nonsense?

Well, these politicians don't care.

None of them will stand up to their party machines. If this were likely, they would not have been selected by Head Office to stand for Parliament in the first place. To do this you have to show 'commitment to the cause' i.e. do what you are told. Churchill would have had no chance.

As we all know, most of the people holding senior posts in any of the main three parties are career politicians. They have gone from Oxbridge into the party machine. They haven't lived in the real world. They haven't a clue what is going on out there. They are careerists (not carers). And their careers are at stake.

So they are all trying to make a mark, rushing through as much legislation as they can in the hope that something worthwhile 'sticks' and their skins will be saved.

And the result is a chronically split society where the politicians who have failed us so badly get on with their yah-boo game playing and their own petty agendas.

There are those of us who get on with our lives and our professional careers in the commercial world, carrying with us the skills, expertise, creativity and energy that the politicians ignore.

And we have the rest – the poor, the sick, the elderly, the needy. People who cannot afford their TV licence fee let alone a computer and who wouldn't know about 'social networking' if it hit them in the face.

What about them?

Who cares?

19
APPENDIX I –
BATTERSEA NEEDS
HUGH!

19.1 WHAT IS WRONG WITH UK POLITICS

31 MARCH 2010 23:11

This reads more like a letter than a blog but, hey, I am going to post it anyway. And as it is Easter, you have got a few days off to read it if you want to.

First of all, many thanks to all of my friends in our industry who have reacted so positively to the announcement last week that I am going to be standing as an Independent MP at the General Election. I have been overwhelmed by your support and am extremely grateful to all who have donated to my fighting fund.

I thought I would take some time to tell you why I am doing this.

As I am not a career politician, I do not find it easy to use words like 'manifesto' and 'policies'. To me, they are the language of a bygone age, a time when politics was defined by ideologies that have been fought and won, a medieval class system that was defined by ownership of land rather than new-money 'rich lists' and a political system that is utterly irrelevant to the modern world. I prefer the word 'principles' but then, perhaps, that word is not very fashionable either.

The Conservatives say we live in a 'broken society' but not how they can fix it.

This is not surprising because if society is broken, our political system is broken too. Please let me explain. Some of this will seem obvious. Sorry, but here we go.

If, at the forthcoming general election, any of the established political parties get a majority vote, they will have achieved all they need for the next five years. With a clear majority, they can do what they like including, as we have seen, set different financial rules and controls for themselves than for plebs like us.

There you are.

The first reason society is 'broken' is because career politicians set different rules for themselves than they do for the rest of us. They assume a certain superiority and invincibility – which, with a majority of votes, is actually a valid truth and which we can do little about.

And I do not like the use of the word 'broken'. Some things that are broken can never be fixed. Not by this lot anyway. I think 'divided' is a better word.

Let me remind you of what Neil Kinnock, then Leader of the Labour Party, said to his Party Conference as long ago as 1 October 1985:

"I'll tell you what happens with impossible promises. You start with far-fetched resolutions. They are then pickled into a rigid dogma, a code, and you go through the years sticking to that, out-dated, misplaced, irrelevant to the real needs, and you end in the grotesque chaos of a Labour council—a Labour council—hiring taxis to scuttle round a city handing out redundancy notices to its own workers. I'm telling you – and you listen – you can't play politics with people's jobs and with people's services."

Well, we are about to be bombarded with 'impossible promises' from all the parties over the next few weeks. And they will all be 'playing politics' with our jobs and what are now called 'front-line' services.

It is going to happen.

Yet, while all this political posturing is happening, even while we are at war in Iraq and Afghanistan, who is going to be telling us about what is good about Britain and about all the positive things that we all agree on and that *unite* us: freedom, human rights, the rule of law, the difference between right and wrong, the importance of education, respect for others, 'do as you would be done by', tolerance, kindness?

How can we converge rather than diverge?

Not one of the established political parties can answer this. This is what John Major said on the Andrew Marr Show last year:

"We have a problem with people becoming advisors to Ministers, learning the jargon, getting selected for seats and getting into Parliament without touching real life on the way."

So, with all their career politicians and carefully selected shortlists, many of whom have not touched real life on the way, the political parties will be feeding back to the electorate the negative concerns they have learnt from focus groups who have been carefully recruited from 'floating voters' in 'marginal seats'.

Then, having learnt (but not lived) these negative concerns, they will be feeding back to the voter the things they know they want to hear.

Unless they do this, they cannot pontificate about 'change' and that, with their skilful expertise and honest management, things can only get better.

In this way, the election can only be a test of style over substance.

With the old ideological wars won and lost, each party – and each party leader – will all be presenting, essentially, the same issues in different ways.

Do not be fooled into thinking there will be any conviction in this politics.

Do not believe what Neil Kinnock called their 'impossible promises'.

Do not accept that these people have any principles which drive them.

The only things that drive them are their own interests and their own careers.

So, why am I standing as an Independent candidate? And, how can I stop this?

Well, as a 'floating voter', who has voted for both Labour and Conservative in my time, and as someone who is not a career politician, I would like to share one thing that has surprised, even shocked me, since I started on the campaign trail to ask people to elect me as their local Independent MP in Battersea.

I have discovered, to a far greater degree than I imagined, and even among my closest friends and family, that many people have what I can only describe as a 'tribal' loyalty to the Conservative or Labour parties.

I have only ever judged people by how they behave towards other people – not by where they went to school, or their religion, or the colour of their skin, or the title on their business card, or the flashiness of their car, or their wealth or their fame.

So, these tribal political loyalties have come as a major shock to me.

It is like being a football supporter. Once you have declared you support Arsenal or Manchester United, even if you have never actually been there, you never change your mind. You have declared your commitment. You cannot back down – that would be a weak admission that you have been wrong for life.

To some people, this tribal loyalty is so strong that they literally hate the supporters of the opposing team. They swear at them. They abuse them. They hate them in principle, not for anything they have done, not knowing if they are caring, loving people, in fact not for knowing anything about them at all. Their sin is to support a different football club. I sat in front of one of these people at Highbury the other day.

Now, in politics, I have had people say to me: "Why are you doing this, Hugh? You're going to split the vote. You're just going to let the other lot in. What on earth are you up to?".

Well, all I can answer is that perhaps the time has come for us to recognise that the 'grotesque chaos' that Neil Kinnock applied to local politics 25 years ago, has now infested politics on a national level.

This is very damaging to our country and a dangerous place for us to be. So, can we all please, please throw away our tribal loyalties to these historic and irrelevant political parties and think of a new way forward?

Really, that is all I ask.

From the constituency I am fighting – Battersea – I can demonstrate a system that is unequal and unfair. Here are the results from the 2005 General Election:

1. In Battersea, there was a total electorate of 69,548 people.
2. Of these 69,548 people 16,569 voted Labour (23.8%).
3. Of these 69,548 people 16,406 voted Conservative (23.6%).
4. So, this means that between them, only 47.4% of Battersea voted for Labour and Conservative combined. And the majority (52.6%) voted for minor parties – or, more likely, did not vote at all.

What did this mean?

This is a very easy question to answer. It meant that with a majority of only 163 people out of a total electorate of nearly 70,000 people, the MP for Battersea had five easy years in the House of Commons, during which time he voted with his whip in 98.3% of the occasions he voted.

Yet 76.2% of the people of Battersea never voted for him in the first place.

I believe this has become much more than a proportional representation argument. Throughout history some very brave and honest people, particularly women and ethnic minorities, have fought, and even died, for the right to vote.

Yet, we are left with a political system that has provided us with scandalous, sometimes criminal, behaviour and a complete lack of integrity of the career politicians who we have elected in the past.

Can any of us seriously accept that not one of these 646 noble and honourable members, including each of the Party leaders, caught even a sniff of the glaring flaws in the expenses system and was prepared to stand up and be counted and blow the whistle?

As someone who was faced with the horrible, and unwelcome, dilemma of having to do this in my own industry (and, I quote, has been defined as 'damaged goods' for doing so and has never worked for a major multinational agency since), I have to say that I cannot accept that this was the case.

So, what can we do about it?

Well, clearly, I accept that it would be impossible for Independent MPs to form a Government.

But I do think that if, say, 20-30 Independent MPs were elected to constantly and forensically interrogate the system and cross-examine the behaviour of our elected representatives from within then that would be a good thing.

Who should those Independents be?

From which constituencies should they come?

I am afraid that all I can say is that I agree with the signees of the Magna Carta of 1215 and have complete faith in the electorate to work out for themselves who these worthy candidates should be.

And I hope I am one of them.

Happy Holidays!

19.2 WHY DID I DO IT?

17 MAY 2010 22:39

I had never been involved in politics, certainly not party politics but, in July 2007, I was asked by a friend, who headed up one of the public sector reviews in Iain Duncan Smith's Centre for Social Justice, to cast my professional eye over the report his team had produced.

We met in a pub, as you do, and I gave him my views. Then he asked me what I thought of the Conservative Party's image and communications. I duly rubbished the 'Are you thinking what we're thinking?' campaign from the 2005 election and agreed to prepare a document demonstrating how I felt the Tories could, alongside my agency, develop and more effectively communicate innovative solutions to help mend the 'broken society' the Centre for Social Justice had identified *(see 3.2)*.

Although this initial work would be pro bono, I was hoping it might lead to a professional appointment (even though I was not a member of the Conservative Party, had not always voted for the Party or even been to a Party party).

I prepared a document *(see 3.2)* in which I argued the case for a more innovative and creative approach to the Role of Government in today's free market economy including:

i) a mission to 'ruthlessly examine every aspect of society and define the part Government has to play'
ii) to 'reassure the electorate that the Conservatives care about each and every UK citizen, including the poor, unhealthy and needy, and have thought through the way 'The State' can help every single one of them'.

Steve Hilton, the Conservative's director of strategy, agreed to a meeting.

Unfortunately, the date offered conflicted with a photographic shoot in The Bahamas I was due to attend for a paying client. Well, however tough the assignment, you have to put your existing clients first, don't you?

In the event, I never got to meet Steve Hilton. He went cold on me. But I sent him my presentation. I have no idea what happened to it – but some of my thinking is surprisingly similar to the Big Society initiative which the Tories have since rather clumsily announced.

Anyway, I enjoyed The Bahamas, as you do, and got on with my life.

Then, early last year (2009), another friend asked if I could help advise a friend of his who was planning to stand as an Independent Candidate in the forthcoming Euro elections. I met and liked the guy. And we went to the launch of The Jury Team, led by the impressive Sir Paul Judge, which was aiming to challenge the Party political system by promoting the value of Independent MPs.

Martin Bell, the former Independent MP, was there. So was Dr Richard Taylor, a standing Independent MP. But I was most impressed by a certain Major General Ramsbotham, one of nearly two hundred 'crossbenchers' in the House of Lords. He said that, on debating every issue, an expert on one side of the House would make his or her case, an expert on the other side of the House would argue an alternative point of view and the crossbenchers would vote for the side which they felt had the most merit.

Yet in the House of Commons, you could argue until you were blue, yellow or red in the face and still the 'career MPs' would be whipped sheepily into their party lobby. This was their job. If they did not do this, they would not have been recruited by their Party Head Office in the first place – and they certainly had no chance of promotion. No debate about it, a majority Government could get what it wanted.

I was persuaded that this situation was daft. The old party political system was as 'broken' as the rest of society. Perhaps, even, one led to the other.

So, I got sucked into this burgeoning case for Independent MPs. Alongside 46 other candidates, I was 'endorsed' by the Independent Network. I passed their tests to show I am a true and proper citizen and I agreed to abide by the Martin Bell Principles of honesty, integrity and trust.

I attended a prospective candidate workshop in Birmingham (Esther Rantzen was there!) and a debate in the Houses of Parliament (where I had never been before). It was all very interesting.

I wrote another paper on the barriers to entry for potential Independent candidates, both emotional – 'will I be seen as the local Screaming Lord Sutch?' – and rational – 'where do I start, how much does it cost, are there any forms to fill in?' (oh, yes there are!).

I also developed my 'Role of Government' ideas and, on a national level, felt that:

i)   I have ideas to help bring UK society closer together
ii) we aren't being very intelligent about how we counter terrorism
iii) there is a role that the media, especially new media, could play in the war in Iraq and Afghanistan. I have blogged on this before *(see 1.1)*.

Appreciating these issues are a bit soft, I had more concrete local policies.

I am very angry about the lack of secondary schools in Battersea – and the consequent behavioural differences of our eleven year old children.

I had the idea that a recently-closed local hospital overlooking the green pastures of Wandsworth Common should be re-built into a vibrant new school.

I also argued the case for changing the name of Clapham Junction to Battersea Junction *(see 19.5)*: Clapham Junction is not in Clapham!

Thus, I found myself standing as an Independent Candidate for Battersea.

This was not one of the target seats that Martin Bell had identified, but I have lived here for twenty years, worked here for over ten and think MPs should come from the area they know and not be parachuted in by the Central Offices of the established parties.

On 5 July 2009, I had watched John Major say on the Andrew Marr Show:

"We have a problem with people becoming advisors to Ministers, learning the jargon, getting selected for seats and into Parliament without touching real life on the way."

Well, I feel I have touched 'real life' so I decided that the time had come for me to stand up and be counted.

I did not know then what we all know now – that the TV leader debates (Gordon Brown and David Cameron's biggest mistakes and

Nick Clegg and the Lib Dem's biggest opportunity), would dominate the election, blow all the Independents out of the water and result in the end (hopefully) of the old tribal party politics we were standing against in the first place!

Before all this, I had developed a marketing strategy for my Independent candidacy in Battersea. Watch this space. My next posts will be headed 'what was it like?' and 'was it worth it?'. I'll get them done asap but sorry, for now, I need to get back to the real world.

19.3 WHAT WAS IT LIKE?

25 MAY 2010 22:17

So, I have this nagging concern that, with the major social battles of the 20th century fought and won – women's suffrage, equal rights, free market economics over socialism – and, especially, with all this new media about – why, in the 21st century, is our society diverging rather than converging?

And why aren't our politicians more sophisticated, more strategic, about how they use these new media opportunities to bring people closer together and unite society – globally as well as domestically.

I have never been very impressed by politicians, certainly not professional 'career politicians'. What have they done? I don't like their air of superiority, their fiddling expenses and flipping houses to avoid capital gains tax. This was going to be a major issue in this election (not).

I must be better than this lot. In fact, I can prove I am. So I decide to stand up and be counted as an Independent MP. I'm the man.

And that's my problem. I'm on my own. I'm Independent. I am not a party. I am a person, warts and all.

I don't have 'policies'. Aren't policies executional (rather than strategic)? Why don't strategic marketers have 'policies'? What was Lowe's Heineken policy? Or the BBH Levi's policy? Or Fallon's Cadbury policy? I don't even like the word 'policy'. It sounds like the police. If you emphasise the second syllable, you can even pronounce it 'policey'.

Call me old-fashioned, but I feel more comfortable with setting objectives, agreeing strategies and developing executions – all in one logical flow.

1. What were my objectives?

There is an easy answer – and a more complicated one.

The easy answer is 'to persuade the constituents of Battersea to vote for me, Hugh Salmon, to be their MP in the House of Commons'.

The complication is that this is an unlikely, unrealistic objective to achieve.

So why bother?

Well, there's the Lottery answer that if you're not in it, you won't win it. And, of all elections, this one is very unpredictable. You never know.

But the chances are still low, so are there any other reasons to justify the time and cost involved?

Well, for me, yes. Remember, my over-arching concern is the divergence, rather convergence, of society. Why are we becoming further apart from each other, rather than closer together?

Maybe, by offering myself up, albeit in a non-commercial environment, I could connect with real people. Not target audiences, not demographic profiles, not focus groups. Real people in the real world.

Where would that get me? I didn't know, but I was keen to find out. If nothing else, it would be a new, interesting and, hopefully, enjoyable experience. And you never know.....

2. What was my strategy?

As I saw it there were three strategic barriers I had to overcome:

i)   how to attract attention but, at the same time, be taken seriously?
ii) how to attract local voters, within my constituency, when they are most influenced by national issues and the established parties (and especially, as it turned out, the national party leaders)?
iii) how to balance offline and online media opportunities?

I decided that I would use offline media and ideas to attract attention and get noticed. And thereby, hopefully (because there was no time to test this), potential voters would go to my website where the content would be full and the tone serious and compelling. My 'manifesto' ran to 27 pages and was posted online.

I was advised to use all sorts of other online strategies but I had set myself a fourth barrier. I was due to move house right in the middle of the campaign, leaving me bereft of broadband for three weeks prior to 6 May. This was going to be a Blackberry campaign if ever there was one.

3. How did I execute this strategy?

Standing in one of the most contested seats in the country (the Labour majority in 2005 was a mere 163 votes), I was aware the Conservative candidate, in particular, had been 'working' the constituency for years.

She had fought Pendle (nowhere near Battersea) in 2005, so she knew the game. She infiltrated Battersea like she has been here all her life.

For unsurprising reasons, the seminal book 'Eating The Big Fish – how challenger brands can compete against brand leaders' has a particular resonance for me.

As, now, a Challenger brand myself, I read it again. The four principal requirements of a Challenger brand stood out (p.60 in my copy):

i) *Self-Referential Identity*

For three weeks, I was going to be me. Introducing myself to people, talking about myself, telling them my views, answering their questions about what I thought about their concerns (and there were some surprises, I tell you).

ii) *Emotion*

To deliver my strategy of getting noticed, I had to find a way to move people emotionally. Ideally, I would be interesting, approachable, welcoming, human, maybe even fun to engage with.

iii) *Intensity*

I needed to offer 'intense projections' and be 'vivid'. Oh dear, this was going to be hard work.

iv) *Salience*

I had to be 'highly intrusive' – unavoidable. I knew I could not compete with the brand leaders – or their leaders. I knew I did not have time to knock on every door of the constituency. I knew they had more money than me.

I had to *think*.

And, I had more reading to do.

The Electoral Commission's 'Guidance for Candidates' runs to 119 pages. Hidden within was the news (to me) that every candidate is entitled to the delivery by Royal Mail of a leaflet to every letter-box in the constituency. So that was a no-brainer. I needed a leaflet, the brief for which was to get noticed in the short journey between the letter-box and the bin. My team and I went for a shot of me and the line 'Battersea needs Hugh'.

Not great, but arresting enough we hoped. On the rear, was a personal 'letter' from me outlining why I would be the perfect vote and a call to action to my content-filled and seriously argued website.

But we could not rely on the leaflet. And we did not have time to follow it round every letter-box in Battersea. We would have to find a way to get noticed – to achieve 'salience' some other way.

Hence renting a milk float bedecked with the line 'DON'T FLOAT – VOTE!' (sorry, the line works better in capital letters than upper and lower case).

We would decorate it with banners and bunting and bottles. We would drive it up and down the roads of Battersea, we would park it on the High Streets, we would drive it past the stations and the supermarkets and in the parks. We would have children rapping on the back and we would wave and smile and have fun. We would be intrusive and salient with vivid intensity and, by having fun, we would 'invite a realignment of emotions'.

We would achieve a self-reverential identity.

And we did.

I'm telling you, we did. Trust me. As the Challenger brand, in terms of impact, the little fish beat the Big Fish. The Tories had but a trestle table!

But no-one was going to the website. According to Google Analytics, we were getting around 50 visits a day, peaking at just over 100 on 6 May itself. In the whole campaign, we did not achieve 1,000 visits to the site.

Yet this was where the serious content had been placed, the arguments discussed, the case made and my 27-page Manifesto housed and hosted (I couldn't afford a print copy).

So I knew, from very early on, that there was no way this level of interest in the website would translate into any sort of meaningful vote.

But, you have made a commitment to the country. You have to carry on. I was out there, my team was out there and the milk float was out there (apart from when it broke down, but that's another story). Whenever I handed out a leaflet, I urged people to take a look at the website – but clearly, this strategy was not working. They just weren't doing it.

Nevertheless, I was enjoying being out there, meeting people, talking to them about the things that mattered to them. There were plenty of surprises, not least that the biggest issue, by far, was Immigration.

MPs expenses, arguably my strongest card, were hardly mentioned.

Immigration came up at the hustings too – those that I was invited to.

Small-minded sprats sidelined me and the 'smaller' parties, using the TV debates as an excuse for restricting exposure to the three major parties. 'What's good enough for the BBC is good enough for us'.

I had had the idea that a recently-closed local hospital overlooking the green pastures of Wandsworth Common should be re-built into a vibrant new school. Researching this idea, I found a group of parents who were after the same thing. But, much to my surprise as I could only help their cause, I found them peculiarly reluctant to engage with me.

Then, I discovered that one of them had been a Labour agent in another constituency and I worked it out. Labour were scared of me!

With a tiny majority to protect, Labour were desperate. By the end of the campaign, the poor Labour candidate was begging for every single vote – and he could hardly bear to look me in the face.

He must have known what was going to happen too, especially after the first TV leader debate on 15 April. But you never know. Nor did he. In the end, although paltry, my vote would have cost him the seat in 2005.

When more open-minded and democratic constituents (including, to their credit, a locally-based trade union) allowed me, as an official candidate, to answer questions at the hustings I really had to concentrate.

The first time I was on top table – alongside Labour, Conservative, Liberal Democrat, UKIP and Green candidates – I realised they all had guidebooks with the answers to give to every 'policy' question asked. Yet again, as I could not resist pointing out to the sizeable audience, I had to think!

As an Independent, how would I run the economy? How would I repay the national deficit? What were my views on Iraq and Afghanistan? What did I think about gay couples being turned away from B&Bs? What were my policies on Immigration?

With every answer, I tried to feature a personal story, a human touch. I wanted to emphasise that, in a Parliamentary democracy, the electorate should vote for the best individual candidate for the people of Battersea – what, later, on 16 May, David Cameron admitted to Andrew Marr is 'a more civilised decision' than to vote by arcane tribal loyalties or the most charismatic party leader.

So, for example, in my answer on Immigration, I asked if people had read 'The Lady In The Van' by Alan Bennett. I said he had let her live in his driveway for nearly 20 years, and it was very generous of him to do so. But he could not let 50 Miss Shepherds live there.

In the same way, I said, as a country, we haven't got room for everyone who wants to live here so it is a numbers issue, and a control of those numbers issue. With my own experience of the civil service and my lack of trust in politicians, did I have faith that the people in charge of controlling Immigration were doing so effectively?

My answer would be a resounding 'no' – however, as their Independent MP, I would be on top of these people and, if necessary, asking them awkward questions in Parliament.

I had lots of answers like this but they are for a book, not a blog, and I'm not a good enough writer to write a book (I've tried).

There is one final 'What was it like?' question that I must address. And that was the count itself. It was in Wandsworth Town Hall, with Battersea (Conservative gain) being counted and announced alongside Putney (Conservative hold) and Tooting (Labour hold).

When you watch these things on TV at home or with some friends, you hear the results read clumsily by the Returning Officer and you smoothly and seamlessly return to the smooth, seamless David Dimbleby to hear considered and interesting analysis by intelligent, well-behaved experts.

Well, it is not like that when you are there, I can tell you. I've never been to Millwall Football Club but this was how, in the past, I have imagined it.

Talk about aggression!

Talk about bigots!

Talk about tribal loyalties!

Talk about uncivilised behaviour!

Talk about divergence!

There were rah-rahs with big blue rosettes sniffing and gloating about their Battersea gain. There were people with big red rosettes (and bright red metallic wigs) pointing at the blues and chanting for Sadiq Khan, the Labour hold, "Yes, we Khan! Yes, we Khan! Yes, we Khan!".

And all this at three in the morning.

Where do these people go all day?

I have every faith that most people are perfectly decent and reasonable.

As advertising people know, consumers are not morons. But, I have to say that some of the people at this count were morons and bigots – and, by the way, I have to say more of them wear blue or red than yellow.

I wanted to experience 'real people in the real world' but this wasn't that.

Frankly, I wondered what on earth I was doing there. I did not feel comfortable at all. After an intoxicating, invigorating, challenging, exciting experience, this was a horrible, unsettling ending.

19.4 WAS IT WORTH IT?

3 JUNE 2010 22:48

By standing up to be counted as an Independent Candidate MP, I certainly learnt some home truths, both professionally (which you might not like) and personally (which you might not care about).

So yes, of course it was worth it. Well, I am not going to say 'no' am I?

From a professional point of view, I know political advertising and marketing is different from specific products or services.

It is very PR-led. Some of the electorate ('consumers') are tied by arcane and irrational tribal loyalties. The political parties conduct the same focus groups with the same respondents from the same target constituencies – so they feed back the same stuff that they know you want to hear, thus encouraging campaigns of style over substance.

I also know that, despite the above, at General Election time the 'market' is volcanic and unstable. And the parties are scared because they know anything can happen – as it did. They just don't know what it might be.

So, here are the home truths, many of which have been acknowledged in other media. I wanted to wait to see if I could add anything new.

As a Candidate MP, you get the chance to connect with real people. Not people in focus groups, not target audiences, not demographic profiles. People in the real world.

A surprising number, clutching a lager, spit at you, an inch from your face and demand: 'what are your policies?', 'what are your policies?', 'what are your policies?'; 'what about me?', 'what about me?', 'what about me?'.

Once, standing opposite the sitting Labour MP on the pavement, I advised our intoxicated constituent: 'that bloke over there has been our MP – why don't you talk to him?'. Sorry, Martin. It had to be done.

But other people have a real grievance or concern they want to share. I met a lady whose 11-year-old daughter is petrified by dogs since being attacked aged eight. I would have had a great creative solution for her.

Another had her daughter taken into care because she didn't have a big enough flat, but she couldn't get a big enough flat without her daughter living with her. Vicious. Neither of these poor ladies knew where to turn.

These weren't the only ones. I met several people in the real world who are completely ignored and untouched by the media world we live in, especially digital media. How many of them need an iPad this week?

Let's be honest, although agencies and media-types like to develop more sophisticated definitions and segmentations, how much of our work is aimed at consumers in what would have been ABC1s rather than C2DEs?

In this real world experience, I have been shocked by how many C2DEs there are out there. You walk past them every day but you don't touch them. In an election, you do. They are all equal. They all have a vote.

But the political parties don't 'target' them. Their game is to trawl the streets for three years, knock on every door and find out who is going to vote their way and who is not. Those who aren't, they try to convert. The key people are the 'floating voters' who haven't made up their minds.

There is such a huge gap between the 'poor, scared, forgotten and alone' and the 'interested and engaged' that, frankly, the former are not courted by our politicians who don't have a clue how to communicate with them.

Why do they matter? They are entitled to vote, but are unlikely to bother, so why bother about them? For that matter, the same goes for marketers.

They haven't got any money so why target consumer products at them?

Others are really interested and engaged by politics and current affairs and are keen to know where you stand and challenge your views. These are the happy moments when you are asked about something you have never thought of and, as an Independent rather than party mouthpiece, you don't have a guidebook to refer to – so you have to think.

But, as we now know, no one had thought of the effect of the TV debates.

Despite not being tactically cute enough to leverage the impact of the first debate into presenting a credible Cabinet team at the time of the second and third, the Lib Dems suddenly became the viable default option.

I was one of 46 Independent MPs 'endorsed' by the Independent Network.

As well as passing tests of character and integrity, we agreed to abide by the Martin Bell Principles. The Independent Network has admitted the Election was undeniably disappointing for independent candidates. Even Esther Rantzen lost her deposit – and she probably had more media exposure than the rest of us put together.

We all thought the expenses scandal would be a major issue and expose our politicians as shabby, untrustworthy jobsworths who spent five years being shepherded into the lobbies in return for their underhand perks.

But, at a national PR launch, I realised to my horror, that the expenses scandal would not be an issue at all. I have a positive track record in this area and my particular point was that the MPs couldn't have worked out individually that they could flip their houses and avoid Capital Gains Tax. The flipping must have been a well-known scam among them – yet not one had the moral compass to raise a hand and say 'isn't this wrong?'.

But, when I made this point to the political editor of a 'serious' national newspaper, he couldn't see the problem. He just said 'of course, they all knew about it – the Commons Expenses Office told them to do it'.

So that's alright then. No point in MPs with financial integrity.

A further motivator for Independent candidates was to fight a political system where majority Governments containing specifically-recruited, spineless, jobsworth backbenchers can whip legislation through without a full and fair debate in the House of Commons. Well, it didn't happened the way we wanted, but it ain't like that now. And I am delighted.

So, in terms of my political objective, although no thanks to me, I believe we now have a 'fairer' Parliament. Hopefully, we'll never have to endure a single majority party again. Nick Clegg is playing the long game. After the referendum on AV, the Lib Dems will get a fairer ratio of seats to votes and these flipping career politicians will have to coalesce for evermore.

Anyway, sorry, I digress. Let's get back to the real world.

Apart from the above, my over-arching motivation in standing had been the divergence, rather than convergence, of society. Why are we becoming further apart from each other, rather than closer together?

This was the fundamental question I was seeking to answer.

So, from a professional (i.e. marketing and media) point of view, here are the home truths as I found them and, I hope, some positive thoughts as to how we might improve things:

1. Better use of marketing, media and creative skills

There are loads of people – probably millions – who we (those of us with Blackberries and iPads) virtually ignore. I know. I've met them.

Political parties like to identify social problems but their solutions, which they call 'policies', are woeful: at best, badly thought-out and poorly communicated (if at all); at worst, self-serving and party point-scoring.

Laughably, the Conservatives once produced a leaflet called 'Breakdown Britain – Citizen's Repair Manual', in which they tried to liken society to a broken motor car with diagrams of broken engines and nuts and bolts. Who is going to read that?!

The poor, scared, forgotten and alone are more disengaged from the media than our London-centric media 'specialists' might think. Their lives are dominated by their own problems and day-to-day survival. And their purchasing motivators are driven by price discounting and affordability rather than cute advertising or fancy media connectivity.

They are not on Facebook and they don't Twitter. In fact, they are unlikely to have internet access at all. They can't read, so why would they?

They may have TV, but the £142.50 licence fee (tax) is a lot of money – a national scandal in my view *(see 14.3)*. They are likely to avoid paying this, which will get them into trouble – or nick the money from elsewhere, which will get them into even more trouble.

Sure, politicians will claim a policy for this and a policy for that, but they are box-ticking – not touching people. Behavioural economics be damned.

If our political system has been working why, after all these Labour years, and with all this great new media technology, have the poor, scared, forgotten and alone become so disengaged from the rest of us?

Can't we, as one of the world's great creative industries, unite to develop genuinely creative solutions to the social problems that these people face?

Can't we develop a professional approach by talking to them other than on a commercial basis, identifying their problems, setting objectives, defining strategies and developing genuinely creative solutions to *help* them?

We would be much better at this than politicians. Why are our skills limited to commercial, rather than social, objectives (I am talking about more over-arching social issues here than the tactical work of the COI)?

If I had been elected, one of my missions would have been to propose a cross-party committee to act as 'client' and lobby Government funding for just such a project.

I do think a Role of Government should be to get the best problem-solvers aimed at the biggest problems in society on a non-party basis.

Politicians claim the high ground in this area ('I am in politics to serve the community, to improve society'). Well they don't. As we now know.

Can't we knock some heads together, whether through the IPA or ISBA or the Marketing Society or the School of Communication Arts, whatever, to set up a non-political working group with an objective to help the lives of people whose demographic profiles fall below the target audiences of our commercial clients?

2. Connecting Government – and people – with charities

For example, for discussion, could we develop a campaign programme to educate these people on where to turn for the help they need?

A Government 'policy' or box-ticking unit is unlikely to be the answer.

Why would you go there, when they might ask you questions that threaten your housing or your dole money? When people need help, they should get it from people who want to give it, not whose job it is to do so.

For example, have you ever heard of Guidestar.org.uk? As a Trustee of a UK charity for nearly 10 years, I had never heard of them. And I bet the poor, scared, forgotten and alone haven't either.

Guidestar was 'set up in 2003 to provide a single, easily accessible source of detailed information about every charity and voluntary organisation in England and Wales'. All 163,000 of them. That's a lot of charities.

Guidestar may or may not be the right people, I don't know. It might be the Citizens Advice Bureau (but I don't have a clue where they are and I haven't ever seen any advertising or messaging from them either). Or, maybe there's room for a grown-up Helpline. I don't know.

I do know that, when I was brought up in Hong Kong, there was a thing called The Community Chest. *Everyone* knew about it. It was so heavily advertised I can recall the corny jingle decades later (that's penetration!):

Give, give, give to the Community Chest
Give, give, give and they will do the rest

Give, give, give just as much as you can
Give, give, give to help your fellow man.
If you're from the East, if you're from the West,
Help your neighbours with the Community Chest.
Give, give, give to help the sick and the poor
Give, give, give and then just give some more.

If there are 163,000 charities in England and Wales, how on earth are the poor, scared, forgotten and alone going to find the right one for them?

They deserve to be told, rationally, that there is one gateway they can go to for help, and, emotionally, that we all care and want to help them.

What is needed is the media skills to identify who these people are and how to reach them, a strategy on how best to do this and creative skills to touch them and encourage them to act. I reckon that is a *great* brief.

And that it is the Role of Government to fund it, not execute it.

I suspect there is also a need to cut across Government departments, including the COI, and connect them to other official or voluntary bodies.

Again, that would have been one of my projects an Independent MP.

3. 'Geek snobbery' in digital media

Before the Election, I approached several 'digital-savvy' friends and contacts before developing my own campaign. To a man (for, sorry, they all were), they promised this would be the first online, social networking General Election.

One of them said he could do me a great deal for £25k.

I am concerned that, influenced by digital media fashions and with more than a touch of 'geek snobbery', we in Brand Republic have developed our own little bubble in our own little world and, in this divergent society, become far more disconnected with reality than we think.

How scared are we to admit that we don't really understand the place – or the future – of digital media?

How influenced are we by the early adopters – the 'geek snobs' – who think, that by knowing how to use a new digital media product, they know how to monetise that technology for meaningful commercial results?

For example, although millions of people use Facebook, do they use it in such a way as to create significant commercial ROI?

Is Twitter an exciting new media opportunity? Or, is it a completely new animal? A cross between – occasionally – an extraordinary news channel (Iran massacre, Cumbrian murders) and a game – a trivial pursuit, if you will – that some people like playing more frequently than others?

And where are the commercial opportunities? I tweet as 'Tweeterbookclub' and today I have 2,790 followers but I know, when I trawl through them (which is very boring), many of them aren't reacting to my tweets – and a frightening number haven't used Twitter at all for months and even years.

They haven't just opted-out of my tweets, they have opted-out of Twitter altogether. Prove me wrong, but I reckon sites like Facebook and Twitter are the definitive 'opt-out' media channels. Commercial messages just get blocked out. And the more the messaging, the more the blocking.

Where's the financial scalability for these sites? Without it, they won't survive.

(Actually, I reckon I know how they could, but I ain't going there now).

4. Client confusion

The explosion in digital media has led to a plethora of digital agencies and a confusion of choice for clients.

More than ever, the agency world has polarised into the multinational groups, with all their advantages of size and international client service, and the local specialists – who are faster-moving, faster-thinking but, for clients, ever-more confusing.

As clients in the last General Election, I am sure all the politicians were being advised to develop digital solutions and that this would be the way.

But it wasn't.

How many clients in today's commercial world are being led down the same line and wasting valuable resources just as I could have done?

I suspect more than the geek-snobs might like to think.

So now, apart from an excuse to post the wordiest blog of all time, I have to touch on how standing for Parliament was worth it from a personal point of view (this will be shorter):

1. It is a privilege to stand outside Clapham Junction with an excuse to talk to anybody who passes by – the more sober, the better. This is a real eye-opener, as I hope I have reflected above.

2. And it was fun. We really engaged with people by driving round with the milk float (DON'T FLOAT – VOTE!).

   This led to some extraordinary and unforeseen experiences. We drove round Parliament Square and I was interviewed by Spanish, Portuguese and American TV stations on College Green. I even predicted the result to the American station. All very random and completely off-strategy for attracting votes from my Battersea constituency.

   Someone asked me for my autograph because they thought I was the actor-singer Michael Ball. Makes a change from Jeremy Clarkson.

   One of my thoughts was to change the name of Clapham Junction, where it isn't, to Battersea Junction, where it is. I was trying to explain this to a potential voter and he said: 'Yes, but it's called Clapham Junction because the station is there'. There's no answer to the wisdom of the electorate.

   Out of respect to them, my website was much more serious in tone and my Manifesto ran to 27 pages.

3. My major local issue was to help persuade the powers that be to convert an unused, derelict local hospital into a badly needed secondary school. It looks like this is now going to happen.

   I have said before that, at a General Election, anything can happen. In a completely different way from commercial marketing, none of the parties know what this might be. They really don't know if, as a local Independent candidate, you might attract a following and tip the balance between one party and another. My vote in 2010 would have done this in 2005.

   But I am convinced that a credible local Independent candidate standing for this issue, and raising its importance, led to Ed Balls (ex-Education Minister) coming to the hospital site and, with a week to go, Michael Gove (future Education Minister) coming too.

   By doing this, and helping to make this an all-party issue, it became a non-issue and it looks like the school is going to happen. Brilliant.

4. Finally, most rewarding of all, was the opportunity to discuss, on an equal basis with the 'main' parties, real issues with real people. You didn't know what they might ask you. Unlike the parties, you didn't

have a crib-sheet of answers supplied by Central Office. You had to think. And I like to think that all of my answers had a more human perspective than the regimented political party dogma.

My website attracted genuine people with genuine concerns. Here is one:

EMAIL FROM BATTERSEA CONSTITUENT

Dear Hugh,

I have read your website with interest and would be interested to know where you stand on the ability of B&B owners to ban gay couples from renting a room together and, please, your views on whether or not the Pope – an apparently committed homophobe and coverer-upper of child abuse – should be allowed a platform in the UK or whether his presence here should be denied as not being conducive to the public good.

Thank you.

MY REPLY

Dear (anonymity respected),

Thanks for getting in touch. I have thought long and hard about these issues. My mother and her side of my family are Catholics.

Personally, I am an atheist and think, through history, religious divisions have done enough damage to the world.

Thank you for taking the time to read my Manifesto. As you will have read, I am for convergence rather than divergence and I will answer your two questions in this spirit:

1.   I, most certainly, am against a ban on gay couples from renting a room together. As I have made clear in all my communications in this campaign, I relate to people on how they behave – not their race, religion, background, wealth or sexuality.

However, in the instance to which you refer, I would prefer to live in a society where the following exchange had taken place:

Landlord: "I am aware that I am legally bound to admit you to my B&B, but I have to inform you that my religious beliefs are such that I would rather you find alternative accommodation at the following hostelries in this area. However, if you cannot find alternative accommodation, then of course you may stay here and you will be as welcome as any of our other guests".

Gay couple: "Thank you for letting us know your position. We do not share your views but respect your right to hold them. We will try and find somewhere else nearby, failing which we will come back as you have proposed".

This way, a relatively simple conflict of views need not have become a national media scandal.

2. Re the Pope, you have used the word 'apparently'. I'm afraid I cannot agree that we deny the Pope a visit on this basis. Overall, I am against the religious divisions in our society, and am certainly against the faith schools that feed them. I do not care if people are Catholic or Muslim, gay or straight, Tory or Labour, or support Arsenal or Chelsea. I have written a book called 'Do As You Would Be Done By' and this does it for me.

I would rather live in a more tolerant world, and this desire is perhaps the defining reason for my standing up to be counted as an Independent Candidate in this way.

I hope this helps.

All the best,

Hugh

CONSTITUENT RESPONSE

Dear Hugh

Thank you for taking the time to respond to me – so thoroughly and promptly too, if I may say so. My partner and I will be voting for you tomorrow and wish you luck......

Your beliefs, are, in my humble opinion, sound, reasoned and reasonable – more power to you and others with independent spirit!

Again, good luck tomorrow!

Regards

END OF MESSAGE

I believe that the opportunity to relate to complete strangers in this way – and this is one of many – has been an absolute privilege and I'm proud to live in a democratic society where this kind of engagement can take place.

I just wish we could do more to recognise all the good things and the good people in this country and somehow do more to recognise, share and communicate the positive values that bind us rather than, as a society, become increasingly divergent which is what seems to be happening not least educationally, financially, culturally – and in the media.

END OF MESSAGE (AGAIN).

19.5 WHAT'S IN A NAME?

12 APRIL 2010 23:19

When does a name become a brand? And at what stage of a brand's development can it rely on the mere transmission of its name to justify expenditure on the exposure of its name alone?

For example, how do marketers justify investment in the presence of their name on the side of a golf ball, or the side-line of a football pitch or the side-pod of the nose-cone of a Formula One car?

I have never really understood this side of our market. These 'sponsorship' brands aren't making a claim. They rely on their name.

To people who do not understand the meaning of the word 'brand', I advise them to substitute the word 'brand' with the word 'personality'.

Once they have understood this, they can then understand that brands rely very heavily on their name. In fact, for most brands, their name defines the brand, although there are some exceptions, such as Nike and Shell, where a visual device says it all. These are formula one brands.

There is an inherent truth behind these brand names. People know what they stand for and what they can get out of them.

Thus, I suppose, 'reminding' people of a brand name alone is money well spent. Personally, I still don't get it, but people do it – so it must be justifiable expenditure.

In the real world, having established a brand like say, Dove, the brand's personality can be extended into new product areas and new income streams. But you need to connect the claim of old brand to delivery in new product.

And in the High Street, signage is very important. The name of the store, even if it is as fatuous as Fat Face, defines the personality of the brand and so encourages shoppers to feel comfortable entering the store.

Unfortunately, these days, it seems the same shops with the same signs and the same personalities are all on the same-looking High Streets in same-looking towns. Wherever you go, the names are the same.

Talking of towns, I have always been interested in the fact that people have a preconceived perception about a place that may not be based on reality, and where they may never have even been. For example, why has

Slough always been defined as such a rotten borough? It can't all be down to one poem by John Betjeman.

Indeed, the place I live and work also seems to be looked down on by certain folk, especially those North of the River Thames.

Why is that the case and how can one change it?

When I moved The Salmon Agency to Clapham Junction 10 years ago, we were paying £12 per square foot compared to over £50 a square foot in Victoria – 7 minutes away on a train.

Because Clapham Junction is a 'main line' rather than a 'tube' station, people think you have to wait for a train or find a timetable – unlike the Underground, where you just turn up hoping a train will turn up too.

Unless you live near Clapham Junction, that is, in which case you will know that trains to Victoria and Waterloo leave every few minutes.

In fact, in terms of frequency of trains to London, to all intents and purposes, Clapham Junction operates as an Underground station – one stop to Vauxhall, two stops to Waterloo and, often, one stop to Victoria.

You seldom have to wait more than five minutes for a train into town.

So I have always told visitors to my office that Clapham Junction raises an interesting branding issue based on people's automatic perceptions of a 'main line' rather than 'tube' station.

But Clapham Junction has another, much bigger branding issue.

Clapham Junction is not in Clapham at all. It is in Battersea.

Clapham is the other side of Clapham Common and Wandsworth is the other side of Wandsworth Common and Clapham Junction is bang between the two – in Battersea.

That brand 'Clapham Junction' is not based on an inherent truth. It is where it isn't.

And it is really boring when you live and work here and tourists come out of the station, often laden with baggage from Gatwick, and ask the directions for a road in Clapham and you have to tell them they are not in Clapham at all.

It doesn't give visitors a favourable first impression of London.

I also think it is really important for the people who live here to have a positive sense of identity about the area they live in.

So I wonder if towns and urban areas like Clapham Junction could identify and admit to their inherent truth (or lack of).

Would Clapham Junction benefit from a change of name to, say,

Battersea Junction and could marketing and communications experts use this to launch and establish a greater sense of pride and identity in a place just like they do with 'brands'?

And, if this could be done, could the new name signal a new direction and a new sense of identity and a new sense of pride and maybe even better behaviour and respect for people within their neighbourhood?

I wish.

19.6 'Man's Inhumanity to Man' on YouTube

I have posted a film version of my earlier post 'Man's Inhumanity to Man' on YouTube.

20

APPENDIX II –
BLOWING THE
WHISTLE

20.1 WHISTLEBLOWERS – BRAVE HEROES OR SOCIAL OUTCASTS?

24 MAY 2012 09:02

The word 'whistleblower' has re-entered my life. I hate this word with a passion.

In the school playground, whistleblowing is called 'sneaking'. As a sneak, you are the person who has reported the misbehaviour of your schoolmates to the teachers. You cannot be trusted. You have behaved in a furtive, underhand way. You are left isolated, alone and friendless (every child's worst nightmare). You are contemptible.

In the criminal world, you are a 'snitch' or 'grass' (derived from 'snake in the grass'). You have reported the criminal activities of others to the police. You are an informant. And you are in grave danger. In retaliation, you risk being kneecapped, 'tarred and feathered' or killed. You are worse than contemptible. You could be dead.

But, in the wider world between the school playground and the criminal underground, isn't 'whistleblowing' a good thing?

For reasons I will come to later, whistleblowing is an aspect of human behaviour that is of particular interest to me. I like to learn about people who have been placed in a dilemma where their social conscience has been challenged to the extent they feel forced to, it says here, 'make public exposure of corruption or wrongdoing'.

In February, I read the obituary of an American rocket engineer called Roger Boisjoly 'whose warnings of catastrophe on the eve of the Challenger disaster went unheeded'.

Working for the company that made the booster rockets for the Challenger Space Shuttle, Boisjoly spotted a design fault that he investigated and reported to his company and NASA. The problem was that in cold temperatures the rubber sealing rings stiffened and became more likely to fail. 'The result,' he warned, 'could be a catastrophe of the highest order.'

His findings were ignored. Shortly after take-off, the spacecraft exploded killing all seven crew members.

Then - and this is the social dynamic I hate – get this:

'In the days, months and years after the Challenger disaster, Boisjoly experienced intense feelings of guilt and depression. Recovery was not helped by the fact that many in the business he loved rejected him as an unwelcome whistle-blower.'

Isn't that dreadful?

What did Roger Boisjoly do wrong? Why did he feel 'guilt and depression'? Why was he 'rejected'?

I take a completely contrary view. I would like to declare that I admire and honour Roger Boisjoly. I had not heard of him until I read his obituary but, to me, Roger Boisjoly is a hero. May he rest in peace.

Whistleblowing also occurs in business. The lead story in the March issue of Management Today featured Michael Woodford, 'Britain's highest profile whistleblower', who was 'sacked as Chief Executive by the Olympus board for refusing to keep quiet about hundreds of millions of dollars of corrupt payments by the high-tech opticals maker'.

But, again, get this:

'And what of Woodford himself? A whistleblower's future is often a difficult and lonely one. Ejected from one pack, Woodford is now a lone wolf in his Thames lair. He has been to head-hunters, but it would be a bold gamble for a big corporation to hire him for a senior management role. It would probably worry that such a highly principled individual, however talented and cash generating, would prove a source of trouble.'

Isn't that dreadful?

And why am I, Hugh Salmon, so interested in the subject of whistleblowing? Why do I feel so strongly? Why do I get so emotional?

It is because, as long ago as October 1998, I featured in a lead story about whistleblowing in the very same magazine, Management Today. Please do not think I am trying to paint myself as a hero – frankly, in my case, I didn't think I had much option.

It seems, from Michael Woodford's case, that in the last thirteen years (despite the best efforts of a worthy charity called Public Concern at Work), nothing has changed.

And this makes me really angry.

As I have discussed before, the biggest challenge we face in the world today is how to make capitalism work for the good of society as a whole.

Surely, in this day and age, if whistleblowers expose financial wrongdoing, they should be encouraged not rejected, welcomed not isolated, applauded not reviled?

It might be that we need a more positive word than 'whistleblower'.

How about 'honest broker'?

'UK: The Whistle blower's dilemma' by Matthew Lynn
Management Today, 1st October 1998.

20.2 THE WHISTLEBLOWER'S DILEMMA – WHAT WOULD YOU DO?

31 MAY 2012 22:07

Further to my last post on whistleblowing, and my own experience thereof, sometimes I get asked to conduct seminars and workgroups on 'Integrity in Business'.

The most rewarding sessions are when I place the participants into a position where the thin grey line between their moral integrity and financial or career ambitions is challenged.

Let's take a hypothetical example:

1. You own and manage a strategic marketing consultancy. You are successful but not rich. You have personal overheads – mortgage, loans, car, children. You know how it is.
2. You are contacted by a long-standing business contact (the 'Contact') who specialises in mergers and acquisitions (M&A) and company turnarounds.
3. He has a client (the 'Client') who owns a small, provincial UK engineering company that is in financial trouble.

On behalf of the Client, your Contact proposes to place the company into administration and then buy it back, restructure the business and re-launch it into an important market, which is where he has asked you to get involved.

The factory and offices are too far for you or your Contact to travel to each day so the Client agrees to fund the use of an apartment nearby. This is where you and your Contact will base yourselves during the week while you rescue, redefine and re-launch this business.

But there is a sting. Because the Client company has gone into administration, and is now trading as a new business under a new name, no estate agent will trust the new company with the lease of the apartment.

So, in good faith but perhaps rather naively, you agree to rent the flat and buy the furniture – subject to an agreement with the Client that you will be reimbursed in full from the revenue generated by the new company.

Your Contact says he knows a cheap furniture store near where he lives and you agree that he will choose all the furniture required and you will pay for it.

The invoice for the furniture arrives. It totals £5,250. You pay it.

However, as an experienced business professional, there is something about the invoice that does not seem right; there is a name but no address; there is no invoice number and, this is the strangest thing, the furniture you have bought and paid for is not specified item by item, piece by piece, price by price. You smell a rat.

So, you call the accounts department at the furniture store and they agree to send you the invoices for the furniture bought and paid for by you.

When you receive these invoices you realise, with disappointment and no little anger, that the furniture for the apartment you have rented has not cost the sum you have paid for it.

In fact, it is revealed that the furniture you have bought and paid for can be neatly divided into two separate deliveries:

1. The furniture that has been delivered to the apartment you have rented near the factory. This consists of an armchair, a sofa, a nest of side tables, two beds, four chests of drawers, a dining table and four dining chairs. The cost of this delivery is £3,100.

2. A separate order which has been delivered to an address in the Contact's wife's name and over 100 miles from the Client business. This consists of a two-seater sofa, a three-seated sofa, a nest of side tables, a lamp table, a wardrobe, two chests of drawers, an extending dining table and six dining chairs. The cost of this delivery is £2,150.

As you can see, the total cost of these two deliveries comes to £5,250. You now face the whistleblower's dilemma.

From now on, whatever you do, all future actions are underpinned by a racing certainty that any trust you may have had in your Contact has been greedily betrayed.

1. Is this theft?
2. Do you tell your Client?
3. Do you report it to the Police?
4. Do you confront your Contact and demand your money back, after which all will be forgiven? If so, will you be able to look your Contact in the eye again, especially while sharing the apartment you have agreed to share with the furniture you have bought and paid for?
5. Do you do nothing, take it on the chin and, desirous of this revenue stream, carry on regardless, avoiding the need to involve the Client (or the Police) but hoping that the ongoing revenue from the Client will make up for your financial loss in the long run?
6. Or, is there another option which, confused and alone, you have failed to consider?

This is the whistleblower's dilemma.

What would you do?

20.3 WHISTLEBLOWING – A CALL FOR NEW LEGISLATION

7 JUNE 2012 08:51

On 24 May, when I posted the first of this trilogy on whistleblowing, I referred to a front page article in Management Today on Michael Woodford, 'the British chief executive who blew the whistle on a $1.7bn (£1bn) corporate fraud at Japanese electronics giant Olympus'.

Little did I know that now, only two weeks later, The Telegraph would report that:

> 'Woodford has brokered an out-of-court deal with the company over his sacking, believed to involve a multi-million pound payout ... At a five-minute hearing yesterday (28 May), Mr Woodford's lawyer Thomas Linden QC said that the two sides had reached an 'agreement' to be rubber-stamped by Olympus's board on June 8. Outside the tribunal, Mr Woodford said he could 'give no guidance' on reports he had received an eight-figure settlement ... 'I'm not at liberty, under the terms of the agreement, to go into any detail,' he said. 'But I genuinely hope, in the interests of Olympus, it helps them go forward and also for my own life and that of my family [to go forward]. Hopefully today is a closure, a line has been drawn. The company can move on and I can.'

What announcement will be made after 8 June? Will all the allegations of fraud, that Woodford has made, be admitted to be true? Will the perpetrators be identified? Will they be punished? Or will the whole thing be washed up in some bland public statement?

Obviously, we do not know. I fear, after 8 June, that we may still not know.

And this – the fact that we may never know – is what worries me and leads me to the point I want to make. For I do hope that, by the terms of this agreement, Olympus will not be able to:

i) 'cover up' the full details of the wrongdoings reported by Woodford
ii) 'protect' the identities of the individuals who perpetrated the 'fraud' (saving them from prosecution and punishment for what may or may not have been criminal activity).

What I do know is that, in my own case against Lintas (reported by *Management Today* in 1998), by settling out of court, Interpublic were able to:

i) deny me the chance to reveal in Court the full evidence I had gathered against the individual managers involved (which I very much wanted to do)
ii) continue to employ them for many years afterwards (rather than face criminal prosecution).

So why did I settle? Good question. I am afraid you will have to believe me when I say that, such is the legal system by which we are bound, I was left with no option. However, I did refuse to sign a 'gagging' clause, which is why I am at liberty to discuss the case now.

So, for the purposes of the case I want to make in this post, let's return to the hypothetical case history discussed in my last post.

In the scenario I discussed, given that there was an outstanding fee involved, it would be no surprise if the Client were to insist that an agreement 'to settle all outstanding claims' would be conditional on you (the Consultant) agreeing to 'gagging' clauses along the following lines:

'The Consultant (you) agrees and undertakes to the Companies and the Directors not to:

i) Make or publish any statement to a third party concerning this Agreement, the dispute settled by it or the circumstances surrounding the termination of the Consultant's involvement in the Companies;
ii) Make or publish any derogatory or disparaging statement or do anything in relation to the Companies, the Directors and any employees of, or consultants to, the Companies which is intended to, or which might be expected to, damage or lower their respective reputations.'

Now this is what I object to:

Why should any company be able to 'gag' a whistleblower to protect their reputations?

The human insight I would make, based on my own painful experience, is that it is the whistleblower – the honest broker who stands up for what he or she thinks is the right thing to do whatever the cost of this stance to their own career or financial interests – who is blamed for being the trouble maker (not the perpetrators of the fraud).

Why is this?

It is my very strong opinion that it should be against the law – a criminal offence – for any company, or the directors of any company and even their lawyers, to draw up 'agreements' whereby paying money to a whistleblower is made subject to that person agreeing not to reveal the financial wrongdoing or fraud he or she has unwillingly discovered.

This is the classic corporate 'cover up'. And far too much of it goes on in business today.

In this vital debate we are having about how capitalism can work for the good of society as a whole, how can business people be allowed to 'cover up' fraud in this way?

It is an absolute disgrace, of which everyone in business should be thoroughly ashamed.

Fraud is fraud. Stealing is stealing. Theft is theft.

Too many businesses get away with it.

And it is so, so wrong.

A TRIBUTE TO MY FATHER

12 MAY 2012 08:45

My dad died ten years ago. As the eldest of his four sons, it fell upon me to give the eulogy at his funeral – the hardest job I have ever done.

You are unlikely to have direct interest in my father as a person but there are two facets of his character, and his life, that you might care to consider.

How many of today's leaders would have volunteered to rebate all income earned outside their salaried job back to their employers, to the extent that by the time of his retirement my father's employers were 'earning' more from him than they were paying to him?

If you have anti-colonial feelings, please consider the possibility that a great many British 'expats' were good people who made a positive contribution to the people and communities they lived with and in. I am proud to say my dad was one of them. I hope you agree:

"He was born on 27 September 1921. In 1940, after only one term at Oxford, he was called up to the army. By the end of the War, he was a Captain and had served in India, Egypt, Persia, Lebanon, Singapore and India again.

After the War, in England but not wanting to go back to Oxford, as a 25 year old and after five years fighting a war, he accepted a job in Calcutta (Kolcata) with Mackinnon Mackenzie, the Far Eastern agents of the P&O shipping company.

Soon, he was transferred to Malaya, where he lived in Penang for three years. And then to Japan, where he lived in Kobe for three and a half years.

In 1954, he was posted to Hong Kong. In 1963, he was promoted to Chairman and Managing Director of Mackinnon Mackenzie Hong Kong and there began 10 happy years.

Professionally, this was his most fulfilling period. Apart from his day job with the P&O, he was Chairman of Mackinnon's Godown, Pennell & Company, Sworn Measurers and Weighers Ltd, Travel Tours Ltd, Shanghai Dockyards and the Hong Kong Electric Company.

He was a Director of the Hong Kong & Shanghai Bank, Mercantile Bank, Union Insurance Society of Canton, Dairy Farm, Hong Kong Tramways, Indo China Steam Navigation Ltd, Union Waterboat Company, Star Ferry, Hong Kong Wharf Company, Douglas Steamship Company, Taikoo Dockyards and Cathay Pacific Airways.

After he retired he revealed to me that, apart from his basic Mackinnons salary, any or all of the fees generated from these directorships were sent back to the P&O in London. He just felt this was the right thing to do.

There were also public appointments. These directly involved him in the Government of the colony. He was a member of the Legislative Council, where he sat on the Finance Committee, the Public Works Committee and School Fees Committee.

Unusually, for a period, he sat on both the Legislative Council and the Executive Council, effectively The Cabinet, at the same time.

He was a member of the Hong Kong Trade Development Council, the Hong Kong Tourist Board, the Port Committee, the Court of the University of Hong Kong and the Tenancy Tribunal. He was appointed a Justice of the Peace in 1968.

There was also voluntary work with the Hong Kong Chamber of Commerce, the Far East Freight Conference, the Federation of Hong Kong Industries, the Joint Associations Committee on Employer/ Employee Relations, the Chinese Language Committee, the Festival of Hong Kong Committee, the Hong Kong Chinese University Committee, Outward Bound, and the Cheshire Homes.

In 1973, he was awarded the OBE for services to the community in Hong Kong.

But I believe it is not what he did in his life that set my father apart, but the way he did it. How he behaved. He was friendly, considerate and courteous. He had a nice word, and a smile, for everybody.

He was modest and completely unmaterialistic. He valued the simple things in life, some of which in his later years, and to his great sadness, were denied him: golf, gardening, bridge, his health and even, at the end, his speech.

He believed in doing the right thing and doing things the right way, even when he knew that doing the right thing would not be easy, or the consequences difficult to face.

He was a man of the world but, more importantly, he was a man of his word. He was absolutely honest. When he said he would do something, he did it. He meant what he said.

And, sometimes, we have to admit, he said what he meant: even if this gave the impression that he could be a little tactless, a little strong-willed, a little stubborn. (Remarkably, none of his four sons have inherited these characteristics!).

Above all, he was enormous fun. In fact, he was probably more fun to be with, and more fondly thought of, than he himself realised. He had a ready smile, a twinkle in his eye, and a healthy sense of the ridiculous, particularly if he felt people were being pompous or taking themselves too seriously.

He was witty, he was warm and he was wise. And he was wonderful company.

There is one final thing I would like to say.

If anyone in this church, or who knew my father at all, ever has a difficult decision in your life, or a personal dilemma, I would urge you to pour yourself a large whisky, or, if it is before lunch, a pink gin; sit down in your favourite armchair; look up from the crossword; look away from the Test Match on the telly; look out through your drawing room window into the garden; and say to yourself: 'What would Gerry Salmon have done?'

Because, if you do this, I know that your decision will be the right one, that you will be a better person, and that he won't have died at all."

ACKNOWLEDGEMENTS

9 JANUARY 2015

I would like to thank all my school teachers for everything you did for me. You dedicated your lives to improving the lives of others and are a noble breed. Especially the late, great Jim Ramage and Hugh Atkins who recognised and developed any writing skills I might have.

I have many people to thank:

In the University of Life, Peter Hunt was a shining star then and forever.

Clive Aldred recruited me twice: for Ogilvy & Mather London in 1979 and then O&M Thailand in 1988. Robert Deighton recruited me twice too: for Foote, Cone & Belding and then Kirkwoods which became Deighton & Mullen. Thank you, gentlemen.

For the glory days of SFX, I must recognise the heroic support of Derek Ralston, Chris Lever, Alison Cruikshank, Tony Monteuuis and, of course, the great Max Bell and countless others.

At O&M Thailand, I would like to thank everyone in the Bangkok office while I was there, especially Simon Bolton for our special friendship then and since.

With my lawyer, the late John Lloyd, we stood up and fought the might of Interpublic, a publicly quoted company in New York. We beat the crooked bastards! Without John, I could never have done it. I will always be grateful.

At The Salmon Agency, the following had special faith in me: Anthony Stileman, Samantha Etheridge and thanks to all the others who came on board, especially my longstanding client The Bahamas Tourist Office. What a country! What a people!

Through sport, I have learnt so much about life:

In cricket, I must thank all my friends in all the clubs I played for, especially the legend that is Chris Potter and my fellow tourists in Sri Lanka 1982-83, South Africa 1983-84 and Australia 1984-5.

In rugby, special thanks to my best man Robin Gale who shared an unforgettable experience supporting England in New Zealand, in 1985.

Plus all who came on that extraordinary tour to Kenya in 1988. Hakuna Matata! And the OWRFC, of course. Special memories too of Greg Stitcher who died in that horrible game, in April 1993. You changed my life, Greg.

Caroline D'Auria gave me remarkable strength, wisdom and support in the 2010 General Election campaign in Battersea. What a lady. We helped achieve the building of a badly needed new secondary school in our borough. Don't Float — Vote!

Lovereading.co.uk has been an interesting journey in which, thirty years after an FCB Management Course in Chicago in 1985, Nick West has shown extraordinary friendship at times when I have most needed a friend.

There have been many doctors and nurses who have treated and tended my old back and helped me cope with constant, chronic pain. You are a noble breed too.

Finally, of course, Ricki, Kris, Nik and Becki of whom I am so proud. What a team. What a family!

Time for the next chapter, eh?